Your End of the Lead:

Changing how you think and act to help your reactive dog

Janet Finlay

To Mirri, who taught me more about reactivity than anyone else could.

You still have my heart.

CONTENTS

ACKNOWLEDGEMENTS

The ideas in this book have developed over more than a decade, through learning and working with many people.

Thanks, in particular, to all my clients and their dogs, students on my Your End of the Lead courses over the years, and members, past and present, of my Canine Confidence Club. Your enthusiasm for discussion and your willingness to try new ideas continues to inspire me. Special thanks to my trusty moderators – Wendy Baker, Ruth Bisgrove and Bernadette Kerbey – for keeping things going when I have been otherwise occupied. You are the best.

I have learned from the wisdom of hundreds of mentors, teachers and colleagues, both in person and through their work, and it would be impossible to name them all. However, there are some who deserve special mention. I have been lucky enough to learn TTouch under the guidance of some incredible mentors over the years: Linda Tellington-Jones, Robyn Hood, Sarah Fisher, Kathy Cascade, Lucie LeClerc, Edie Jane Eaton, Debbie Potts, Marie Miller, and Tina Constance. Thank you all for sharing your knowledge and experience: TTouch has transformed how I work with animals. Thank you also Sarah Fisher for your ACE Free Work and detailed observations, which are so powerful in helping us to understand our dogs; Leslie McDevitt for Control Unleashed, which has been a huge influence on my training for the past decade; Professor Susan Friedman for continual inspiration and clarity of thinking on behaviour science; Sarah Readings for teaching me about coaching and changing so much of my thinking; and Jane McGonigal for the brilliance that is Superbetter. Other influences are acknowledged in the references.

For the past three years I have been an authorised trainer on the Facebook group Reactive Dogs UK and have watched it grow from a few thousand to well over 18,000 members. Thanks to founder Nic Crampton, the admin team, my fellow trainers and all the members of RDUK: I have learned a lot from your questions and from your answers and have nothing but admiration for your commitment to your dogs and to the group. Go ninjas!

Many fellow trainers and TTouch colleagues have supported me over the years and our discussions have enhanced my knowledge and understanding. Particular thanks to Morag Heirs, Tracey McLennan, Louise Downing, Morag Sutherland, Isla Fishburn and Jo Churlish: I really appreciate your work, support and friendship.

Thanks to those who have helped with the practicalities of making this book a reality. I owe a huge debt of gratitude to Andrea Rayner for her meticulous editing of the manuscript. It is much better for her attention: any errors remaining are entirely mine. Thanks also to members of the Canine Confidence Club and, especially, to Laura Mawson for helpful discussions on the cover. Thanks to Melody Todd, of Springer Loaded Creative, for producing the final cover design and to Kate Sweeney, of Kate Sweeney Dog Photography, for the lovely cover photographs and permission to use them. Thanks to Toni Shelbourne for taking many of the photos in the book and to Penny Leedal and Mia and Alex Wilson and Mischief for modelling for them. Other photographs and images have been contributed by Kate Sweeney, Robyn Hood, Bernadette Kerbey, Cameron Laing and Esther Dix – thank you all. Thanks also to the guardians and dogs whose photos feature.

At the beginning of 2018 I launched this project, with an option to 'buy in', while it was still no more than an idea. Special thanks to the 220 people who had enough faith and interest in this book to buy a copy before a word had been written. You gave me the motivation I needed to keep going as well as great feedback along the way. I hope it is worth the wait! You were promised a mention in the book so here you go:

Jacqui Griffiths, Clare Hargate, Lynne Turpin, Sue Brunton, Kate Riley, Monica McGill, Diane Gregory, Correna Taylor, Maureen Bywater, Christine Kiefer, Maria, Gloria Davies, Debbie, Debby, Carole, Julia Lewis, Christine McMillan, Patricia Templeton, Jo Blake, Sarah Gordon, Ruth Bisgrove, Carol Ashmore, Allyson Giel, Luisa Dormer, Bonnie Patricia Wright, Camelia Geary, Theo Jak, Kathie Ward, Laura Mawson, Ros Kinloch, Natalie Richards, Mandy Collins, Trisha Harding, Angela Thompson, Sandra Bellingham, Heather Cunningham, Diane Self, Susannah O'Hanlon, Jane Taylor, Victoria Clements, Brenda, Katrien Alewaeters, Valerie, Mandy Wilson, Lucy Phillips, Linda Hilliard, Wendy Baker, Rhiannon Kay, Tracy Grossmith, Joanna Coupland, Sarah Relf, Barb Owen, Sally Thompson, Tess, Angie Marchant, Margaret Anthony, Cathy Withall, Deborah Wilkes, Susan Martin, Charlotte Garner, Karen Davies, Gretta Ford, Ruth Evans, June Skilton, Carol, Alan Collins, Sarah Baker, Zoe Biscombe, Trish Mahon, Kate Segal, Veronika Danielson, Rachel Birt, Alison Campbell, Lola Carey, Joanne Denton, Michelle Fowler, Hannah Jarvis, Bernadette Kerbey, Anne-Marie McNulty, Jan Spencer, Pam Thornton, Jan Aldous, Rho, Sarah Brookes, Adam Barrett, Julie Barclay, Jacqui Sahin, Carolyn Hopper, Sue Palterman, Alison Kamffer, Viv Raundorf, Margaret Crowe, Maggie Irving, Gwynne Wright, Pat Penny, Kirstie Thulin, Helen Harvey, Debbie Noon, Gail Laurence, Kevin Morgan, Nancy Webb, Andrea Rayner, Alicia Long, Jane Harvey, Frederique Fremont, Jane Richardson, Jayne Samuel-Walker, Ang Reynolds, Mary McPherson, Sylvie Fradette, Michelle Holloway, Marion Ostler, Sara Di Crescenzio, Lisa Benshoff, Beatrix Kersten, Susan Oakes, Ella Burt, Jacqueline Salisbury, Ada Ng, Sue Valler, Maria Weiss, Tilly Termijn-van Bekkum, Sandra Lawrence, Christine Magness, Andrea Richards, Susan Sanderson, Kathryn Bagnall, Catherine Mackay, Daniela Albisser, Naomi Hillman, Fiona McLean, Janet Wilson, Hilary Eldridge, Neet Lawrence, Gill Vlahovic, Angela Warren, Val Polson, Jo

Millin, Samantha Paxton, Sally Ann Salt, Marjorie Fisher, Amy Kellaway, Jennie Wall, Penny Leedal, Jo Law, Julie, Jenni Pass, Alexandra Kitching, Sandra Duncan, Tara Hunter, Kirstie Dear, Diane Beech, Andrea Paterson, Ann Corcoran, Gill Kimber, Matty Al-irimi, Debbie Lister, Camilla Goran, Joanna Pienescu, Lesley Glover, Diane Milner, Pauline Burlace, Alex Chapman, Harriet Herley, Stephanie Deville, Sonia Hayes, Julie, Anna Petto, Linda Hemming, Kate Sweeney, Robbie Sarkisian, Claire, Jackie, Tracey, Debby Morris, Nicola Windsor Smith, Marga, Catherine, Doreen Jevons, Rachel Richards, Elizabeth Johnson, Steve Taylor, Carol, Alison Bunn, Franciane Breda, Claire Guttridge, Judith Atkinson, Joanne Frame, Emma Rodell, Jill Maddocks, Kitty Herbert, Jacqueline Surdu, Deena Haragan, Kim, Shelly Jagger, Sasha Dugdale, Meredith Laycock, Sal Philpott, Clarice, Christine Spencer, Cakbob, Sue Williamson, Linda van der Riet, Marian Rickerby, Jody Broughton, Barb Beschta, Melanie Tyler, Emma Rennick, Lottie Bennett, Clare Swanger, Wendy Hayward, Dawn Holroyd, Izzy Johnson, Vikki Dykstra, Stefanja Gardener, Kareen aufm Kampe, Rachel Owers, Paula L Loewen, Louiza Baker, Rona Gregory.

Finally I want to thank all my family and friends for their patience and support in the months it has taken me to complete this book, as well as the years spent following my dream to work with dogs and their people. Special thanks to Ann Finlay, for being an excellent student and ally; Michael Finlay, for suggestions on design and typography; Alison Campbell and Fiona Dix, for encouragement discussions and ideas; Rachel Cowgill, for unfailing support throughout my whole Canine Confidence adventure; and Janet Atkins, for the time we have shared enjoying dogs and friendship over more years than I suspect either of us care to remember! And of course to the dogs with whom I have been privileged to share my life – Bruno, Florence, Grace, Ambrose, Orsa, Jake, Mirri, Lewys, Martha, Roo and Otter – you have been and are my greatest and best teachers. Thank you.

PREFACE

"If you want to change your dog's behaviour, you have to
change *your* mind."
Linda Tellington-Jones

This book is about you and your reactive dog. We will go into more
detail in the next chapter about what we mean by 'reactive' but, if
you are reading this, I would hazard a guess that you know already.
You have already experienced living with a dog whose response to
other dogs (or sometimes people or vehicles or strange objects) is
to lunge, bark or growl, or to freeze or panic. You know what it is
to worry about your dog, to be frustrated by their[1] behaviour, to be
embarrassed by the racket they make, to be anxious about the
possible repercussions and secretly to long for the days when you
could walk your dog easily and lightly and without needing a level
of preparation worthy of a military operation.

If you recognise that scenario and have experienced those
feelings, the chances are that you have also consulted many books
and other resources in your search for a solution. So why would
you need to read one more?

Because this book is different.

There are many excellent books out there that will teach you how
to train your reactive dog. Some focus in detail on specific tools

---

[1] A dog is not an 'it' so I have chosen to use 'they' as a pronoun when talking
about our dogs, whether singular or plural, rather than choose a gender that
excludes half of our dogs or use the clumsy 'he or she'. It may not be strictly
grammatical but it is clear and fits much better with the way I – and I am sure
you – think about dogs.

and techniques. Others give you a step-by-step guide to help you shift your dog from crazy to calm. Still others give you case studies of particular dogs and how they have been helped. All of these are useful and I absolutely recommend that you read some of them in addition to this one.[2] But what these books have in common is that they focus primarily on the dog and how to change how the dog behaves.

Well of course they do, you may be thinking. What else would they focus on? It is the dog who is reactive after all, isn't it?

When we think about changing our dog's behaviour, we usually think about training, or management, or counter conditioning, or some other approach that focuses on the dog. When we have a challenging dog, we tend to focus on that problem and we see it as a dog-focused issue that we need to address. Our dog is reactive or fearful or over-exuberant and we need to change their undesirable behaviour.

Certainly, our end goal is to have a dog who does not feel the need to react inappropriately, who is confident enough to handle the situations they face on a day-to-day basis. But our dog is not a problem. Our dog *has* a problem just as we do. Our dog is struggling in some way with a situation or situations they are experiencing. They are finding their world a challenge. And we are part of that world.

There are two ends to any lead and my premise is that your end of the lead is just as important as the dog's end. All the training tools in the world will not help if you do not have the right mindset to take on the challenge of your dog's behaviour. The best techniques and equipment will be useless if you don't have the confidence to use them effectively. And, perhaps ironically, you will only make real progress in changing your dog when you learn how

---

[2] You'll find a recommended reading list at the end of this book.

to live with them as they are today.

So this book focuses on reactivity from your perspective. It will help you change your mindset and how you think about the problem of reactivity, about yourself and your dog, about handling and training, about walks and all those annoying people with 'friendly' dogs, who make your life so challenging. It will help you change how you respond and teach you a core set of skills that will enable you to live happily with your dog while you work on changing that reactive behaviour. And ultimately it will help you shift from anxiously surviving each encounter, to actively enjoying your walks again.

If you are ever anxious or stressed when you are out with your dog, if their reactive behaviour has ever made you feel despondent, defeated or demoralised or if you feel that your anxiety contributes to that behaviour, this book is for you. It will teach you how you can "be the change" that your dog needs.

BE THE CHANGE

So am I saying that your dog's reactivity is somehow your fault or that it is you who is making it worse? Absolutely not.

You may feel that it is. You may find it impossible not to grip the lead tightly when you see another dog coming towards you. You may find your heart rate increases and you start to panic. And people may helpfully suggest that if you could just "relax a bit" all would be well!

But think about it for a moment. I am pretty sure that you did not start out like this. Your anxiety has been triggered by your experiences of your dog's reactivity and you have learned these responses as a way of coping with a situation you find challenging. It is not your fault – any more than the stress we are feeling is our dog's fault. It is simply that when we live closely with any other living being, we will influence them as they will influence us.

But the good news is that we can change our response. We can choose to do things differently. Change in our dogs needs to start with change in us and that is only fair. After all, the way they are behaving works just fine for them. They shout and the scary thing generally goes away. Job done. It is we who want them to learn to respond in a way that is more acceptable to us.

So we need to be willing to change ourselves first – our expectations, our habits, our routines, our beliefs, our mindset – so that we can help our dogs to change their behaviour. And if we change the way we see things, change our responses and our expectations, then we will influence our dogs to change also. In the words famously attributed to Gandhi, we can "be the change we wish to see" in our dogs.

Are we holding our dogs or ourselves back because of our negative thinking? How aware are we of what our dog needs and what they are trying to communicate? Do we have realistic expectations of both our dog and ourselves? Are we using our bodies in the most effective way to help them be more physically balanced? Are we inadvertently triggering tension in the equipment we use or the way that we respond? When we start with these things, change in our dog will follow.

THE LENS WE USE

There is widely used adage, attributed to such diverse sources as Anais Nin, Steven Covey and the Talmud that "we don't see things as they are, we see them as *we* are." We do not see the world objectively; we see the world through the lens of our experience, our expectations, and our perceptions. It explains how two people can experience the same event and interpret it very differently.

Reactivity is a case in point. One person with a reactive dog will see a dog who is misbehaving, their behaviour as embarrassing, the priority as stopping the 'acting up'. Another person will see a dog who is frightened, their behaviour as information, and the priority as making them more comfortable. Exactly the same behaviour, but very different responses.

I believe we need to be willing to think differently about every aspect of how we live and work with our dogs. Changing our thinking leads to changing what we do and we can't change how we act until we change how we think.

Your End of the Lead cycle: Changing how you think about...

The structure of this book, summarised in the diagram, reflects this. In the linear book, we start with the problem and work through to progress. But it is actually a continuous cycle of reflection and re-examination. As we change how we think about one thing, we will start to think differently about something else.

My own lens on reactivity is a relational one. When it comes to it, all of what we do with our dogs is about relationship and connection. Relationship and connection with our dog, as we build trust and help them learn to live successfully in our world.

Relationship and connection with our families and friends, as we negotiate how we expect them to be with our dogs and what they can expect from us. Relationship and connection with neighbours and strangers, as we try to maintain peaceful relations all round. And relationship and connection with ourselves, as we strive for self-acceptance and self-belief.

Behavioural science is one ingredient in building that relationship and connection but we also need to look beyond this. My work with reactive dogs and their guardians and the approach presented in this book draws on many modalities and disciplines, from Tellington TTouch, to transformational coaching, games research, self-acceptance, psychology and productivity. We can learn a lot by looking beyond our usual horizons.

As you read this book, you will encounter ideas that, at first glance, may not seem to be directly relevant to your dog's reactivity. Be open to this and focus on how these might influence what you do with your dog. If you are prepared to 'think outside the box' and use what you learn in this book, you will see change.

Chapter One

WHAT IS REACTIVITY ANYWAY?

The word reactive simply means "responsive to a stimulus" but when talking about dogs we tend to understand it as a dog barking, lunging, growling, or otherwise responding 'inappropriately' to another dog (or person or object).[3] A dog that does this frequently is often called a 'reactive' dog. But it is important that we understand what that actually means and what it doesn't.

Reacting to scary things is normal survival behaviour. Any animal that fails to react to something that is genuinely threatening would likely die. They would be eaten by the bear or run over by the bus or shot by the hunter.

So reacting to threat is, in and of itself, appropriate. When we talk about our dog being 'reactive', we actually mean 'over-reactive', and our judgement of what is an over-reaction is very human-focused. Our dog is reacting to something that we and other humans do not consider dangerous or life-threatening, so we consider their response inappropriate. Our dog likely does not share our view!

How our dog reacts to scary things is not a character flaw and it does not define our dog. It is simply a reaction.

My work with reactive dog guardians started in earnest when I adopted a small, black lurcher named Mirri. I was already a

---

[3] In this book, we will discuss primarily dog-dog reactivity as it is the most common issue. However everything we cover also applies if your dog is reactive to people, traffic, children on bikes or anything else. You may need to adapt exercises to your own context but the tools and principles will apply.

TTouch practitioner and pet dog trainer, and in that capacity had worked with dogs who barked and lunged at other dogs. But it was Mirri who challenged my thinking and changed my perspective on the whole issue.

Mirri definitely found other dogs a challenge. She would bark and lunge if she was too close, particularly if the other dog was running. She could scream like a banshee when alarmed and throw herself against the end of the lead with the best of them.

But she was also a joyous, affectionate, fun-to-be-with dog, who loved people and her close doggy friends, and she wriggled her way into my heart.

So was she a 'reactive dog' or was she my loving, joyful 'dog of a lifetime', who also barked and lunged at other dogs when she felt threatened? This is an important distinction. The first defines her; the second describes her behaviour under specific circumstances.

Describing a dog as 'reactive' can be a useful shorthand to avoid clumsy phrasing but we always need to remember that we are talking about behaviour not about character. Reactivity does not define your dog. It is simply a behaviour in response to an emotional trigger or a behaviour that they have learned helps them to cope with situations they find difficult.

Mirri's reactions were simply an expression of her fears in particular situations: emotions and behaviours that we were able to change over time. Her loving, joyful character was a constant throughout.

How reactive is your dog?

We can get some perspective on our dog's reactivity by considering how much of the time our dog is actually reacting. Ask yourself:

☐   For how much of any 24-hour period is your dog reacting?

☐   Is it measured in hours or minutes or even seconds?

☐   What is your dog doing the rest of the time?

Sometimes, when we stop and think, there has not been a reactive incident in days, weeks or even months. Yet we label our dogs 'reactive' as opposed to affectionate, playful, mischievous, lazy, clever or a host of other adjectives that might more accurately describe what they are doing much more of the time.

The reason is that, of course, those few moments are often excruciatingly painful and difficult for us both. However, it is worth remembering that our dog is many things besides reactive and that reactivity is just one of a whole range of behaviours that they display.

When we talk about 'reactive dogs' in this book, note that we are talking about a particular set of behaviours, not a character trait. And, fundamentally, we are talking about a dog who does not feel safe. So before we go any further, it will help to consider what is happening in the body when we feel threatened.[4]

THE PHYSIOLOGY OF SAFETY AND THREAT

To understand reactivity, whether in our dogs or in ourselves, we need to understand a little about our mammalian physiology. We are biologically designed for survival. Our nervous system is fine-tuned to keep us safe, seek out opportunities and respond to potential threats. This is managed by our autonomic nervous system, so called because it operates without our conscious involvement.

Traditionally, there has been a two-branch model of the autonomic nervous system. We have the sympathetic nervous system, which is activated under threat, leading to fight or flight responses, and the parasympathetic nervous system, which is our resting, safe state. This two-branch model tends to lead to a

---

[4] Of course, dogs and humans are both mammals and share much of the same mammalian biology. The physiology of threat and safety is fundamentally the same.

perception that these two systems are discrete, opposing states. They are either off or on. We are in one or in the other. But the reality is a little more complex.

Activation of the sympathetic nervous system does not always mean we feel threatened or are distressed. It is also associated with excitement and play. Similarly, the parasympathetic nervous system enables relaxation and restoration, but it can also lead to our body shutting down and can even, in extreme circumstances, stop our breathing. So what is going on?

In the 1990s, Dr. Stephen Porges proposed a three-branch model of the autonomic nervous system, based around the function of the vagus nerve.[5]

The vagus nerve connects the brain stem to the rest of the body. It is long and meandering: in fact its name comes from the Latin word meaning 'wandering' or 'rambling' and that gives a good picture of what it does. It runs from the brain to the digestive tract, branching off to the lungs, heart, throat, voice box, and ears. It carries instructions to regulate heart rate, blood pressure, breathing rate, digestion as well as facial expression and tone of voice. Crucially, it also passes sensory information back from these systems to the brain: in fact this accounts for around 80% of its function.

In Porges' model, known as Polyvagal Theory, the parasympathetic nervous system has two circuits, representing different pathways of the vagus: ventral and dorsal. These originate in different parts of the brain stem and connect to different parts of the body: the ventral vagus connecting to systems above the diaphragm (heart, lungs, voice and facial muscles) while the dorsal vagus primarily connecting to systems below the diaphragm, relating to digestion.

---

[5] Porges, S. (2017). *The Pocket Guide to The Polyvagal Theory.* NY: Norton.

Together with the sympathetic nervous system, these determine our autonomic response. Rather than these being either 'on' or 'off', we can think of them all as dials that can be turned up low or high. It is the combination of these levels of activation that determines our response.

In Polyvagal Theory, the primary functions of these three circuits are distinct:

- **Sympathetic nervous system:** active, mobilised defensive behaviours, such as fight, flight, fool around.
- **Ventral vagus circuit:** social engagement.
- **Dorsal vagus circuit:** immobilised defensive behaviours, such as freeze.

The ventral vagus circuit is activated when we feel safe. It is where learning happens. We feel connected to others. We are able to grow and heal. This is the optimal state for health and where we ideally want to be most of the time. It can also regulate sympathetic activation, acting like a gentle brake, to enable mobilisation without defensiveness in play, excitement and exploration. In this safe state, the dorsal vagus circuit manages our 'rest and digest' functions.

If we feel threatened, our sympathetic nervous system prepares us for defensive action. It tells our body to take in more air, to pump more blood, to release more glucose to the muscles, to stop wasting energy on things like digestion. This is primarily our fight or flight response but it also includes fool around, where we use appeasement strategies to reduce threat.

If the threat continues and fight or flight cease to work, then the dorsal vagus circuit will go into high tone and act as an emergency brake and take us to defensive immobilisation. This is the freeze or shut down response that we sometimes see in terrified animals and people. They stop fighting or trying to run because it is not working and they move to a state where they can do nothing.

As part of this process, our nervous system is constantly

evaluating how safe we are. It does this automatically and at a subconscious level, through a process Porges calls *neuroception*. Key elements that are monitored for potential threats include the environment, how safe those around us are feeling, and whether danger is present in communication signals that we are receiving, such as the facial expressions and tone of voice of others. The vagus also passes information from our body back to our brain so factors such as pain, temperature, hunger, respiration and heart rate will all influence this safety evaluation.

So for us and our dogs to feel safe, we need to keep our autonomic nervous system in a non-defensive balanced state, where the parasympathetic circuits are regulating sympathetic activation to enable social engagement and play, growth and learning as well as "rest and digest". We can facilitate this in many ways, including addressing factors that reduce our own and our dog's sense of safety, ensuring a safe environment and providing safe ways to communicate and interact. We can also strengthen our vagus nerve itself. We will look at all these later in this book.

But first let's look at little more closely at how these responses to threat manifest themselves as the reactive behaviours that we are familiar with in our dogs.

TYPES OF REACTIVITY

As we have seen, we may response to threats in different ways, depending on the activation of our autonomic nervous system. The same is of course true of our dogs. And reactivity is not always what it seems. So let's consider the types of reactive behaviours that we may experience and the variety of triggers that may be involved.

Different reactive responses

We have described reactivity as an inappropriate response to the sight of another dog (or other trigger) and this most often shows itself as lunging, barking, pulling towards the other dog and other seemingly 'aggressive' behaviours. But our dogs may react in different ways so it is worth us spending a little time outlining these.

As we have seen, when our dogs feel threatened their stress response is activated and their autonomic nervous system can take them into one of four main responses:

- ☐ Fight. This is perhaps the most common response we see and certainly the one we are most likely to think of when we hear a dog described as 'reactive'. The dog barks, growls and lunges at the end of the lead or, if off lead, chases or attacks. The function of this behaviour is rarely to do actual harm but to chase off the scary stranger.

- ☐ Flight. These are the dogs who panic, struggle to run away, hide behind you and do all in their power to avoid the other dog. A flight response can be particularly upsetting to see in our own dog.

- ☐ Fool around. These are perhaps the most misunderstood of all, as they can, at first glance, appear happy and active. Their tail may be wagging (often frantically) and they may be rushing about, licking other dogs or people, or rolling on their backs. This giddy response is just as much a stress reaction as the others but it may look as if the dog is having fun. This can mean that we don't always remove the dog from situations that they find difficult.

- ☐ Freeze. As we saw in the last section this is the immobilisation response that is usually triggered when the other responses fail (although some dogs will go straight to this based on their learning history). It can be less obvious but it is still a reaction to a scary trigger. The freeze dog may refuse to move forward, may be unable to respond to our voice as they are 'shut down'. Dogs who freeze are very often misunderstood and thought to be 'stubborn' or difficult. Their lack of response can even be misinterpreted as calm, leading to them being exposed to more rather than less of whatever is threatening to them.

These responses are not absolutes. Dogs will often display different responses depending on context; so, for example, a dog who displays flight when off the lead may revert to fight when on lead and unable to get away.

Fear or frustration?

We've talked about fear-based reactivity but some of these responses, particularly fight and fool around, can also occur as a result of frustration. A frustrated dog is often much better with other dogs off lead than on: the dog who screams at another dog when on a lead but plays happily when off, is often showing lead frustration. However, this is not always the case as these dogs often have poor social skills so may find appropriate play challenging as well. But while the fearful dog wants others to go away, the frustrated one may want to interact.

The same can be true of reactivity to people. Some dogs are afraid and behave aggressively to keep the strange human at bay, while others may be more conflicted, wanting to interact but finding it challenging to do so. With reactivity to people it is best to assume it is a fear response and only allow interaction if it is clearly initiated by the dog. One difference between reactivity to dogs and people is that you can instruct people how to behave around your dog. They may not always do as you say, of course, but it is important that you try to protect your dog from unwanted advances. We will look at this more in Chapter 5.

The key thing to remember is that, while the root causes may be different, the end result is the same: a threat response in our dog,

triggered by the presence of something they find challenging. Our
aim is also going to be the same: to help our dog feel safer in that
context. How we do that will vary and when we change how we
think, we are able to see our dog more clearly and make choices
that are appropriate for them. We are not dealing in 'one size fits
all' solutions!

Different triggers

We call the thing our dog reacts to the 'trigger'. Common triggers
are other dogs, people, vehicles and unusual objects. These may be
very specific (reactive to black dogs or men in hats or bicycles) or
more generalised (reactive to all strange dogs, all people or to all
moving vehicles).

We will talk a lot about dog-to-dog reactivity that occurs outside
of the home, that is, dogs who react inappropriately to strange
dogs, who they meet while out and about. Such reactivity may be
quite specific (reactive to young dogs, black dogs, big dogs, running
dogs or dogs of a specific breed for instance) or a more generalised
reactivity to all dogs. It may also be context-dependent: for
example, only reactive to other dogs when on lead or when off
lead, or when the other dog is on lead or off, or only when seen in
open spaces. However, triggers for reactivity go beyond these
primary triggers and can be quite complex, which often leads to a
confused and frustrated guardian. We will talk more about this in
Chapter 4.

Most the ideas, tools and techniques discussed in this book are
equally relevant if your dog is reactive to people or vehicles or
anything else. Obviously these bring their own challenges as well,
not least the additional worries you may have about the legal
implications of your dog reacting to people in public, or the risk
involved if your dog was to escape and chase a car. We will discuss
these as they arise. But please assume that whenever we discuss

reactivity to other dogs, we are talking about other triggers as well. It is just rather clumsy to write out a whole list each time!

When is reactive not reactive?

As we've seen, reacting is a natural and normal response, and we need to be careful about interpreting every reaction as inappropriate. I often hear people say "My dog is only reactive when another dog gets right in her face" or "My dog only reacts when the other dog jumps on him".

I was walking on the beach with my collie Martha recently when she attracted the attention of an enthusiastic young male hound. He was perfectly friendly but, in spite of my efforts to keep him away, he kept running up to Martha and bouncing around her. She did not share his enthusiasm and tried to ignore him but he didn't take the hint. When he finally tried to mount her she sat down, turned her head and air snapped at him over her shoulder. He backed off.

Was this reaction inappropriate? Not at all. It was an entirely appropriate and proportional communication, which the other dog understood clearly. There is nothing inappropriate about one dog telling another dog to get out of their face or one expressing displeasure at another dog jumping on their back. Dogs are social creatures but they have rules of engagement that determine what is polite and what is not. Rushing head long into another dog's face is rude. Jumping on another dog without invitation is rude. In these contexts, appropriate responses include a grumble, growl or air snap. The intruder is told to mind their manners and then left alone as long as they back off. This is not 'reactivity'. It is normal dog behaviour and we need to accept that canine communication includes a range of vocalisations and displays that we may find much more alarming than our dogs do! Had she pursued him after he backed off or attacked him, it would have been inappropriate!

Of course it is better if we can intervene so that our dogs do not have to respond in this way, since there is clearly a level of stress for them in doing so. However, it does not mean that your dog is reactive.

Age-related reactivity

It is not unusual for younger dogs to go through a 'reactive' stage as they are entering their teenage phase. Dogs experience what is known as a second fear period any time between 6 and 14 months where they can develop fears of things that have previously not bothered them. People often worry that their dog is becoming reactive but they can usually pass through this stage unscathed, with careful management. A key thing is to allow them to investigate things, safely, in their own time. No dog should be forced to face or come close to things they are wary of. Just take a step back and allow them time to process, making encounters as positive as possible.

This period also coincides with hormonal changes in our dogs: an increase in testosterone in young entire males and first seasons in females. The complex influence of hormones on behaviour is beyond the scope of this book but if you feel your dog's behaviour has changed due to hormonal factors do discuss your options fully with your vet or behaviourist. Neutering may appear to be the solution but it can have a negative affect on fearful dogs, so it is important to seek qualified advice.

Older dogs may also begin to react if they have pain issues or are feeling less secure or physically stable. This is normal and we need to support them by addressing their physical needs first and foremost, while ensuring they get the space they need to feel safe.

WHERE DOES REACTIVITY COME FROM?

One of the most common questions people ask about reactivity is: where did it come from? You may be asking that yourself.

Reactivity can be bewildering to us. We can't understand why our dog is reactive. We don't know where the reactivity has come from.

The truth is that often we simply can't say. Sometimes we can identify an incident that led directly to the reactivity. Our dog was attacked and they became fearful of all dogs afterwards. But even then, the situation is probably more complex than it seems. After all, many dogs are attacked and simply shake it off, showing no reactivity afterwards. So there are additional factors, such as genetics and resilience, at play.

Often our dog is already reactive when they come to us, and we can only guess at their history. Sometimes they develop reactive behaviour without anything notable happening to them. We can find no obvious starting point.

We got them as a puppy. They have not been treated differently from our other dogs, who are not reactive. We have raised and educated them in the same way. We know they have never been traumatised or had a bad experience, and so we start to doubt ourselves. Then people trot out the old chestnut "there are no bad dogs, just bad owners" and we feel we must have done something wrong.

But the truth is much more complex. Two children from the same family, with the same genetic background and the same parents, can have very different personalities. And so can our dogs. They are individuals. Some can be brought up 'by the book' and still find life difficult. Others can sail through life in spite of difficult experiences.

What we do with our dogs is important but it is only part of the story. We always need to remember we are living with individuals. They don't all see the world in the same way and they vary in their personality and resilience. We can do what we can to stack the odds in their favour but some dogs will still struggle in spite of what we do.

REACTIVITY AND US

So much for our dog's reactivity but what about ours? When we are out with our dog, we often find that we are also reactive. We may not scream and yell or leap about (unless seriously provoked!) but we still feel anxiety and fear. Our breathing becomes faster. We feel our heart pounding in our chest. We tighten our grip on the lead and feel overcome with panic.

We start to dread our walks, to feel helpless and out of control. We are embarrassed and ashamed that our dog behaves as they do. We feel isolated and alone. And all of this affects how we feel about our dog and the relationship we have. Will our dog ever be 'normal'? When will we get our life back? Are we even doing them any good?

WHY DOES REACTIVITY BOTHER US SO MUCH?

So why is reactivity such a difficult set of behaviours for us to handle? How is it that our dog's behaviour affects us so profoundly? There are many reasons but here are a few of the most common ones.

We are embarrassed

Our society has high expectations of dogs. They have been designated a 'social' animal and so they should like every other dog and person they meet. And if they are scared they should stay quiet and well behaved and not show it.

None of this is true of course. Our dogs are as entitled as we are to have preferences for how and when they socialise. Some dogs want to be friends with everyone. Others are perfectly happy with just the people and dogs they know and like their space to be respected. Still others are genuinely afraid of other dogs or strangers. And vocalising when we are scared is behaviour we share with our dog!

Yet still we feel embarrassed when it happens. We feel that our dog's behaviour reflects negatively on us. We have not trained them sufficiently. We are being judged and found wanting. If we happen to work with dogs, we can expect these feelings to be magnified tenfold!

We know rationally that we have nothing to be embarrassed about, but the feeling is still very real for many of us.

We are scared they will hurt someone

Reactive behaviour can look and feel scary. It is hard to feel in control when we are hanging on to a raging, snarling, screaming dog with all the strength we have. We worry that those friendly dogs will get too close and that our dog will hurt them. We worry that another guardian will get involved and get bitten. We worry that our dog might bite us while in this frenzy. If our dog is scared of people then these worries are magnified even more. What if someone approaches or ignores our warnings? The fear that our dog may do damage is very real for many of us.

We may also be afraid of what might happen to our dog. What if they react to a dog, who then attacks them? This can be a particular fear when your dog is little. What if someone reports my dog for barking and lunging at them or their dog, especially with dangerous dog laws becoming more widespread and ever-less forgiving? What happens then? Might I lose my dog?

Again these are very real fears for many of us.

We are worried about our dog

We are also concerned for our dog. We see them frightened or stressed and we want to protect them from it. We feel that they are missing out because of the things that they are not able to do.

Often our concerns are based on our assumptions of what dogs need. Dogs need to run free and our dog can't go off the lead. Dogs need social companions and our dog can't play with other dogs. These concerns can haunt us when we feel that our dogs' lives are constrained.

We are grieving for what we have lost

When we get a new dog, whether as a puppy or an older dog, we have visions of how our life with them will be. We may have plans to take part in canine sports, like agility, flyball, obedience or gun dog work. We may have seen ourselves taking long walks in the country or watching our dogs play with others in the local park. We may have imagined stopping at the café, with them snoozing under the table, or taking them with us to the pub on summer evenings. We may want them to accompany us on holidays at home and abroad or visit family and friends with us. Whatever we hoped for or expected, the chances are it was not quite what we now have!

It is perfectly normal to have feelings of disappointment or even grief over the loss of the life we had hoped for. When those 'normal' activities are beyond what our dog can cope with, we find ourselves on a different path from the one we had planned and we may never be able to do the things we had looked forward to doing. This can cause disappointment, frustration, grief and even anger.

We feel we don't deserve this

Sometimes we are just confused by our dog's reactivity and feel we don't deserve this. We have followed all the best advice on training and socialisation and still our dog behaves this way. We have had dogs all our lives and none of them has ever behaved like this. What did we do wrong?

It may seem unfair that our dog is like this when others are not. We just wanted a dog to enjoy life like everyone else. We see lots of happy, social dogs playing in the park. Why is our dog different?

Again these feelings are perfectly understandable.

WE CAN CHANGE

The bottom line is that it bothers us because it matters. We love our dog. We want them to be happy. We want to enjoy the time we have with them. We want to keep them safe. Instead we feel threatened and frightened.

Plus we feel guilty. We must have not done something or not be doing enough! All of this adds to the stress we already feel.

If this rings true to you, I have two things to say.

First, your response is normal. Having a dog who can be reactive is not easy and it does change your life. But the fact is, the new path you are on may prove to be a more satisfying one after all. It is hilly with a lot of ups and downs, it may challenge all your expectations and resources, but you will learn more about yourself and about dogs, from living with and loving this 'challenging' dog than you would have done had your 'perfect dog' arrived.

Second, your dog's reactivity is not your fault! However stressed and 'reactive' you are now about your dog's reactivity, I am willing to bet that you were not born a reactive dog walker. You were probably quite relaxed when you first took a dog for a walk. Possibly even when you first took this dog for a walk! Your reaction is an emotional response to what is happening and, just as it does not define your dog, neither does it define you.

If you have been dealing with it for a while, chances are you have now learned certain behaviours that help you cope with what you are dealing with. You have learned to be reactive. These may not always be the best habits, but they have helped you cope up to now.

The good news is that you *can* change your response to your dog's reactivity and your behaviour. You can choose to think and do things differently. Risk can be managed and mitigated and you can learn to keep everyone safe. You can enjoy your dog again.

WHY NOT JUST FIX THE DOG?

You may be thinking: "This concern about me is all very well but isn't it better just to fix the dog? After all, if the dog stopped reacting then I wouldn't have a problem!"

It's a fair question, and wouldn't it be great if it was that easy? But sadly it is based on two false assumptions. Let's look at these.

The Myth of the Quick Fix

The first and most important assumption is this: that there is a quick and easy way to fix reactivity, a silver bullet to make it all ok, and this is just not the case. At least it is not the case if we are committed to keeping our dog safe and working in ways that respect them.

Fear-based behaviours are not resolved overnight. There are trainers who will offer you a quick fix but when you look at what is being suggested closely it will always involve some form of shock, surprise, punishment or flooding. The dog reacts and you throw something at them. The dog reacts and you zap them with a collar or check them with a lead. The dog reacts and you spin them round and hold them tight. The dog reacts so you put them in a field with lots of other dogs until they stop reacting. They will tell you they are 'interrupting' the behaviour or 'refocusing' the dog but however you dress it up, they are using something that the dog finds unpleasant to change the dog's behaviour.

Others will advise you to 'push through' reactivity; that your dog will 'never learn' to like other dogs unless they meet other dogs close up; that you need to make them face their fears.

Pushing through in this way doesn't work. They'll actually 'never learn' if they are frightened or so over-aroused that they are no longer thinking. This approach may overwhelm your dog to the point that they temporarily appear to behave better. But you are storing up trouble further down the line.

These methods may seem to work as the dog outwardly reacts less. But think about the underlying emotion: has the fear been addressed? Think about that for a moment. Imagine something you are afraid of. Now imagine that you are forced to face it close up or, worse, slapped down if you utter so much as a whimper. Would that make you feel more or less afraid?

I can answer this from experience. I have had a lifelong phobia of spiders. The kind of fear that sends you running from the room screaming when you find one in the bath and tentative to go back in, even when assured it had been removed.

One time, in my early twenties, a work colleague laughed and told me I was stupid. I needed to face my fears she told me, as she held pictures of huge spiders in my face. It was horrible and I left. I was no less afraid of spiders but I have to say I hated that woman, viscerally, for many years. Even now, decades later, I still feel a wave of anger if I see her.

Later on, I did get over my fear of spiders. In fact, for months I had one on my windowsill and refused to let anyone sweep away her web. Each morning I chatted to her and admired the beautiful colours on her back. And I can now remove them safely and calmly from my bath. So what did bring about this change?

TTouch practitioner training clinics sometimes include the chance to work with exotic animals, including spiders. The first time they were there, I could barely be in the room. I couldn't even look towards the corner where the spiders were. But no one laughed. No one forced me. Instead they put up barriers so I didn't even see a spider accidentally.

After a couple of sessions I started to get curious. I started to look over to see what was happening in that corner. And gradually

I moved a little closer, all the time knowing that I could retreat whenever I wanted.

By my sixth session I knew I was ready to meet a spider. Everyone supported me. The spider expert talked to me about spider behaviour, showing me how I could influence a spider's direction of movement. This gave me control of the situation and made me feel safe around them. When I was ready, he held one for me to touch and then held my hand steady as I held her myself.

I have a photo of me that day, smiling as I hold a tarantula in my hand.[6] These days I can support other people working through those same fears.

There is a right way and a wrong way to address fear. The wrong way is to dismiss it as 'unacceptable', to force someone to face what they fear and to repress and punish any expression of it. The right way is to give space, to give choice, to give control, to challenge safely and to take time to change the emotional response.

The wrong way may change behaviour quickly but it doesn't remove fear. It will very likely remove trust in the people involved and there is every chance the fear will be expressed even more violently at some point in the future. The right way takes time and patience. It builds trust and changes the relationship between the one who fears and the object of that fear.

So, working with reactive dogs is not always quick. You may be working with your dog for weeks, months or even, in some cases, years to help them feel more comfortable. So we need to learn how to live joyfully with our dogs as they are right now.

Changing us *is* changing the dog!

The second assumption is that changing ourselves – how we think

---

[6] I won't include the photo here as I know it is a common phobia, but you can see it on www.yourendofthelead.com.

about the problem and how we behave – is not an essential part of 'fixing the dog'. Change starts with us, and when we get our thinking and responses right, we will make faster and more consistent progress with our dog.

We may not be responsible for our dog's reactivity but there is no doubt that they are sensitive to our emotional state. When we are frustrated or angry or stressed it affects their behaviour. When we anticipate something bad happening, they will also be more on edge and worried.

When we learn how to build our own confidence, we can help our dog build their confidence. When we learn how to calm ourselves, we can help them calm themselves. When we become more resilient, we can help them become more resilient.

Everything we cover in this book has practical application to how we change our dog's behaviour and how we live and work with our dog's reactivity. By looking at ourselves we are not avoiding working with our dog.

We are in partnership with our dog. The problems we have are shared problems and the solutions must come from us both. It is not fair to expect that all the change will come from our dog, when we can make it easier for them by changing things about ourselves.

In short, this book will help us become the best guardian we can be, so we can help our dog become the best dog that they can be.

Chapter Two

CHANGING HOW YOU THINK ABOUT THE PROBLEM

THREAT OR CHALLENGE?

When we have a reactive dog it is very easy to become overwhelmed. Our world closes in. Every time we leave the house we feel under threat, sometimes even within our own home. We set out on walks, planning everything carefully and expecting danger at every turn. As this becomes our world, it starts to influence our thinking. We start to feel that we can't, that we don't have the resources to handle this situation, that it is not fair that we should have to. We take on a threat mindset.

When we have a threat mindset, our focus is on preventing damage, rather than seeking a positive result. We feel out of control, unable to influence our own situation, and this, in turn, reduces our confidence and resilience.

It is a common and understandable response to a stressful situation but it is not helpful if we want to make progress. And it can be physically damaging. As we saw in Chapter 1 when we see something as a threat, it activates our sympathetic nervous system, our 'fight or flight' mechanism. This is helpful if we are genuinely under attack, if we need to run fast or fight for our survival. However, when it becomes a constant or regular state of being, our health suffers, both physically and mentally.

Our sympathetic nervous system is not designed to be activated day in and day out. It is designed to help us survive when we need it but it is not healthy for us if sustained. Our heart has to work harder as our arteries constrict, making us more prone to heart attack. Our body has to deal with excessive levels of the stress hormone, cortisol, which can compromise our immune system. It makes us more likely to become depressed and anxious, less able to work under pressure and more socially isolated. It is not a healthy state to live in.

Yet this is exactly how many of us feel about our dog's reactivity. It is a threat to our safety and happiness. It is a danger to be survived. This way of thinking is uncomfortable and puts our physical and mental health at risk.

Thankfully there is an alternative: a challenge mindset. Here, instead of looking at the difficulty that we face as a threat that we have to survive, we view it as a challenge, something we can do something about, that we have, or can develop, the resources to meet and address.

Having a challenge mindset enables our parasympathetic nervous system to regulate sympathetic activation, reducing our anxiety and enabling us to think and act more rationally. Shifting to a challenge mindset fundamentally improves our health and well-being, enables us to handle stressful situations more easily and encourages optimism and self-efficacy.

The great news is that we can control which mindset we adopt. We can focus on the threat or choose to accept the challenge. When we choose to see things as a challenge it changes everything.

I had a major breakthrough with Mirri and her reactivity when I stopped seeing her behaviour as something to be survived and started viewing it as a challenge that I could do something about. This was my shift from a threat to a challenge mindset. My challenge was not to change her behaviour but to help her succeed.

I started to do things more playfully, setting myself mini goals.

Keep enough distance. Play 'Look at That' with new dogs.[7] Practice my leading techniques so the lead was never tight. These were all things I could do to help her to succeed. My aim was always to do better than the day before. I even invented a scoring system: how many reactions we had against how many dogs we met, which gave me a success rate that I could measure! Being a competitive soul, I started to enjoy the challenge of trying to beat our highest score.

It made all the difference. Before long, instead of dreading walks I was looking forward to taking her out. Eventually I was even disappointed when we didn't meet other dogs, because I had no opportunity to beat our highest score! It was a far cry from the dread I used to feel.

I was still learning and experimenting. I did not have all the resources in place that I needed to succeed in all the situations we met. We were still finding our way.

What had changed was not my skillset, but my mindset. I was thinking about her reactivity differently. This in turn led me to improve my skillset as I looked for ways to achieve my goals more effectively, but it was the mindset change that came first.

MOVING TO A CHALLENGE MINDSET

So how do we go about shifting from a threat to a challenge mindset? What can we do to move our thinking so that we are able to perceive our dog's reactivity as a challenge to rise to?

It turns out that one of the most powerful ways to do this is exactly what I intuitively did back when I was working with Mirri. I turned it into a game. Adopting a playful, gameful approach is a natural way to shift your thinking from threat to challenge.

When we play a game we naturally adopt a challenge mindset.

---

[7] We will cover the techniques I used later in the book so you can use them too.

We have to actively accept the challenge to play. Playing games focuses our attention and gives us goals and mini challenges to keep us motivated and engaged.

There is plenty of research to support the fact that, far from being a time-wasting activity, playing games is a powerful force for changing mindset and, ultimately, behaviour.

Games have been used to change thinking and behaviour in very difficult scenarios. For example:

☐ Playing an immersive computer game reduced the experience of pain in patients with severe burns.[8]

☐ Playing a game empowered young cancer patients to become more consistent at taking medication.[9]

☐ Playing a simple visual game like Tetris within hours of a traumatic event stopped the involuntary flashbacks associated with Post-Traumatic Stress Disorder (PTSD).[10]

☐ Playing games together enabled people from conflicted social groups not only to change their attitude toward the individual they were playing with, but also how they perceived all other people who were like that individual.[11]

All of these work, not because of some kind of magic within the

---

[8] Hoffman, HG, Chambers, GT, Meyer, WJ, Arceneaux, LL, Russell, WJ, Seibel, EJ, Richards, TL, Sharar, SR, Patterson, DR (2011) *Virtual reality as an adjunctive non-pharmacologic analgesic for acute burn pain during medical procedures.* Annals of behavioral medicine: a publication of the Society of Behavioral Medicine, 41(2): 183-91.

[9] Kato, PM, Cole, SW, Bradlyn, AS, and Pollock, BH (2008) *A Video Game Improves Behavioral Outcomes in Adolescents and Young Adults With Cancer: A Randomized Trial.* Pediatrics, 122 (2): 305-317.

[10] Iyadurai, L, Blackwell, SE, Meiser-Stedman, R, Watson, PC, Bonsall, MB, Geddes, JR, Nobre, AC and Holmes, EA (2017) *Preventing intrusive memories after trauma via a brief intervention involving Tetris computer game play in the emergency department: a proof-of-concept randomized controlled trial.* Molecular Psychiatry, 23: 674–682.

[11] Chua, PH, Jung, YO, Lwin, M, Theng, YL (2013) *Let's play together: Effects of video-game play on intergenerational perceptions among youth and elderly participants.* Computers in Human Behavior, 29: 2303–2311.

game, but because playing and gamefulness unlock the power of our mind. We all have the power to control our attention, thoughts and feelings, to motivate ourselves, to make connections, but often we have so much noise and distraction in our lives that we are unable to use this power to its full potential. Playing games is one way to activate these powers and our challenge mindset.

GAMES TO CHANGE YOUR MINDSET

So what games can we play to change how we think about reactivity and set ourselves on the path to viewing it as a challenge?

Well, we can play pretty much anything that encourages setting playful goals, that is motivating but light-hearted, and that will maintain interest. Here are three that I, and my clients, have used successfully.

Tracker games

The simplest game is what I did with Mirri. Make a game of tracking your progress. There are different ways you can do this.

How many dogs?

The game I played with Mirri was *How many dogs?* I simply counted up all the dogs we saw and noted all those she passed calmly. Then, for each walk, I calculated our success rate as a percentage. Let me give you an example.

We go out for a walk and we meet 12 dogs. Mirri reacts to 5 of them and passes 7 calmly. So our success score was 7/12 multiplied by 100 to give a percentage, in this case 58% success! You can of course simply record the ratio (5 out of 12, 2 out of 7 and so on) but turning it into a percentage makes it easier to compare from day to day.

This simple game gives you a measure of how you are doing and trying to improve on your own best score is motivational. You can even play with buddies if you are the competitive type!

Streaks

Playing *Streaks* is a great way to build a positive habit. Choose something that you want to do every day with your dog. It may be practising something specific or it may be simply doing some training or playing with your dog. Then record every day that you succeed in doing your task. Your 'streak' is your longest an unbroken run of days. It can become quite motivational to keep that streak going, especially if you are the competitive type.

It is very simple to play. Your tracker can be a calendar where you tick off each day; a page in your journal where you colour squares; or a chart on the fridge door where you stick gold stars. You can even get an app to manage it for you (there is one called *Streaks* that works very well).

Set clear goals for how often you want to do the thing you are tracking - ideally daily or every other day. Once your streak gets going you will want to keep it up - and that will be added motivation on the days when it is tough to fit it in.

But be warned. It can be very demotivating to lose a streak, especially if it is a long one. So build a realistic amount of slack into your game. Aim for 5 days out of 7 or 7 days out of 10 or simply allow a certain number of streak 'repairs' each month, which activate if you miss one day but come back the next.

Simple tracking games are a great start to developing a playful, challenge-focused mindset about your dog's reactivity.

Prediction games

Making predictions is good for us. It activates our brain's reward systems, releasing dopamine, which promotes feelings of pleasure and enhances memory and focus. Each prediction we make has one of two outcomes. Either we are right, which gives us a positive boost, or we are wrong, which helps us to predict better next time. This opportunity to learn actually also gives you a dopamine boost so making predictions is a win-win.

A gameful way to use prediction and reframe reactivity as a challenge is playing Reactivity Bingo.[12] You have a blank Bingo card: 9, 16 or 25 squares, depending on how ambitious you are feeling. There are two ways to play: ideally play both games regularly to get double benefit.

Worst-case reactivity bingo
Predict all the bad things that might happen when you are out and about with your dog: rude responses of other owners, unexpected meetings with other dogs, meltdowns. Write one in each of your blank squares. Then mark these off if they happen when you are out on a walk.

The process of predicting possible events gives you a dopamine boost and the gamefulness of the approach takes the sting out of your worst-case scenarios and helps boost your resilience. Plus it is a game you cannot lose! If you get 'Bingo!' then you can reward yourself for surviving a 'line' or a 'full house' full of worst-cases. If not, then you have the reassurance of knowing that those bad things didn't happen. Either way it is a win-win.

Best-case reactivity bingo
Predict and write on your card all the good things that might happen: all the successes that you may have. The times your dog copes with triggers. The times other people are co-operative and help you. The times you see your training paying off.

Again you get the dopamine boost from your predictions and the challenge-focus from being gameful. But here, as you mark off the

---

[12] You can download some cards to get you going at www.canineconfidenceacademy.com/reactivity-bingo.

squares, you also get clear proof of the progress you are making!

Immersive games (Superbetter)

If you are looking for a game that will really support your move to a challenge mindset, then you can do no better than playing Superbetter, a real-life game that applies the principles of computer gaming to addressing issues with a challenge mindset.[13]

Developed by games researcher, Jane McGonigal, as part of her recovery from a traumatic brain injury, Superbetter has been used successfully by over half a million people to address situations ranging from running a marathon, writing a book, going through a divorce and living with cancer. It has been the subject of a clinical trial at the University of Pennsylvania, where it was shown to be effective as a complementary treatment for depression. Superbetter players experienced significant improvement in symptoms as well as reduced anxiety and increased self-efficacy.[14]

Superbetter is a real-life, immersive game, which adopts concepts from computer gaming. Players strive to complete quests as they seek to achieve their goal. They activate power-ups to make them stronger or more effective. They join forces with allies to encourage and help them. They battle the bad guys who try to stop them from making progress. They celebrate epic wins when they have reached a significant milestone. And they adopt secret identities to help them to access their inner strengths. Let's look at those elements in a little more detail.

---

[13] McGonigal, J (2016) *Superbetter: The power of living gamefully.* London: Penguin.
[14] Roepke, AM, Jaffee, SJ, Riffle, OM, McGonigal, J, Broome, R, Maxwell, B (2015) *Randomized Controlled Trial of SuperBetter, a Smartphone-Based/Internet-Based Self-Help Tool to Reduce Depressive Symptoms.* Games Health Journal 4(3): 235-246. Worthen-Chaudhari, L, McGonigal, J, Logan, K, Bockbrader, MA, Yeates, KO, & Mysiw, WJ (2017) *Reducing concussion symptoms among teenage youth: Evaluation of a mobile health app.* Brain Injury, 31(10): 1279-1286.

Find and complete quests

A quest in Superbetter is a small but purposeful action that moves us closer to our end goal. Quests are powerful because, as we complete them, we give ourselves lots of tiny successes. Each success is a positive experience that increases our resilience (see Chapter 3 for more on how to build resilience).

Physical and social quests are generally easier to accomplish than mental and emotional quests, but all will move us forward. So on difficult days our quest might be something simple and physical: get showered and dressed, go round the block or play a game with our dog, eat some fresh food. Alternatively, we might choose a quest to make contact with others: speak to someone; send a text; post on a support group.

On easier days we can move on to quests that challenge us mentally or emotionally: learning something new, practising a new skill, addressing a limiting belief, taking our dog into a challenging environment.

When playing Superbetter, we aim to complete at least one quest a day.

Activate power-ups

A power-up is any small action that we can do that makes us feel better, stronger, happier, or more energised. We collect power-ups by identifying them as things that will work for us and we activate them by doing them. Power-ups are very individual - we need to find the ones that work for us - and they may well be different from someone else's. But we will recognise them as the things that give us a boost. These can be as simple as drinking a glass of water, going for a walk or singing along to our favourite song.

The best power-ups are those that we can access easily and freely whenever we need them, things that we can choose when we need to feel a bit better or stronger. Once we have a collection, we will have a resource to help us to feel a little better no matter what we are facing.

Some of the power-ups identified by guardians who have played Superbetter for reactivity include:

- ☐ Watching our dog sniff
- ☐ Stroking our dog
- ☐ Eating blueberries (a superfood)
- ☐ Reading a post on our support forum
- ☐ A deep breathing meditation.

Power-ups are simple but powerful ways to boost the positive in your life. We aim to collect as many as we can and to activate at least three a day.

Battle bad guys

A key element of Superbetter is identifying and battling bad guys: the things that hold us back, that obstruct our progress, that limit our horizons, that darken our mood. Even just the process of naming them can start to loosen their hold over us. We feel better from doing this, even if we don't completely overcome them. Examples of bad guys that we face with our reactive dogs include the *Should Monster*, who shames us for what we are *not* doing by saying "You *should* be able to...", and *Paralysing Panic*, who stops us in our tracks and renders us incapable of responding as we want to a tricky situation.

We can adopt various strategies to battle bad guys. We can avoid them by choosing to ignore them. We can use our strength and skills to resist them. We can adapt what we do to work around them. We can lessen their power by challenging them. Or we can ultimately find the benefit in them and turn them into a power-up. Battling bad guys, even if we don't always succeed, helps us to move forward towards our goal.

Connect with allies

In Superbetter, our allies are people who will help us to meet our goals in the game. They may help us by suggesting quests, activating power-ups with us, helping us with strategies to battle the bad guys and celebrating our Epic Wins. Allies will check in with us as we play, listen when we are finding things difficult, encourage us to keep playing and recognise our successes.

Anyone can be an ally as long as they are supportive of our aims. They don't need to know anything about Superbetter. We can recruit them simply by sharing our challenge and asking them to help. Getting friends and family on board as allies can make it easier for us to succeed.

Adopt a secret identity

One of the fun things about the Superbetter game is how it uses the concept of secret identities to create a little distance and refocus us on the strengths and qualities we need for the task at hand. A secret identity is a heroic alter ego that we can use through the game, an avatar that we adopt when playing. We can choose a superhero or heroic character that we identify with - or we can create our own.

When we are facing a challenge, it is easy to focus on the difficulty and think about our weaknesses and what might go wrong. But when we consciously remind ourselves of our strengths we are more successful, happier and, crucially, handle challenges more effectively. When we choose a secret identity that embodies the strengths and values that we need for the challenge, we start to focus on those strengths. It is a fun and playful way to keep our strengths at the front of our mind. And when we focus on them, we can draw on them more easily.

A secret identity also helps give perspective. It allows us to view challenges as if they were happening to someone else and to see things more objectively. This can really help us when we are dealing with things we find difficult: we can ask ourselves what would our alter ego do or say in that situation? We can choose any secret identity and we don't have to share it with anyone unless we want to. To decide on a secret identity, we need to think whom would we choose as our alter ego? What strengths and values do we want to draw on right now? What superhero would help us to focus on those strengths?

Secret identities that reactivity Superbetter players came up with recently include:

- Ariel the Gatekeeper of animals and courage (being brave in safeguarding her dog)
- Explorer Byrd and his dog Igloo (exploring alternative ways to do things)
- Lodestar, a superhero lighting the way for travellers (keeping the way safe for dogs and their humans)
- Aeriel any Styx - an anagram of Anxiety Slayer (beating fear of what might happen)
- Shell the Shielder (protecting her dog from danger).

Celebrate epic wins

An epic win is a special goal, something that moves us more than a single step forward and that constitutes a breakthrough moment or something measurable. It should be realistic and achievable but not trivial. We need to feel challenged to achieve it - perhaps needing new skills or strength - but it should also make us feel excited and energised, rather than burdened. It is a game, so it should be fun!

Completing an epic win builds our motivation and encourages us to move forward with new enthusiasm. When we achieve our epic win we realise what we are capable of and strive to do more. Epic wins are to be celebrated!

The reactivity adventures

When I first heard about Superbetter, I had already been using and teaching simple games to help with reactivity and Superbetter seemed like the natural next step. I was sure that we could apply the Superbetter concept to becoming 'superbetter' at handling reactivity! So I wrote a set of adventures, with daily quests, baddies to battle, and power-ups, to help us on our journey with our dogs.[15]

The adventures model our life with our reactive dog as a journey and cover:

- Fit for the Journey: Looking after the Traveller
- A Fit Travel Companion: Looking after my Dog
- Meeting other Travellers
- Travelling Safely
- Navigating the Unexpected
- The Road to Mastery

We have played it successfully in my online membership with great results. We have seen big changes in mindset and consequently significant progress towards our goals. And we have had a lot of fun!

So playing games is the key to changing from seeing our dog's reactivity as a threat to seeing it as a challenge. This in no way trivialises the seriousness of the problem you may be facing, but it will help you to change how you think and feel about that problem, so that you can start to find solutions rather than feeling overwhelmed.

But in addition to our thinking about the problem of reactivity, we need to address unhelpful patterns of thinking about ourselves. We will look at this in the next chapter.

---

[15] The reactivity adventures are available within the Confidence Game/Superbetter Challenge as part of the Canine Confidence Club subscription membership. http://www.canineconfidenceclub.com

Chapter Three

CHANGING HOW YOU THINK ABOUT YOURSELF

We have looked at the importance of adopting a challenge mindset with respect to our dog's reactivity but sometimes it is our thinking about ourselves that gets in our way and blocks us from following through effectively. We talk ourselves down and find ourselves mired in guilt about what we feel we *should* be doing or we feel helpless and become trapped in a feeling that we simply can't move forward with our dog. These negative patterns can prevent us making progress.

In this chapter, we look at our natural bias towards negativity and self-criticism and some of the ways we inadvertently put blocks in our own way. We will look at how we can remove those blocks and instead become our own inner coach, so that we stop sabotaging our own progress and build up our resilience.

OUR NEGATIVITY BIAS

It may not be any great surprise that our tendency as humans is towards negative thinking and language. We focus on what has gone wrong, what might go wrong, what we did wrong or what others did wrong.

This is another well-known biological response. Our brain reacts faster to negative things and they are more 'sticky'. Negative inputs are transferred into long-term memory faster than positive ones. Psychologist Rick Hanson describes it like this: "The brain is like

Velcro for negative experiences but Teflon for positive ones."[16] So we are hard-wired to overestimate threat and underestimate opportunity.

This is called the negativity bias and there is a good evolutionary reason for it. If you underestimated a threat in the days when that threat was likely to eat you, it could easily be the last thing you did. That rustle in the bush could be the wind or it could be a tiger – but you really don't want to get it wrong! Likewise if you overestimated the opportunities for finding resources such as food, you might not make enough effort. Sitting about waiting for food to land in your lap isn't a great survival strategy either! So this negativity bias worked very well for our hunter-gatherer ancestors, where the most important thing was surviving to pass on genes.

However, today, our focus is on having a good, healthy, enjoyable life and not merely surviving long enough to reproduce, so this bias towards negativity is less helpful to us.

In this chapter we look at how our negativity bias influences our thinking in ways that can trip us up and stop us moving forwards, and some techniques we can use to shift our focus.

But one general rule we can adopt to keep on top of our negativity bias is the Reality Check. Remember that the negativity bias is designed to keep us safe so negatives are not always bad. But also remember that we are hard-wired to overestimate the negative. So we need the Reality Check to make sure the threat is real.

When we think of something that worries or scares us, we can ask ourselves the following questions:

1. What is our worst-case scenario?
2. How likely is our worst-case scenario?
3. How would we handle our worst-case scenario?

---

[16] Hanson, R (2013) *Hardwiring Happiness*. London: Penguin

4.   Can we avoid our worst-case scenario?

5.   Can make our worst-case scenario less damaging?

Let's look at a couple of examples.

☐   **Scenario 1:** We worry that our dog-reactive dog will pull the lead out of our hands and get away. On occasions that a dog has approached ours, our dog has chased but not harmed them. The worst-case scenario is that our dog will chase another dog. Our dog is strong and we have trouble holding them when they lunge suddenly. So the worst-case scenario is quite likely to happen. In the event of our worst-case scenario we would retrieve our dog as quickly as possible with apologies to anyone whose dog has been concerned. We can improve our chances of avoiding our worst-case scenario by working on our dog's recall and attention to us around other dogs so that we are not reliant on the lead to keep them with us. This is a long-term strategy. We can make the worst-case scenario less damaging (and less likely) by attaching the lead to a strong hip belt or using a bungee connector to take some of the power out of our dog's lunging.

☐   **Scenario 2:** We worry that the police will seize our dog because of their behaviour. Our dog barks at people but has never made contact with them. The worst-case scenario is unthinkable. However the likelihood of this happening is very low. While theoretically possible under current legislation in the UK, it is highly unlikely to happen without a bite or injury to a human. If it did happen we would need legal advice from the best canine legal team and we can formulate a plan in advance if that helps us feel more secure. Our strategy for dealing with this threat is to manage our dog carefully, making sure that they are always on a long line and communicating to strangers that they do not bite. We can improve our chances by working on ways of refocusing them in challenging situations and we can make it less likely by training our dog to wear a muzzle and ensuring they are not able to get close to a person.

Many of the things we fear most may be very serious threats but highly unlikely to happen. While we cannot think our way out of feeling threatened, we can challenge our assumptions and acknowledge the influence of our negativity bias. When we do this we can often see a way through to reduce the risk or we may realise that the risk, though scary, is highly unlikely to happen. We can identify steps and precautions that we can take to make the thing we fear even less likely.

BELIEFS THAT HOLD US BACK

The way we operate in the world is governed by our beliefs. I'm not talking here about explicit beliefs that we might hold, such as political or religious beliefs. These will certainly influence what we do but we usually make conscious choices about these.

I'm talking about the beliefs that we adopt to explain the way our world works: beliefs about ourselves, about other people and about our dogs. They are often unconscious: the stories or explanations that we create from a young age to make sense of our world or to protect ourselves from having to face failure, pain or self-blame.

Sometimes they come from other people – parents, teachers, or other authority-figures in our lives. Sometimes they come from our social groups or societal norms. Sometimes they come through the repeated words of others. Sometimes they are created through our immature and incomplete reasoning as a child.

Some of these have been with us for many years and have been reinforced over and over. If we have been repeatedly told that we are no good at something, then we will often adopt that as a belief. If we hear people we respect expressing particular beliefs, we will

47

often adopt these without necessarily being explicitly aware of it.

We also adopt beliefs based on our experiences. We construct explanations to make sense of what we observe. We do this all the time: from how we think the physical world operates, to what we can and can't do, what our dogs can and can't do and why other people do what they do.

Sometimes our beliefs are realistic and constructive. They can empower us and help us make good decisions and move forward. Sometimes they can help protect us in situations of deep trauma. But often they are destructive and damaging and then they hold us back and can stop us even trying. These beliefs are known as limiting beliefs.

An example: sketching lost and found

A limiting belief I held growing up was 'Failure is bad'. I would never have expressed it in those terms but that belief nonetheless strongly influenced what I did. For years, I chose to do things that I was very sure I would be good at and walk away from things where I was not so sure. My limiting belief stopped me from trying.

It also robbed me of things that I enjoyed. As a child I loved to draw. I remember having a gallery around the walls of my primary school classroom, where I proudly displayed my charcoal sketches of animals. Then, aged 16, disaster struck. I failed my Art 'O' Level. I suspect it was the first significant failure in my life (remember I chose what I did carefully) and it devastated me. I stopped drawing. Clearly I was rubbish at it. I was not going to fail again.

It took decades before I started sketching again. By this time I had worked through my limiting beliefs and realised that, far from being bad, failure is a great way to learn, that getting things wrong often teaches you more than getting things right. So I picked up my pencils again and drew for fun. It no longer mattered whether I was any good – whatever that meant – it only mattered that I enjoyed it.

INNER CRITIC VS INNER COACH

The threat of our Inner Critic

If left unchecked our limiting beliefs can form an incessant, negative commentary on our appearance, our character, our abilities and our intelligence. This voice tells us we are not good enough, that we don't deserve to succeed, that we are stupid or incapable, that someone else would be better for our dog than we are. This is the voice of our Inner Critic.

Most of us are familiar with this voice. We only have to look in the mirror to start to hear its critical words. *You've put on weight. Why are you wearing that? You're looking tired. You should do something about your hair.*

But it doesn't limit itself to our appearance. It will criticise our efforts. It will berate us for failing to reach its exacting standards. It will tell us that we are not good enough, not as good as our friend or our colleague or the person we see in the park.

Our Inner Critic reminds us of our limiting beliefs and makes them devastatingly personal. You are rubbish. You are a failure. You will never be able to do that.

A telltale sign that we are hearing our Inner Critic is when we use words about ourselves that define us rather than describe our behaviour. Words like: I can't/can only; I never/always; I am/am not.

These words make things personal. They are not about what we do, but about who we are. They are not about a particular situation or incident. They are absolutes that define us. They are designed to make us feel bad about ourselves.

We may think that words don't matter that much. Or even that it is good for us to be self-critical. But there is a world of difference between critiquing what we *do*, which can be constructive and positive, and dismissing who we *are*.

What we believe about ourselves matters. For example, there are studies that have shown that:

☐   Making a person think about their daily work as 'exercise' leads to actual weight loss and reduction in blood pressure, without any change to the work done.[17]

☐   Giving someone a 'fake' knee operation can be as effective as a real one, if they believe they have had the real one.[18]

☐   Having a positive perception of ageing actually makes you live longer.[19]

☐   Teaching children that being 'smart' is not a fixed characteristic but an attitude can radically improve their performance and results.[20]

What we believe about ourselves can make us try harder and push on through challenges. It can set our expectations, which determine so much of what we experience, including things that you would imagine would be entirely based on physical elements such as fitness, visual acuity and fatigue. It can even change our brain chemistry and circuitry, determining which neurotransmitters are released and, ultimately, which neural pathways are strengthened.

So when we listen to our Inner Critic we are cultivating that negative, threat mindset again. We are making ourselves less powerful, less able to cope.

---

[17] Crum, AJ and Langer, EJ (2007) *Mind-set matters: exercise and the placebo effect.* Psychol. Sci. 18(2): 165-71.
[18] Moseley JB, O'Malley K, Petersen NJ, et al. (2002) *A controlled trial of arthroscopic surgery for osteoarthritis of the knee.* N Engl J Med. 347(2): 81–8.
[19] Levy BR, Slade MD, Kunkel SR, Kasl SV (2002) *Longevity increased by positive self-perceptions of aging.* J Pers Soc Psychol. 83(2): 261-70.
[20] Yeager DS, Dweck CS (2012) *Mindsets That Promote Resilience: When Students Believe That Personal Characteristics Can Be Developed.* Educational Psychologist. 47(2): 302-314.

Cultivating our Inner Coach

Our Inner Critic comes with the territory of being human, of having a negativity bias. But we do not have to accept its destructive narrative. We can instead cultivate an Inner Coach, who is constructive, builds us up and helps us move forward. We can make choices that allow us to hear our Inner Coach's voice over the Inner Critic.

Our Inner Coach has a very different agenda from our Inner Critic, an agenda concerned with us reaching our potential and being the best that we can be. Rather than seeking an unachievable perfection, our Inner Coach recognises that excellence does not mean never making mistakes and sees things going wrong as opportunities for learning.

When we mess up, our Inner Coach will say "Perhaps not your finest hour" and not "You are so stupid". When something doesn't go as planned, they will say, "That didn't work" rather than "You always fail". When we make a mistake, they will say "What can we learn from that?" and never "You are useless".

There are steps that we can take to cultivate our Inner Coach and banish our Inner Critic.

1. Challenge the Critic

Our Inner Critic will highlight our limiting beliefs and personalise them. So we have to deal with them head on: challenge them and then replace them. Until we actually shift these beliefs, they will keep influencing what we do.

We can start by examining what is going on. Whose voice is speaking? Is it our voice or that of someone else from our past or our imagination? Is our life or our dog's life enhanced by this belief? How well does this belief serve us?

Go back to the evidence. Ask yourself:

☐ What evidence is there to support that?

☐   What evidence is there that the opposite is true?

☐   What would I say to someone I loved who said that about themselves?

When we challenge the truth of our limiting beliefs we can start to dislodge them and quieten our Inner Critic.

2. Gather evidence

Our Critic hates evidence because evidence brings down absolutes. But sometimes, at first glance, we may feel the evidence is supporting what the Critic says. Our negativity bias can lead us to focus on the negative things that happen. So if our Inner Critic is telling us we are useless at managing our dog, and we have a walk where our dog reacts to another dog, the chances are we will naturally focus on that one incident. Instead we can choose to remember the four dogs we passed calmly, and store them up as evidence to defend ourselves against the Critic. If you are unconvinced take a sheet of paper and draw a line down the middle. On one side, make a list of the evidence that seem to support the negative thinking. On the other make a list of all the evidence that is against it. Which list is longer? Keep gathering that evidence.

We can also refute an absolute assertion, such as 'you never', with a single example that contradicts it. So when you find yourself saying, "I *can't* do…." something, challenge yourself to do that thing, just a little. When you find yourself saying, "I *should* do…" something, see what happens if you don't, just this once. Every small win we have is evidence to use to defend ourselves against the Inner Critic.

3. Change our language

Make sure that the words you use are those of your Inner Coach and not your Inner Critic. If you want to develop a positive mindset about yourself and your dog, talk about yourself and your dog in positive terms, both to others and to yourself. Surround yourself with people who will encourage you rather than those who insist on talking to you in negative terms.

Words matter. They reinforce our thinking and determine which voice we hear most clearly: our Inner Coach or our Inner Critic. We will discuss this in more detail in the next chapter.

4. Admit the possibility

When your Inner Critic says 'You can't' or berates you because your dog 'can't cope with' something, reframe the statement. Replace "I can't" with "I haven't …yet". This simple tool, suggested by psychology professor, Carol Dweck[21], shifts us from feeling that we have no power to change things, to feeling that there are possibilities.

- ☐ "I haven't enjoyed a trip to the park with my dog…yet!"
- ☐ "I haven't kept my hands relaxed on the lead…yet!".
- ☐ "I haven't stopped feeling anxious about going out with my dog…yet!"

Try it. Replacing the negative *can't* with the much more factual *haven't* and adding that simple word *yet* becomes a way to turn your Inner Critic into your Inner Coach because it shifts your entire focus from the impossible to the possible. It turns a fixed and immovable negative into a possible future that we can work towards.

Once we have made that shift we can start to work out how we will make the 'yet' a reality. But it begins with the shift in focus that 'yet' gives us.

5. Embrace imperfection

Our Inner Critic thrives on perfectionism and uses it to chip away

---

[21] Dweck, C (2014) The power of believing you can improve. TED Talk
https://www.ted.com/talks/carol_dweck_the_power_of_believing_that_you_ca
n_improve

at our confidence. But nothing and no one is perfect. We are all imperfect members of the human race. Mistakes are normal and allow us to learn.

This is easy to assert and less easy to feel deep down. Whether it is working with our dogs or addressing our own struggles with reactivity, we may know in our heads that it doesn't have to be perfect, that mistakes are part of being human, that things need practice and repetition before we get them as we want them, but we may still feel pretty rubbish about it when things don't go to plan.

But we can still make that assertion. Making that assertion is the first step to accepting its truth. When we focus on the things that have gone wrong or that were not as good as we had hoped, we are giving power to our Inner Critic. When we make the assertion that we did our best, that we are OK, that we are imperfect but learning, we are empowering our Inner Coach.

The secret lies in the choices we make about where and how we direct our attention. We can consciously choose to focus on the possibility and learning in any situation. We can choose to examine all the evidence rather than simply accepting the negative side, which we naturally tend to believe. We can choose to be as kind and encouraging to ourselves, as we would be to a friend going through the same experience.

We may not be able to do it perfectly and that is OK too. Elizabeth Gilbert, author of the best seller *Eat, Pray, Love*, says, "As long as you're still here, you're still a student."[22] Being a student frees us from always getting it right. It only requires that we are open to learning.

6. Reframe your fears as challenges
Our Inner Critic uses our fears to hold us back. *"What if..."* the

---

[22] Gilbert, E (2017) *Test everything against love.* Presentation at the Self-Acceptance Summit, September 11th 2017, Sounds True.

Critic whispers in our ear. What if... it all goes wrong? What if... they react? What if... people stare at us? What if... they hurt someone? What if... someone hurts them?

Fear of 'what if' can stop us doing the things we would like to do. They can interrupt our efforts to move forward. They can suck our energy so we no longer have the heart to try. But worrying about 'what ifs' is unproductive. We will never make something less likely to happen by worrying about it.

Our Inner Coach takes a different approach. The Coach recognises our fears but reframes them as challenges, turning 'what ifs' into 'what cans'.

- ☐ What if... they react? What can I do to make that less likely?
- ☐ What if... people stare at us? What can I do to make that matter less?
- ☐ What if... they hurt someone? What can I do to make sure that can't happen?
- ☐ What if... someone hurts them? What can I do to protect them as much as is possible?
- ☐ What if... it all goes wrong? What can I do to take control so it doesn't?

This reframing leads us to practical solutions. We can look for more space or work on alternative responses to triggers. We can reframe how we respond to other people. We can muzzle train our dog or use a long line. We can learn to use barriers and ensure we engage other owners to get them on side. We can practise so that we become more and more competent.

These are of course simply examples. The actual solutions matter less than the reframing: you will choose the solutions that work for you and your dog in your context. But the key is to start by listening to your Inner Coach and turning each 'What if...?' into a 'What can I do...?' This reframing will make all the difference.

Instead of feeling helpless and worried, you are empowered to take action on your next challenge.

THE TYRANNY OF SHOULD

There is one category of limiting beliefs that deserves special mention. We think they are ours but they actually belong to someone else: for example, a parent, a community, a leader or a friend. They are easy to spot as they include the word 'should', which often indicates that we are taking on beliefs from someone else. Some of these may be things we aspire to but others may limit our progress and bring additional stress.

Our Inner Critic loves 'shoulds' and uses them to make us belittle our accomplishments and feel inadequate and small. 'Should' encourages comparison with others and tell us that there is an established standard out there that we are not meeting.

Consider the way you talk and think about your dog's behaviour and what you want to change. How many times does the word 'should' feature? You know the sort of thing:

- ☐ My dog should play with other dogs.
- ☐ My dog should have off-lead running every day.
- ☐ My dog should be able to be touched by strangers.
- ☐ My dog should ignore other dogs on walks.
- ☐ My dog should focus on me on walks.
- ☐ My dog should be walked for several hours a day.

You will probably find several about yourself as well:

- ☐ I should walk my dog every day.
- ☐ I should be able to train my dog not to be reactive.
- ☐ I should be able to take my dog everywhere.
- ☐ I should be able to let dogs/people approach my dog.
- ☐ I should be able to walk all my dogs together.
- ☐ I should be able to let my dog off the lead in public.
- ☐ I should take my dog to training classes.

Example: Joanne and Fly

Fly was a rescue greyhound who had always been afraid of other dogs. On the day Joanne took him home from the shelter he threw himself to the end of his lead and screamed like a banshee when he saw a dog across the playing field. Joanne was shocked but was determined to help him. With hard work over several years she and Fly got to the point where he could walk calmly past another dog and lie next to her without reacting if one approached. I was impressed and congratulated her on her progress. But Joanne still felt a complete failure: "Fly should be able to play in the park with other dogs", she told me. When we explored where this 'should' came from, she realised that it was the voice of her friends who had more social dogs. Joanne herself was happy with Fly ignoring other dogs.

The good news about 'shoulds' is that, coming from outside, they are relatively straightforward to reframe. They do not have the same emotional power over us as some other limiting beliefs.

If you find yourself saying you should do something or your dog should be a particular way, activate your Inner Coach. Ask yourself:

- ☐ Where does the belief come from? Is it based on facts?
- ☐ Whose voice is saying these words? Is it mine? Or is it my trainer, the bloke down the pub or some random person on Facebook?
- ☐ How important is it to me? What would happen if I didn't do it?
- ☐ How important is it to my dog? Would it make their life more fulfilled?

Unless you find that it is evidence-based and that you believe it would help you and your dog, you are at liberty to dismiss it. This doesn't have to be confrontational. Others may believe this or find it helpful, but you have assessed it as not being important for you.

Where you do find evidence, or where it represents something you want, then reframe it. Rather than using the word 'should', which suggests obligation rather than choice, use 'want' or 'choose' or 'am working on'. I want to walk my dog off the lead. I choose to walk my dog three times a day. I am working on taking my dog everywhere. That shifts you from being driven by the requirements of other people, to making a conscious decision that something is important to you.

NURTURING OUR RESILIENCE

Challenging our Inner Critic and cultivating our Inner Coach will significantly help to reduce the stress that we experience, but we will never avoid stress altogether. Resilience is our ability to handle the stress that life brings. The more resilient we are, the less we will be affected by things that happen to us and the more we will be able to adopt a challenge mindset in the face of difficulty.

But what makes us resilient? Is it something that we either have or don't have, or can it be developed?

Vagal tone is key

It turns out that our resilience is directly related to our physiology. Remember the vagus nerve that we met in Chapter 1? Through research going back decades, Dr. Stephen Porges has identified that the health of our vagus nerve is a key indicator of our ability to deal with stress.[23] The good news is that we can make our vagus nerve stronger. So if our resilience is currently low, we can indeed nurture it and build it up.

Having a healthy vagus nerve is known as having high vagal tone and it is this that has been measured and correlated to how well our

---

[23] For example, Porges, S (1995) *Cardiac Vagal Tone: A Physiological Index of Stress.* Neuroscience and Biobehavioural Reviews, 19(2): 225-233 and Porges, S (2017) *The Pocket Guide to The Polyvagal Theory*, NY: Norton.

bodies deal with stress. High vagal tone is not only associated with resilience but with healthy heart and lungs, strong immunity, good memory and the capacity to build strong relationships.

Vagal tone is so important that doctors are using electrical stimulation of the vagus nerve to treat depression, chronic pain and epilepsy. We, of course, can't stimulate our vagus nerve directly but it turns out that there are things that we can do that will exercise it naturally over time. Remember all the places our vagus nerve passes through on its wanderings? Simple actions in these areas of the body can activate the function of the vagus nerve and improve vagal tone.

Here are five of the many simple things that we can do to help:

1. **Slow our breathing.** Slowing the breathing stimulates the vagus nerve. One way to do this is Box Breathing, a simple deep breathing approach used by the US Navy Seals. Start with a long exhale to empty the lungs, then breath in deeply through the nose to a slow count of four, hold your breath to a count of four, breath out slowly and noisily through the mouth to a count of four, hold for a count of four. Imagine that you are breathing around a square or a 'box'. Repeat several times.

2. **Embrace cold.** Cold stimulates the parasympathetic nervous system and activates the vagus nerve. Splashing cold water on your face, drinking ice cold water, taking a cold shower or, if you are brave, swimming in a winter sea can all help!

3. **Have a foot massage.** Working the feet in a Reflexology massage reduces the sympathetic nervous system response, activates the parasympathetic nervous system and so increases vagus nerve activity.

4. **Take Probiotics.** Probiotics have been shown to produce positive changes in the brain in animals, leading to reduced

anxiety.[24] This is mediated by the vagus nerve, which connects gut to brain. It is therefore likely that probiotics will have a similarly positive effect on us.

5. **Sing, Chant, Hum or Gargle.** The vagus nerve passes through the vocal cords and the muscles at the back of the throat so anything that engages these muscles can help to stimulate it. Singing, chanting, humming and gargling all produce the vibrations necessary to spring the vagus nerve into action.

Vagal Tone and the Positivity Ratio

So we can help promote a healthy vagus nerve through exercising it but there is more. Professor Barbara Fredrickson and colleagues have shown that the ratio of positive emotional experiences that we have is a strong predictor of high vagal tone and, most importantly, that this also applies in reverse.[25] What does this mean? It means that we can improve the health of our vagus nerve by ensuring that we have a high ratio of positive to negative experiences. And since high vagal tone correlates to our resilience, a high ratio of positive to negative emotional experiences will also increase our resilience.

These positive experiences don't have be huge things; in fact lots of smaller things are more effective than one big one. Quantity definitely trumps size! Plus it is ratio that matters: we are not looking to eliminate the negative, just to increase the proportion of positive to negative. This is great news as it gives us a practical way

---

[24] Wang, H, Lee, IS, Braun, C, & Enck, P (2016) *Effect of Probiotics on Central Nervous System Functions in Animals and Humans: A Systematic Review.* Journal of Neurogastroenterology and Motility, *22*(4): 589–605.

[25] Fredrickson, BL (2013) *Updated Thinking on Positivity Ratios.* American Psychologist 68(9): 814-22.

Kok, BE, Coffey, KA, Cohn, MA, Catalino, LI, Vacharkulksemsek, T, Algoe, SB, Brantley, M, & Fredrickson, BL (2013) *How positive emotions build physical health: Perceived positive social connections account for the upward spiral between positive emotions and vagal tone.* Psychological Science, May 2013.

that we can nurture our resilience: we can increase the number of small positive emotional experiences that we have. And where have we come across small positive experiences before? Think back to the Superbetter game in the last chapter. Power-ups! To increase our resilience we can activate plenty of power-ups.

Remember power-ups are small positive things, that we can do easily and relatively quickly, that make us feel better, stronger, happier or more connected. They are perfect for boosting our positive to negative ratio! As we saw in the last chapter, power-ups are very individual. What works as a power-up for me, may not work for you. But this list of some of mine will give you ideas. Note that none of these things take much time or effort to do, so we can activate them at any time. This makes them very powerful.

- ☐ Drinking a glass of cold water
- ☐ Doing some exercise or moving around
- ☐ Singing (or dancing) along to my favourite song.
- ☐ Eating fruit or drinking a smoothie
- ☐ Playing with my dog
- ☐ Smiling at someone
- ☐ Laughing
- ☐ Getting outside in fresh air or the sun
- ☐ Reading something inspirational
- ☐ Cheering someone on.

This is just part of my list. Collect the power-ups that work for you. Write a list and put it somewhere you will see it, then choose a few to do each day. Write each one on a slip of paper and put these in a jar. Whenever you need a power-up (aim for at least three times a day) pull out a piece of paper and give your resilience a boost!

Savour these positive experiences. Remember our negativity bias? It is estimated that, while negative experiences are quickly stored in long-term memory, positive experiences need at least 12 seconds to get there. So make a point of savouring each and every positive experience. Write it down. Go over it in your mind. Note every detail. Share it with someone you trust. Develop a gratitude practice and be thankful for each positive thing that happens.

Spending time deliberately focusing on the good things that happen helps us to remember. Positive experiences have a natural disadvantage in the memorability stakes, so do what you can to make them stick and make sure they count towards your positivity ratio.

SELF-COMPASSION AND SELF-CARE

So we have looked at how challenge our Inner Critic and cultivate our Inner Coach, how to reframe 'shoulds' and build and nurture our resilience. But there is one more area we need to look at that is key to changing how we think about ourselves: self-compassion.

My guess is that everyone reading this book is an animal lover. You are committed to kind and fair treatment of animals. You are upset by reports of animal cruelty. You encourage others to treat their animals with gentleness and compassion. You are patient with your dog's learning and reinforce generously the things they get right. And that is all exactly as it should be. But how much do you show the same compassion to yourself?

The truth is we expect extremely high standards of ourselves but often fail to give ourselves time to learn and practise. If we make a mistake, we give ourselves a hard time and never let it go. When we get something right, we dismiss it: it was just a fluke or it was the least we should expect so not noteworthy. When we receive a compliment on something we have achieved, we brush it off as someone 'just being nice'. Yet, of course, when we hear criticism, we take it into ourselves, pore over it and treat it as fact.

Just for a moment, imagine a person who treated their dog this way. Punishing mistakes. Refusing to reinforce success. Giving no space to learn. Nagging and criticising. It would be hard to watch wouldn't it?

Yet many of us treat ourselves like this every day.

Self-compassion is often difficult for many of us to 'feel'. We can have almost impossible expectations of ourselves. We face constant nagging from our Inner Critic and find it hard to believe our Inner Coach.

But self-compassion is not primarily about feeling, it is about action. It is practical rather than theoretical or emotional. We can practise self-compassion through committing to active self-care.

Self-care is not an optional extra or only for the 'touchy-feely' types. It is not selfishness. It is not a one-off thing that we'll do if it ever reaches the top of our 'to do' list. It is not ticking off a few 'good for us' things off that list and considering it done. It is not even doing fun things to spoil ourselves like having an occasional bubble bath or getting a massage every now and then. Those things could be part of self-care but when we think of self-care only in those terms, we trivialise it.

Self-care is choosing to give ourselves whatever we need to feel energised and restored. It is choosing to prioritise our power-ups as well as making sure that we do more substantial things to help ourselves thrive. It is essential not only to our own well-being but to our ability to care for others, including our dogs. We have to 'fit our own oxygen mask' before we try to help someone else.

Think of what you can do for yourself that makes you feel really positive. What increases rather than drains your energy? What leaves you feeling fitter and more alive? Build this kind of conscious self-care into every day until it becomes a habit.

Some areas of self-care to consider:

- Health and well-being: Are you eating food that gives you energy and makes you feel well? Are you drinking enough fluids to keep you hydrated? Are you getting appropriate exercise? Are receiving appropriate treatment for any health issues? Would you benefit from seeing any other health professionals? Are you protecting your mental health?

☐ Rest and relaxation: Are you getting enough sleep and does it leave you rested? Do you have enough down time? What do you do to relax? Do you practise mindfulness or meditation or another practice that helps you be present? Are you taking regular breaks from technology, social media and work?

☐ Work-life balance: Do you have a healthy work-life balance? Do you make time for interests outside work? Do you have a hobby? Is your work enjoyable and satisfying? Can you improve on this?

☐ Social interaction: Do you spend enough time with friends and family, including canine family? Do you interact with people every day? Do you have an active support network? Do you also give yourself the attention that you need? Do you take time out to relax with those you love?

☐ Self-compassion: Do you build yourself up or knock yourself down? Do you take time to learn, to read or listen to new ideas? Do you forgive yourself when you mess up?

☐ Environment: Is your living environment enabling you to think and rest and relax? Do you have spaces where you can unwind and take time out amid the bustle of daily life?

Remember our power-ups? A good way to begin to integrate self-care into your daily life is through daily power-ups. They are manageable and don't take up much time but they can make a huge difference to our experience. Why not start by making your own list of small, easy-to-do power-ups and aim to activate at least three every day.

Self-compassion on bad days

We all have bad days. Days when nothing goes as planned. When we have a fight with a loved one. When we've had a tough day at work. When we are in pain. When all hell breaks loose on a walk. When we don't get enough sleep. When we get frustrated.

And when these things build up, we make mistakes. We forget what we know. We take risks we wouldn't normally take. We lose our temper.

It is when we have days like this that we are tempted to forget self-compassion and start giving ourselves a hard time. But this is exactly when it is important that we remember to be kind to ourselves.

We need to cut ourselves some slack. Making mistakes, getting things wrong, reacting out of fear, pain, exhaustion and stress, dealing with our life experiences – all of this is part of who we are. Our tendency is to deny it, to bury it, or to beat ourselves up over it. The image of the perfect guardian with beautifully behaved dogs is all around us in the closely-edited and managed world of social media but it is a myth that helps no one. We can even use the 'only positive reinforcement training' mantra as a stick to beat ourselves with. How can we call ourselves 'positive' when we just lost our rag and yelled at our dog?

But being a positive trainer or guardian does not mean we get it right all the time. It does not mean we never lose our temper and never get frustrated with our dogs. It does not mean we won't sometimes feel we are too exhausted to continue.

What it means is that we are committed to finding ways to help our dog that respect their being, that seek their best, that do not use fear and pain in the name of training. It means that we will do the best that we know how to do, within the physical, emotional and mental resources that we have. Sometimes it means we will be willing to work through our own demons so that we are able to help our dogs and ourselves heal.

So instead of berating ourselves, why not ask what we would say to a friend who was feeling this way? Would we be berating her?

Of course we wouldn't. We would be offering support, seeing if there was anything we could do to help, even if just making a cup of tea. We would be reminding her that it was just one day. That she is still making progress. That she has not ruined everything. We would be giving her permission to take things a little easier. To make time to recharge her batteries. To take a break.

Treating ourselves as we would a valued friend is really what self-care is all about.

Feeling safe

As we have seen, safety is a fundamental need of all of us. It is not good for us to spend our life anticipating harm or hurt at every turn. It is healthy to be aware of risk but not to expect bad things to happen all the time.

Trauma can, of course, change that in an instant. When something traumatic happens, suddenly the premise that our world is fundamentally safe is shattered and we may feel unsafe all the time. This is part of post-traumatic stress.

I have no doubt that some dog guardians experience this. Those who have witnessed their dog being attacked, or who have seen their dog do something that shocks them or puts them at serious risk, often experience the flashbacks and panic attacks associated with post-traumatic stress.

But, even where this is not the case, most of us have some fear of what might happen. We have already looked at the role of our negativity bias in how we perceive threats and how a Reality Check can help us get perspective on our worries.

But sometimes we have good reason to feel unsafe with our dogs. Our Reality Check has shown that there is a good chance that something will go wrong or we feel that our fear is affecting the progress we can make.

It is important for our own well-being that we don't ignore this. Self-compassion leads us to safeguard our own safety.

This might mean involving other people, such as professionals, to help us restore a safe environment, or allies who can help us with practicalities to help us feel safer. It might mean changing the context to scaffold our own safety or that of others. It might mean working out a plan to avoid certain triggers until we can address the issue in another way.

If you are avoiding something or fearful about what might happen, then think about what you can do to make yourself feel safer.

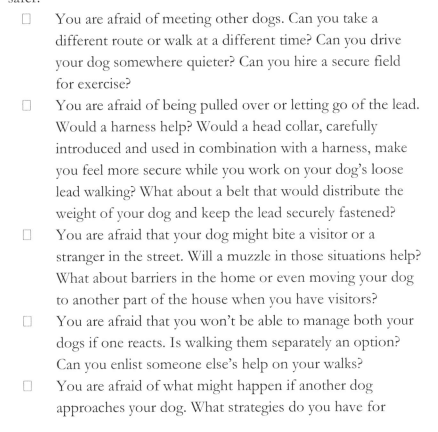

- [ ] You are afraid of meeting other dogs. Can you take a different route or walk at a different time? Can you drive your dog somewhere quieter? Can you hire a secure field for exercise?
- [ ] You are afraid of being pulled over or letting go of the lead. Would a harness help? Would a head collar, carefully introduced and used in combination with a harness, make you feel more secure while you work on your dog's loose lead walking? What about a belt that would distribute the weight of your dog and keep the lead securely fastened?
- [ ] You are afraid that your dog might bite a visitor or a stranger in the street. Will a muzzle in those situations help? What about barriers in the home or even moving your dog to another part of the house when you have visitors?
- [ ] You are afraid that you won't be able to manage both your dogs if one reacts. Is walking them separately an option? Can you enlist someone else's help on your walks?
- [ ] You are afraid of what might happen if another dog approaches your dog. What strategies do you have for

making a quick getaway or for blocking and distracting an approaching dog? We will look at this more in Chapter 5.

☐ You are afraid that your dog might bite you. Do you have a safe way to handle him? Are you aware of his signs of concern and any triggers? Can you keep everyone in the house safe, particularly the most vulnerable?

Don't dismiss your own need to feel safe any more than you would ignore your dog's need. Remember that our (and their) nervous system is monitoring how safe those around us feel as it evaluates our own threat level. You will not be able to help your dog until you feel safe yourself. Taking these measures now does not mean you have to take them forever. It simply means that you are creating a safe space where you both can learn.

Once *you* feel safe, you can start to focus on the needs of your dog. We will look at these in the next chapter.

Chapter Four

CHANGING HOW YOU THINK ABOUT YOUR DOG

In the last chapter we looked at how we could think differently about ourselves and shift from a negative, threat-based mindset to a more positive challenge mindset. We met our Inner Critic and our Inner Coach and we learned how we could boost our resilience and take better care of ourselves.

But our negative thinking goes beyond how we view ourselves. It also affects how we view our dog. We may have limiting beliefs about what our dog is capable of and we may be finding it hard to see the positive beyond their challenging behaviour.

Now don't get me wrong. I know that you adore your dog. You wouldn't be reading a book like this if you didn't. This isn't about how much you care. But if you didn't have some negative thinking about your dog, you probably wouldn't be reading this book either. You wouldn't need to.

The reality is that when our dog is reactive or fearful, most of us do feel frustration or exasperation or disappointment and some of that is directed towards our dog.

Let me reassure you right now. It is normal to love our dog more than anything and still be exasperated by their behaviour. It is normal to go from laughing at their antics to feeling desperate, wishing everyone else could see what we do. It is normal to feel that we can't imagine them not being in our life, while sometimes hankering after the life we might have without them.

All of this is perfectly human. Life is messy. We may want it all to be clear-cut and black and white but it rarely is. We can feel grief and joy in the same moment. We can experience desperation and hope.

The truth is that our reactive or fearful or over-exuberant dog is challenging for us and it would be surprising if we didn't have some negative thoughts about them at some point. We may also have beliefs about them that are limiting our progress, in much the same way as we have limiting beliefs about ourselves. We may be perpetuating these beliefs by the words that we use and the way that we interpret their behaviour.

However, when we look more closely at what is going on with our dog, when we learn how to observe what is actually happening rather than what we think is happening, when we understand what contributes to those challenging behaviours, we will see that we do not have a problem dog. We have a dog who has a problem and we can help them.

Changing how we think about our dog changes how we speak about them and how we interpret what they do. This helps us be more effective in helping them change their behaviour.

LIMITING BELIEFS ABOUT OUR DOGS

In Chapter 3 we learned about limiting beliefs, the faulty thinking that holds us back from making the progress we are capable of making. We learned how our Inner Critic uses these beliefs to undermine our confidence and stop us trying.

Many of these limiting beliefs are about us and what we are capable of but we may also have limiting beliefs about our dogs. These are beliefs about what they can and can't do or what they should or shouldn't do, that constrain how we work with them and the choices we make for them.

Just as with limiting beliefs about ourselves, we can often spot these beliefs about our dogs by the words we use: they can't, they can only, they never, they should, they shouldn't.

Limiting beliefs about your dog do not have to be huge to hold you back and they can grow so easily out of just one or two negative experiences.

Martha the travelling dog

To illustrate, let me tell you about Martha. Martha arrived a few years ago at four years old. She was seriously sick on the journey home. Next time we tried to get her in the car, she slunk away from it, frightened to even approach. At the time, we lived on a small farm and had walks from the door, so it was rarely necessary for Martha to travel. Car travel for Martha wasn't a priority for me to sort out and gradually "Martha needs to learn to enjoy travelling" became "Martha hates the car and can't travel" in my mind. It was always a limiting belief. It meant that Martha never came on trips or went far from home but for a long time it did not concern me too much. She was happy at home.

Then our circumstances changed and it became clear that 'Martha travelling' would be a necessity. Initially I felt desperate. She can't travel. She hates the car. What was I going to do?

By necessity, I started working to help her be more comfortable with the car, feeding her closer and closer, until she would jump in and out of it happily while stationary. Then we started short trips – just two or three minutes followed by a walk – yet she was still sick. I installed a large memory foam cushion, which seemed to help a little. Over several months we gradually built up the journeys, through very careful short trips, until she managed a couple of longer rides without any sickness. However, I still saw this as luck rather than progress. I still believed Martha hated the car and would always be sick so taking her out was still a negative thing in my mind.

Then we had another breakthrough. I had booked her into a

workshop, mainly because I didn't want to leave her home alone. It was an hour away, mostly on the motorway, and she was not sick on the way. She got in and out of the car throughout the day, as she took turns to work and then to rest. Each time she happily jumped back in and she rested quietly and comfortably in the car. She did bring up her sausage treats, a quarter of a mile from home, as we hit the local, windy, bumpy roads but overall it was beyond my expectations.

I realised I had been holding us both back with my beliefs about Martha and the car. The evidence told a different story.

Martha clearly did not hate the car. She could be comfortable hanging out in the car and would jump in and out willingly. She was not always car sick. She could get car sick when she had eaten lots of treats and the roads were windy.

Challenging my beliefs just a little took me to a new place. A place where we needed to think about timing of her meals and treats and about the routes we took and the way we drove, rather than not travelling at all. A place where the car could be a safe space for Martha. Ultimately, a place where Martha's opportunities for trips and activities were hugely expanded.

I realised, as I was working through this, that I had bought into a limiting belief: Martha can't travel. Martha having concerns about travelling had become Martha will *always* have concerns about travelling and, therefore, Martha *can't* travel. So I stopped working on it for a while.

Martha now travels happily in the car several times every week. Recently we completed a 1,000-mile road trip in a camper van and Martha took it all in her stride. Next we are planning to drive around the entire coast of Britain. *Martha can't* has definitely become *Martha can and does*!

Limiting beliefs about our dogs can come from many sources. They may, like mine about Martha, develop on the back of negative or traumatic experiences. They may come from our expectations and past experiences. We may compare our dog to past companions and develop a limiting belief about our dog not being able to do something, when in fact they are simply different. We may have expectations about what dogs should and should not do, or what a particular breed is or is not like, and these become embedded in our thinking as limiting beliefs.

We may also develop limiting beliefs based on the expectations and beliefs of others: trainers, family and friends, strangers in the park and, of course, the internet! A dog who does not want to play with other dogs or be handled by perfect strangers must be anti-social. A dog who does not behave perfectly in every situation must be badly trained. A terrier/sighthound/livestock guardian/husky (delete as appropriate) cannot be reliably trained. A rescue dog is going to find life difficult.

In all these keep an eye out for *can't* and *should* and *must* – and for absolute statements and generalisations. If you are not sure if you have limiting beliefs about your dog consider the following questions. Examine your immediate reactions. Do any of these hold you and your dog back from making the progress you want to make? If so, you may have uncovered a limiting belief.

- ☐ Do you feel your dog should be able to play with other dogs or meet unknown people?
- ☐ Do you think you'll never be able to enjoy a walk on the beach with your dog or go to the pub together?
- ☐ Do you expect your dog to behave in a particular way because they're large... or small... or a terrier... or a particular breed... or a rescue?
- ☐ Do you think your dog is difficult to train?
- ☐ Do you think your dog is stubborn or dominant or naughty?

☐   Do you think your dog's past limits their future?

☐   Do you tell a story about your dog that defines them in a constraining way?

The way we address limiting beliefs about our dogs is similar to how we dealt with those we held about ourselves. We challenge the belief and gather evidence to refute it. We ask what is actually going on? We address our language to make sure we are not inadvertently reinforcing the belief and we work towards what we want.

In the rest of this chapter we will look at how to get a detailed rather than a limited picture of what is going on with our dog. We will find evidence through careful observation, which focuses on what we actually see and not what we think we see. We will examine how we speak about our dogs and look at how we can use more positive language. We will explore the many factors that can contribute to our dog's reactivity and learn how changing any one of them can help us to make progress towards our goals. Let's get started.

DEVELOPING YOUR OBSERVATIONAL SKILLS

Observation vs. history

Evidence is key to dispelling limiting beliefs and when it comes to our dogs, the most reliable evidence comes from observing them and what they do. Ideally we will listen and respond to the dog in front of us and observe their body language and behaviour, without complicating matters with our interpretations, at least initially.

This is harder than you might imagine. We always want to interpret the behaviour we see. Their tail is wagging; therefore they are friendly. They hesitate to approach; therefore they 'don't like' someone. They won't go down a particular path; therefore they are stubborn. They flinch away from hands over the head; therefore they have been beaten.

Some of these interpretations may, of course, be true, but jumping to interpretation without more evidence can mean that we miss important information. Making assumptions based on what we think we know, including from our dog's history, can lead us to misinterpret what we see.

Does this mean that our dog's history is irrelevant? Of course not. Learning history and experiences, genetics and breed characteristics, as well as medical and care history are all important but we do not always have accurate information and these elements do not always play out the way we expect.

We can't know for certain the reasons for specific fears or behaviours, or whether they are the result of particular experiences. We can speculate about this of course – and it can be interesting to us to do so – but if we start to rely on the stories we construct, and believe them to be truth, it can start to limit our expectations of our dog.

For me, history, where we have it, is part of the observation process. It gives me clues about what might be going on. It highlights potential physical issues and gives me an idea of what training methods have been used and how. It tells me what the dog's routine is like and whether pain or discomfort is likely to be a factor.

However, it is only part of the process. Very often, when I meet a dog, they present quite differently to what I am expecting based on the history. This is not because they have been misrepresented in any way. It is simply because dogs vary from day to day and from context to context and because, when you live with a dog, your perspective can sometimes be very different to that of someone coming in and observing through a different lens.

So while history can give us important information, we need to handle it with care and remember that the dog in front of us is not defined by their history, nor does it necessarily limit their future.

Just because our dog has experienced trauma, their potential for recovery is not necessarily limited. Just because our dog responded in one way in the past, does not mean they cannot behave differently in the future.

Let's look at a common example: a dog who flinches when you reach towards them. It is easy to assume that the dog has been hit. We might think that the hand coming towards them reminds them of this and they are getting out of the way or bracing themselves. We often hear people say, "He's *obviously* been hit", when they see this kind of behaviour. Yet it is not at all obvious and such assumptions can be very hurtful to caring guardians who have had their dogs from puppyhood and still see this behaviour.

There are several other possible explanations for this behaviour. Here are just three:

- It may be a startle response, much as we might jump away from something we see out of the corner of our eye. It can be a protective response to the unexpected.
- The hand may be associated with some other 'friendly' handling, such as being stroked on the head or picked up. If they are not keen on this, they may flinch when a hand approaches.
- They may be in pain and be avoiding contact.

The most important lesson about this is that when we make assumptions we can miss important information. So by assuming that our dog has been hit (in a former life perhaps) we miss the real cause for their behaviour: that our dog is startled by or uncomfortable with how we are approaching them. By making assumptions about what cannot be changed, we may not act on something that we can easily adjust to improve our dog's experience.

If we rely on searching our dog's history for answers we can also become perplexed. Perhaps we can find no obvious starting point.

We have had our dog from puppyhood. Our dog has not been treated differently from our other dogs, none of whom were reactive. They are the same breed and we raised and educated them in the same way. We know they have never been traumatised or had a bad experience, and so we start to doubt ourselves.

How we raise our dogs is important but it is only part of the story. We always need to remember we are living with individuals. They don't all see the world in the same way and they vary in their personality and resilience. We can do what we can to stack the odds in their favour but some dogs will still find things difficult.

So by all means think through your dog's history to glean what you can from it, but don't get hung up on it. It is just one part of what you can observe about your dog. If you don't know your dog's history, or can't pinpoint any 'cause' for your dog's reactivity, be reassured by this. We do not need to know a dog's history to be able to help that dog. We only need to learn how to observe what they are telling us now. All the history we need is there in our dog's behaviour if we learn to see it.

So focus on what you can observe. What is your dog doing? How are they holding their head, their ears, their tail? What is their posture? What communication signals are they offering? How are they vocalising? Keep a diary and see if you can spot patterns. And then work from there. Once we have a clear picture from our observations, we can make more informed interpretations. We are acting on the evidence rather than on assumptions.

So let's look in more detail at what we can observe and how to do it.

What are we observing?

There are four key things to look at to get a fuller picture of what is going on with our dog:

1.   Physical tension

2.   Posture
3.   Physiological signs
4.   Communication signs

Let's look at each in turn.

Physical tension

When we are physically tense it affects everything else that is going on. We can't concentrate, we may be grouchy or withdrawn and we have less interest in what is happening around us. We may experience pain or discomfort. Physical tension may indicate illness or injury, but it can also arise from the way we hold ourselves or the way we move. The same is true of our dogs.

I recommend that you have a vet check your dog, to see if there is a physical factor involved, particularly where there is any sudden behaviour change. However, it is important to note that a vet check will usually only diagnose clinical issues and physical tension can still be present when there is no underlying medical condition. On a day-to-day basis, our dogs may be feeling 'out of kilter' for very similar reasons to us – an awkward jump, an unusually long walk, a new physical activity, an uncomfortable posture, or being protective over low-level bumps and bruises.

When our dogs are holding physical tension, their range of movement is restricted and they are tight and inflexible through their body. This will, in turn, influence how they feel, how other dogs perceive them and, ultimately, how they behave.

If we can release the tension in the body, we make them more comfortable and balanced, so they feel better. As their emotional response changes so can their behaviour.

Tension patterns can be defined as areas of tightness in the body that may affect posture, movement and coat.[26] They may influence

---

[26] Sarah Fisher's work on tension patterns is key here and her 2007 book *Unlock Your Dog's Potential* is essential reading on this topic. Later articles and

a dog's level of comfort and, ultimately, their behaviour. They can occur for lots of reasons. Injury or medical issues, whether major or minor, can cause a dog to compensate or be protective of a particular area, which can lead to uneven posture, even after the initial condition is resolved. Experiences of training, equipment and environment can also create tension patterns, for example if a dog pulls forward constantly or holds their head in an unnatural position, they can develop tightness in the shoulders and neck. Sometime tension patterns are congenital: dogs are simply born that way.

Emotional state also perpetuates tension patterns: for example, adopting a posture with tucked tail and hindquarters will lead to further tension in that area. This is one reason why reactive and fearful dogs are often tense in the hindquarters.

We can spot tension patterns through physical signs that we can observe, such as:

- Changes in coat pattern, texture and colour.
- Concern about being touched in a particular area or muscle twitching on touch.
- Changes in temperature that cannot be explained by external environmental factors, such as sleeping by a radiator, or by the location of major organs.
- Weighting the body forward or backwards.
- Limited movement through the back.
- Uneven gait, where one or more legs are favoured, where movement is laboured or tight, or where one limb moves differently from the others.

We will look at how to observe these things in the next section. Observing physical tension patterns in our dogs can tell us which

presentations are also available and her Dog Detective and ACE workshops are highly recommended to learn more about this work. See https://www.facebook.com/tilley.farm for details.

areas of the body need attention and act as a barometer for how our dog is changing over time. Change is often subtle but sometimes it can be quite dramatic.

Gus was a huge bundle of silky golden enthusiasm who loved everyone and everything – except his kitchen floor. He was a confident dog but he point-blank refused to cross the threshold onto the laminate in the kitchen. The first thing I noticed when I met him was his lion's mane. His coat was silky and smooth – except over his shoulders and neck, where it was coarse and curly. This change in coat pattern suggested physical tension, so I worked with Gus using TTouch[27] over his shoulders, neck and spine. I introduced his guardian to the TTouch Confidence Course, which gave him a positive experience of different surfaces and encouraged balance and movement through his body in both directions. We also changed the environment to make it easier for him, by laying down runners into the kitchen, and we reinforced him for any steps he made in that direction.

A few weeks later I spoke to his guardian. Gus was now happily running in and out of the kitchen but that was not all. The mane around his neck and shoulders had gone. The coat had become silky and smooth again, just like the rest of his body, and everyone they met was commenting on it!

Observation helped us to identify where Gus was holding tension and observation enabled us to see the result of releasing that tension. We need to observe in order to make change happen and to recognise it when it does happen.

Posture

Posture reflects our dog's state of mind and can indicate concern, fear, high excitement or arousal. Most of us can recognise the

---

[27] For more on TTouch see Linda Tellington-Jones (2013), *Getting in TTouch with Your Dog* (2nd Edition), VT: Trafalgar Square Books.

difference between a frightened dog with tucked tail, lowered head and flattened ears and an alert dog, standing up on tip toes, leaning forward with ears up. However, as with everything, there are many more subtle variations. The dog with head lowered but leaning forward may be more threatening than the one leaning back and hunched. The dog who is alert but not leaning forward may be less likely to react than the one leaning forward.

It is important to know your own dog's postural norms so that you can differentiate between interest, alertness and over-arousal, for instance, or between minor concern and fear.

Remember the stress responses we met in Chapter 1: fight, flight, fool around and freeze? We can get clues to them all through our dog's posture. Flight is not just the dog that is fleeing across the park to escape but the dog that is leaning back, trying to avoid, or hunching up to make themselves small. Fight is not just actually fighting but more often is an aggressive posturing, standing up on toes, leaning forward, or lunging. Freeze is usually associated with a lowered head and tail, planted feet and no engagement. If you get stillness with an upright, forwards, on-the-toes posture, the dog is likely to be about to attack or react. Fool around is constant movement: the dog that wriggles, rolls on its back, can't stand still and wags manically.

Being aware of these responses helps us to understand reactive behaviours in the context of stress and, in particular, to recognise responses such as freeze and fool around for what they are. These two tend to be less disturbing to us: the dog is 'quiet' or 'friendly' so we do not worry as much but the stress our dog is experiencing is just as real.

Ideally we want to intervene before the stress escalates to the point when our dog reacts in one of these ways. We can do that if we learn to observe how dogs communicate early signs of discomfort. We will look at this more later.

Physiology

Stress is designed to protect our dog from threat and prepare their body for action. This results in physiological changes that we can observe.

The body releases stress hormones in response to a threat: adrenaline, to prepare our dog for the immediate danger, and cortisol, to regulate vital body functions. As a result their heart will beat faster and they will breathe more rapidly, they may drool and may sweat through their pads. They may also lose their coats.

We can observe physiological indicators to help us monitor our dog's stress level. Any increase in respiration, heart rate, level of salivation, amount of sweat secreted through the pads or rate of shedding should be noted. We need to know our dog's resting levels so that we can see how much these change in different contexts.

Communication signals

Dogs may not have auto-translators, like the dogs in the wonderful film, *Up*[28], but they can still communicate quite clearly if we learn to listen. The language dogs use most is body language: the position of their head, how they use their eyes, how they hold their tail, and so on; all communicate what they are feeling, as we have seen. They also have a language of specific signals to communicate intention and appeasement. These are known as "calming signals" and have been well documented by Turid Rugaas in her classic book.[29]

So a dog that turns its head away from us is being polite – quite often in response to human 'rudeness' in staring directly at it! Blinking is a sign that says "I am not threatening". Licking lips indicates concern and shaking off is often a way to release tension.

---

[28] *Up* (2009), Pete Docter (director), Pixar Animation Studios/Walt Disney Pictures.

[29] Rugaas, T. (2006) *On Talking Terms with Dogs: Calming Signals* (2nd Edition). WA: Dogwise Publishing.

Tail wags can be complicated: a relaxed and level wag is friendly, a rapid and manic wag is excited, but a high, slow wave is suspicious or threatening.

There are about thirty calming signals, some of the most common ones being licking lips, turning the head away, rapid blinking, yawning, shaking off, sniffing the ground, scratching, approaching in a curve, and play bow stretch.

We can't simply look for one sign, of course, and say this means that. We need to take it in context, observing the whole picture not just the one signal.

I remember having an interesting encounter on the beach, when Otter was a puppy. She was playing when she was approached by a similarly-sized but older terrier. They met head on with tails high, wagging slightly. Their bodies were a little stiff and they were on their toes. They were both very alert and not entirely relaxed so I called Otter away after a few seconds. The young girl with the terrier confidently informed me that it was OK because their tails were up – that you only needed to worry when the tail is down.

It was neither the time nor the place for a lesson in the nuances of canine body language, so I simply said that I wanted to keep things calm between them as Otter was still young, and sure enough, a few seconds later they had shaken off, circled round, play bowed and raced around the beach in a chase.

The girl was, of course, partially right. If either of them had held their tail very low or tucked, it would certainly suggest that the encounter was not working for them. But a higher tail carriage on its own could mean anything from playful arousal to tension, not to mention being the characteristic tail carriage of terrier types, and, of course, tail carriage is just one small part of the larger picture.

So we need to remember that canine body language is complex. Not only are there multiple elements for us to learn to observe: tails, of course, but also ears, eyes, mouth, feet, body posture, neck position, coat, vocalisation, and behaviour. Each of these has a huge and subtle range of variations and, to make it even more complicated, what we see is always contextual. I swear if you saw and heard Otter playing with her friend, Raffi, sometimes you would think they were tearing each other limb from limb but it is play (albeit high arousal play, which can switch very quickly into cross words between them, so intervention is sometimes needed).

Sarah Fisher, TTouch Instructor and very talented canine observer, always says that the only canine experts are those with four legs and she is, of course, spot on. When it comes to learning our dog's language, we are all students. We need to learn the vocabulary of their language – the different elements and their variations, as well as the grammar – and how all these combine together to pass on a message.

But if we want to do more than just recognise a few words, if we want to really grasp the richness of the language and move towards fluency in understanding, we need to immerse ourselves in it, spend time with 'native speakers' (our dogs), and observe the nuances of communication.

How and when to observe

We have looked at what we can observe about our dogs, but how do we go about it and when do we do it? We can practise observation with our own dog both as separate activity, where we focus on watching and noting as much as we can about our dog, and as part of our practice while out on walks and interacting at home. We can also practise observation as a learning exercise away from our dogs to hone our skills in reading dogs. Let's look at each of these.

Observing a snapshot in time
In TTouch we use observation continually as we work with a dog,

but we often start with an initial observation session, that gives us a snapshot of how that dog is in that moment. We use visual and hands-on observation, as well as listening for any vocalisation. This is a guide to how to do this. Remember at this point you are just observing and taking notes.

Start by really looking at your dog. Note any changes in coat pattern, texture or colour, such as swirls in the coat, changes from silky to rough or changes in shade. How does your dog hold their tail and ears? Are the ears symmetrical or uneven? Is the tail held more to one side? What about the pelvis and the shoulders? Is one side higher than the other? Note any areas where the muscles are unevenly developed. Check the head and jaw. Is the mouth tight or dry? Are the sides of the mouth 'sucked in'? Are their eyes soft or hard? Wide or narrow?

Look at how they sit and lie down: is it straight on or to one side? Do they stand four square or weighted unevenly? Next watch them moving: are their limbs underneath them or thrown out when they move? Do they extend through the shoulder and hips or is the stride short? Is there any stiffness in their movement and how much do they bend their legs? Are they able to turn easily in both directions? When they do this, do they bend through the back or shift their rear end round to follow their front?

Next do a hands-on observation, using the back of your hand and observing very carefully your dog's response. Stop any time your dog shows discomfort, moves away or sits down and note where you were touching when they did this. Feel for changes in temperature throughout the body and for areas of tightness. Watch for muscle twitching when you touch an area and note any areas that your dog is concerned about you touching. For each leg, gently hold it near the top and lift it off the ground. Is it easy to lift or not? Are the legs equally easy to lift or is one much heavier than another? Look at their pads and nails. Is the wear even?

Remember that we are observing, not diagnosing. Changes in coat pattern, unbalanced posture, sensitivity to touch and lack of flexibility through the body are all things that can indicate physical tension or pain and merit further investigation. If you notice these, it is worth considering consulting a TTouch practitioner or chiropractor.

Focused attention

Observing our dogs can sometimes seem overwhelming. There are so many physical, postural, physiological and communication signs that we can observe. How can we possibly monitor all of that continually? The answer is that we can't – but we don't have to. What we need to do is find the signals that our own dog uses, the signs that our own dog is becoming concerned or worked up or stressed and become skilled at recognising these.

One way to do this is through focused attention.[30] Initially, don't try to monitor everything. Instead give your focused attention to just one thing.

How does that work? Next time you go for a walk, choose just one thing about your dog and give it your full attention. This might be how their ears move or whether their mouth is open or closed, or how they are breathing, what their tail is doing or whether the hair on their neck is raised. It could also be something about your interaction with your dog: when the lead tightens or when they look at you.

The key is to choose just one thing at a time. Another day you can choose something else but each day just choose one thing to observe. See when it occurs and what precedes it. Do you notice any patterns? You are not trying to change anything here, you are simply learning to really observe.

---

[30] This use of focused attention is based on the work of Tim Gallwey in his book The Inner Game of Work, NY: Random House, 2001.

You can do the same for your own behaviour: observe your breathing, your heart rate, how tightly you are holding the lead. You will be able to think of other things. The only rule is focused attention on one thing at a time.

Spend a week giving focused attention to a different thing each day. Then choose the one that you found most interesting and continue to practise this over a few more days and see what happens. Often with focused attention things start to change. It is not that your dog is changing but that you are adjusting your behaviour to optimise theirs. So, say you observed that your dog's ears went forward just before they became agitated; you may find yourself anticipating and taking evasive action automatically. But don't try to change your behaviour; just focus your attention on the one thing you are observing and see what happens.

Practising observational skills
Canine body language, posture and communication are rich areas and it is well beyond the scope of this book to discuss all the nuances of them. But the good news is that there is a wealth of material out there to help you to develop your observational skills and, if you are serious about helping your dog, I strongly recommend that you spend some time learning more about this.

Turid Rugaas' book, already mentioned, is a great introduction but if you want to understand more, check out one of the more detailed illustrated books[31] that will help you to learn the vocabulary and grammar of the language that dogs use.

However, photographs can only show so much. We really need

---

[31] These are all excellent illustrated books on canine body language and communication. The first is a very useful and easy to read explanation of posture and body language, with illustrations and photographs. The second two are more detailed reference books on the subject. Gutteridge, S (2019) *Canine Communication: The Language of a Species*. Independently published. Aloff, B (2005) *Canine Body Language, A Photographic Guide*. WA: Dogwise. Handelman, B (2008) *Canine Behaviour, A Photo Illustrated Handbook*. WA: Dogwise.

to watch dogs in action to make this come alive. Watch them live playing and interacting. Watch videos, ideally in slow motion. Video allows us to see how the interactions play out. Slow motion allows us to see the things that happen so quickly that we miss them at real-life speed (though, of course, they are not missed by our dogs!).

You will find groups on Facebook dedicated to observational analysis of canine behaviour and it is something we occasionally do in my own groups. Getting involved in these discussions can be of huge value as not only do you get to watch many different dogs interacting, but you also get the benefit of a group of observers and their experience. This is the kind of activity that can really help us with our canine language learning!

Once we become skilled at reading our dogs and the other dogs that we encounter, we will be able to understand their responses and adjust what we do to make them feel safer. We will be responding to what we are seeing rather than what we are assuming and we will have gathered evidence to challenge our limiting beliefs.

WATCHING OUR LANGUAGE

Positive vs. negative language

As we saw in Chapter 3, language is powerful. Our brain acts on the language we use and hear, both positive and negative. The words we use determine our expectations and those of other people, but they also impact on us physiologically. Negative language actually produces physical stress responses: the release of stress hormones. Just contemplating lists of negative words can influence sleep patterns, memory, appetite and mood. Negative language has this effect both on the speaker and the listener: stress hormones are released in both. What is interesting about fear and negativity is that our brain and neural system respond to it as if it is real. So if we imagine all the things that might go wrong, our brain will react as if it is a real threat – and release more stress hormones!

Positive language, on the other hand, gives our brain a picture of what we want to achieve. It can encourage a sense of control and action. Researchers have found that even hearing a word related to physical action in a positive sentence will increase the force with which a person grips an object, but not when the word is heard within a negative sentence.[32]

We can use positive or negative language about ourselves and about our dogs. When we use negative language we often reinforce our limiting beliefs. If we want to challenge the limiting beliefs we hold about our dog, we need to watch our language.

There are two specific ways that we tend to adopt negative language about our dogs without really thinking about it: labels and nicknames.

Labels

We have already touched on labels in Chapter 1 when we talked about 'reactive' dogs. We have a tendency to label our dogs: reactive, challenging, aggressive, stubborn, dominant, submissive and so on, but it is not always helpful. At best labels are an attempt to describe complex behaviour in a single word, a kind of shorthand. At worst, they become an excuse to use force. "He is dominant, so show him who is boss". "She is just being stubborn, so make her do it". Our dogs deserve better than to be reduced to a label.

We do, of course, need ways to describe our dogs that allow us to communicate in a sensible way: descriptors if you like. 'Reactive' can be used as a descriptor, when we are clear what it means. It can

---

[32] Aravena P, Delevoye-Turrell Y, Deprez V, Cheylus A, Paulignan Y, Frak V, et al. (2012) *Grip Force Reveals the Context Sensitivity of Language-Induced Motor Activity during "Action Words" Processing: Evidence from Sentential Negation.* PLoS ONE 7(12).

be used to describe a particular set of behaviours, rather than to label your dog. Similarly, a word like 'rescue' can be a descriptor, describing a factual aspect of a dog's history. However, even these are not as straightforward as they appear. One person's idea of the behaviours involved in 'reactive' can be very different from another's so just using the word as a descriptor of behaviour, without defining it, can mean we are talking at crossed purposes. Even 'rescue' has different connotations for different people, for some suggesting the dog has been removed from a damaging situation, for others simply that the dog has been rehomed.

The ideal is always to be explicit about the behaviours we see; this is why observation is so important. However, a descriptor can be helpful as a shorthand, as long as we are clear about its definition and we remember that it is only a descriptor. It describes one set of behaviours our dog displays. It does not describe our dog.

The problems really start when labels are used to characterise our dogs. When we are told or believe that our dog is dominant or stubborn or pessimistic or shy or social or submissive or compliant or even reactive. So why is this a problem?

Well, we are no longer describing what we see. As soon as we label in this way, we are setting the lens through which we interpret what we see and we will be much more likely to interpret our dog's behaviours as confirming the label we have applied.

So, for example, if we label our dog as stubborn, we will find more and more examples of 'stubborn' behaviours. Our dog stops and won't move forward? They are being 'stubborn'. We don't even consider the possibility that they are scared or in pain or interested in going the other way where there is a fascinating smell.

When they act outside the expectations set by the label, we are also less likely to notice or believe it. Our 'shy' dog approaches a stranger? It was 'out of character' or 'just a fluke', rather than an example of their varying sociability in different contexts.

Labels also set other people's expectations. You have a 'social' dog? Other people will respond to that dog differently than to a 'shy' dog. Yet perhaps your 'social' dog is really only social in some situations and would prefer space in others?

Sometimes positive labels can be as problematic as negative ones. If we label our dog as 'friendly', 'outgoing', 'liking other dogs', it can make it harder for us to notice when our dog is anxious. When our dog doesn't want to be handled or chooses not to interact with a dog, it can be harder to see because we have in our head that our dog is friendly.

So it is better to avoid labelling as much as possible. Simply changing the way we talk about ourselves and our dogs can make a difference to our thinking and our responses. Talk about the behaviour, the context and about what you are actually seeing, rather than applying a label.

Remember we are living with complex, emotional beings. Just like us, how they feel and respond is contextual. Some days they will be optimistic. Some days less so. In some situations they will be social. In others less so. They may have behavioural and emotional tendencies, of course, but even these are multiple and complex. Our dogs are not defined by them, any more than we are.

Nicknames

In the days when I lived on a smallholding, I remember once being deeply offended by someone on the radio, mocking the fact that a vet receptionist had asked her for her chicken's name. "Name?" shrieked the speaker, "Name?! She's a *chicken*" – as if this fact was enough to make the idea of naming her beyond insane.

Every animal on our smallholding had a name: the dogs and feral cats, each of our forty sheep and, yes, the chickens. Names are important. They give identity and personhood. They make a difference to how we perceive and are perceived.

In 2017, a storm named Doris brought chaos, damage and, tragically, death to the UK. Afterwards, commentators wondered why people had not taken more precautions, when they had been warned that the storm was coming? The point was made that it had not been taken seriously enough because the name was more suggestive of tea with your granny than a severe and potentially dangerous weather front.

So what has this to do with our dogs and their reactivity? Think about what you call your dog. Not only their given name, but the actual names you use when you talk to them and about them. Think about the nicknames, the shortenings, the lengthenings. What message do those names give to you and to the people you meet?

When we have a dog whose behaviour frustrates us, we tend to reflect that in the nicknames and descriptions we use. We often do it jokingly. Our dog is "Naughty-dog" or "Idiot-dog" or a "Devil-dog" or, even, "Little s**t" (insert your favourite expletive). I am guilty of it myself. In the aftermath of the boat-naming fiasco[33], Martha gained the nickname Barky McBarkface – and it stuck.

We may feel that this is all just harmless fun but we know that what we call things influences how we see them. So each time we call our dog Idiot or Devil or Naughty we are telling our brain that this is what they are. What will the impact of that be over months and years? At the very least it is going to make it harder for us to see them as the bright, willing, co-operative creatures that they are. Martha's nickname may be amusing and descriptive, but it has certainly not helped us change her habit of over-vocalising!

Remember the Superbetter game back in Chapter 2? One of the

---

[33] https://www.theguardian.com/environment/2016/apr/17/boaty-mcboatface-wins-poll-to-name-polar-research-vessel

elements of that is to adopt a secret identity and it has been wonderful to see the creative and positive alter egos players have come up with for themselves and their dogs. Fantasy heroes. Super heroes. Crime fighters. Some with vulnerabilities but all with powers for good. Even going through this process of naming can lighten how we feel about our dog's issues.

So why not try giving your dog a nickname that reflects what you love about them or how you'd like them to be rather than what frustrates you? You may find it changes more than just the name!

UNPREDICTABLE OR TRIGGER-STACKED?

My dog is so 'unpredictable'

A very common label that we often use about our dogs is 'unpredictable'. So many guardians tell me that things wouldn't be so difficult if their dog was more predictable, if they always responded in the same way to the same trigger. Instead, one day they may react to a dog and the next day pass by quietly without a care in the world. How can we move on with helping our dogs to change, when they are so unpredictable in the first place?

It is a completely understandable response – we like things to ordered and certain. We like to know what is going to happen and when it will happen. However, unfortunately for our sense of order, living beings are not very predictable; that goes for our dogs and for us! We are not computers, where we will get the same output for the same input. Instead we, and our dogs, are *contextual*.

This is both good news and bad news. The bad news is that it means our dog's behaviour will not always be the same, given the same input. So one day, our dog might see a man in a hat and be fine about it. The next day, the same man in the same hat could trigger a riot!

The good news is that when we understand that our dogs are

contextual creatures, we can start to make more sense of their behaviour. We can then start to make more accurate predictions.

So take the Man in the Hat. He is only one part of the context. He is what we tend to notice because he is the focus of our dog's outburst. But there are many other factors that contribute to why our dog barks at him one day and not another, including:

- Weather: Is it particularly hot or cold? Is there thunder in the air? Does our dog cope better with some weather conditions more than others?
- Location: Is the location different? More echoey? Less visibility? Element of surprise?
- Health: Is our dog feeling well? Any pain? Discomfort, including low level 'niggles' that might not halt activity but may reduce patience? Is our dog hungry or thirsty or needing the toilet?
- Energy levels: Is our dog tired? Or are they full of energy and raring to go?
- Our Energy levels: Are we tired? Or full of energy and raring to go?
- The Man in the Hat's Energy levels: Is he tired? Or full of energy and raring to go?
- Mood: Are they calm and relaxed? Wound up and stressed? Over-excited?
- Our mood: Are we calm and relaxed? Wound up and stressed? Over-excited?
- The Man in the Hat's mood: Is he calm and relaxed? Wound up and stressed? Over-excited?
- Other people: Is there anyone else present? Any other dogs?
- What happened yesterday: Any barking incidents? Any highly charged fun activities? Plenty of rest?

I could go on but you get the idea. Context is everything and contexts are rarely the same from day to day – even if you are in the same place meeting the same person.

We have a term for this in dogs: *trigger stacking*. It refers to the cumulative effect of stress triggers, where each one builds on the next until tolerance is exceeded and the dog 'loses it'. We all get trigger-stacked sometimes. It is really just part of being a sentient, living, breathing being, whose mood is affected not only by specific scary things but by the environment, how safe we feel, whether we are hungry or in pain or tired and much more besides.

Trigger stacking means that reactivity is a bit more complicated than 'not liking other dogs' or 'being scared of people', and there are a couple of important things we need to keep in mind.

Firstly, the thing that triggers the reaction may not always be the primary cause of the reaction. It may simply be the thing that tips the balance. Sometimes our dog may suddenly react to something new or have a bigger reaction than they have had before, and we can get demoralised. Is this going to be yet one more thing to try to avoid? Not necessarily. It may simply be a relatively minor trigger coming on top of other more significant anxiety or upset.

Secondly, sometimes every day things can be triggers, even things that our dog enjoys. Remember that adrenaline and cortisol are released in response to excitement as well as to threat and, when combined with other factors, excitement can tip our dog over into a reaction in much the same way as fear or frustration.

I once went to the beach with Martha and Otter, my sister and her dog, Raffi, and a new dog she was looking after. As we came onto the beach all four dogs were running round playing and Martha was barking with excitement. The beach was quiet and the only other person was a long way off, walking along the shoreline with her small dog. I tend to keep an eye out for other dogs, as Otter can be tempted to go and see them, but this dog was a long way off and Otter was totally focused on Raffi and their new buddy. We continued along the top of the beach when, suddenly, Martha took off across the sands, towards the woman and her dog. I called her back and she didn't come. I was horrified. Martha is my shadow. She rarely goes more than a few feet from me and (until then at least!) always recalls reliably. So what happened? How did my normally 'velcro' dog take it into her head to leg it across the beach to investigate another dog?

This is a perfect example of trigger stacking. As we had come onto the beach she had been slightly spooked by a tent that had been pitched at the bottom of the steps. So she started the walk with a burst of adrenaline. She was then super-excited by the little dogs playing and all the additional fun of having a larger group than normal. More adrenaline. By the time we were parallel with the dog, her arousal level was already much higher than normal. She hadn't had any major upsets but the combination of factors, including some positive ones, meant that her behaviour took me by surprise and her heightened arousal meant that she did not respond as normal. However, it was not unpredictable. The excited barking was a sign that she was more aroused than normal. I just missed its significance on that occasion.

So when we think about our dog's 'triggers', we need to consider everything that contributes to how our dog feels on any given day and not just the specific things our dog reacts to. This may seem like an enormous task but it is also an opportunity, as we will see.

The positive side of trigger stacking

Trigger stacking can be frustrating and make things more complicated for us, but it also gives us a great opportunity. Sometimes we can feel that tackling our dog's reactivity is too difficult, especially if we have a dog who reacts at pretty much any distance to their primary triggers. How do we even get started? Trigger stacking can help us in two ways.

1. We can identify and address each trigger individually to reduce our dog's overall stress.

2. We can use our observations about trigger stacking to inform our judgements about when and how to work with our dog.

One trigger at a time

As we have seen stress is cumulative, the product of combining many different factors. So we can reduce stress by addressing these one at a time. We do not need to wipe out stress altogether to make a difference; that would be a daunting prospect. Instead we need to 'turn down the heat'.

Think of your dog's stress as a big pot of water. Underneath it are dozens of separate flames: the factors that contribute to the stress.[34] So one might be the weather, another pain, another your mood, as well as the primary triggers such as seeing another dog or an unknown human. Some are large flames that heat the water quickly. Some are smaller flames. The more flames that are lit the faster the water will boil and the longer it will take to cool down. Each one that we extinguish will slow down the heating process and, if we can get rid of enough of the flames, then the water will never boil.

These flames are the factors that contribute to our dog's reactivity. We can start to address it by "extinguishing" any of the contributing factors. Some of these will be relatively simple to remove, like replacing uncomfortable or aversive equipment with something more appropriate. Others will take more time but can be dealt with separately from working on the reactive behaviour, such as physical tension, injury or illness, or indeed our own anxieties

---

[34] This analogy comes from TTouch Instructor Edie Jane Eaton, who used the analogy of triggers being 'candles' that we can blow out. Sarah Fisher has also extended the candles analogy.

and responses.

We can also reduce the 'temperature' with 'cooling' additions, such as relaxation exercises, TTouch and calming supplements. These will make it less likely that your dog's stress will ever 'boil over' into reactivity.

The good news is that many of our dog's triggers can be removed or their impact reduced individually, and every one that we deal with will help lower our dog's overall reactivity. This may not mean that they no longer react, but it will mean that they are slower to react and quicker to recover. When our dog is reactive on sight of another dog, addressing secondary triggers in this way can make all the difference to being able to work with our dog effectively.

Adjusting to triggers

The second way that trigger stacking can help us is by informing our judgements on walks. When we work on our observational skills and recognise the role of trigger stacking, we can make choices to help rather than hinder our dog. Rather than assuming that our dog will always be happy to meet the Man in the Hat, we will note that they become less comfortable when the Man is also carrying a stick or when it is hot or when they have had a bad day the day before.

Some of these things, of course, we can only judge in the moment: the things about the specific scenario. But some of them we can know in advance and make allowances for.

If we notice that our dog is always more 'grumpy' the day after a long walk, we can choose to go somewhere quieter the next day, or keep them on a lead, or give more space, or even take the next day off from walking (see Chapter 7 for ways to do this effectively).

If we realise that our own mood really affects how our dog reacts, we can make sure we only walk them when we ourselves are feeling calm and relaxed.

If we find they are more reactive when they are hungry, we can time walks to be after meal times[35] and avoid walking just before they are due to eat.

Understanding trigger stacking can help us make better decisions and keep perspective.

Stacking the odds in our favour

We have seen that our dogs are not unpredictable. It is just that each day many things combine to determine how they feel and react. So can we stack the odds in favour of good days? Of course. Do this three-step exercise for your own dog to help raise your awareness of the triggers and factors that are likely to affect them.

1.   Write a list of all the things that you know your dog finds hard whether it is things people do, other dogs or animals, weather, noises, being left alone, disruption to routine and so on. Just the act of listing them will raise your awareness and help you to spot when those things might be adding up so that you can make allowances for them.

2.   Think about the things that make your dog really excited. These are not bad, of course, but they will add more adrenaline to the mix. Writing these down will make you more aware of when you need to take them into account.

3.   Consider your dog's physical needs. Is there anything there that you need to address? In particular, think about:

☐   **Diet:** There is growing evidence that gut health has a significant influence on behaviour, so look at how you can maintain digestive health. Ensure that you are feeding an appropriate and healthy diet and see your vet or consider supplements such as probiotics

---

[35] Always allow a good hour after eating to avoid bloat, especially in susceptible dogs.

if your dog has any digestive issues.

☐ **Sleep:** We all need good sleep to remain healthy and interrupted or insufficient sleep can be a factor in unexpected behaviour. So, if your dog reacts unexpectedly to something, it is worth thinking about their recent sleep patterns. Have they been awake more than usual? Is anything disturbing their sleep? There are lots of reasons this might happen and they are often not negative things. Perhaps they have had a day out at an event or been away with you on holiday? Perhaps you have been off work or you have visitors staying and there has been more going on than usual? Perhaps they have spent more time playing with the kids or had playdates with doggy friends? All of these are likely great fun for your dog but may still mean they have slept less than usual. So if you have a change to your normal routine, make sure that you allow plenty of rest time afterwards. With young dogs and those who love to be in the thick of it, this may need to be actively encouraged, as they may not see the need, much like a tired toddler who resists going to bed! So, sometimes, moving them to a quiet space, giving them a chew toy, and letting them settle themselves away from distractions is what they need. Once rested, they will be back to their normal self.

☐ **Exercise:** All dogs need appropriate exercise. What this entails depends on your dog's breed, age and energy level, but remember that if your dog has pent-up energy they are more likely to react. This does not mean that you need to exercise your dog like an athlete – unless you want a canine athlete!

But it does mean providing sufficient regular physical activity to keep them fit and well.

☐ **Enrichment**: At least as important as physical exercise is mental exercise. Dogs need the opportunity to use their brains, to investigate their world, to problem solve, to use their nose, to learn new things. Again what they need depends on the individual dog: enrichment for a livestock guardian may look very different from enrichment for a gun dog. However, bored dogs are likely to be frustrated dogs and therefore more likely to react.

☐ **Pain and illness:** We have already seen how pain and illness can affect our dogs. If your dog has a chronic condition, you may not be able to eliminate these altogether but you can work with your veterinary team to minimise pain and discomfort and address health issues as quickly as possible.

It is so important to take a holistic approach to understanding our dogs. They are not robots, receiving instruction and executing commands, unaffected by the outside world. They – like us – have good days and bad days: days when they want to work or play and days when they are not in the mood; days when they are lively and days when they are quieter; days when they are tolerant and days when patience wears thin.

By observing them carefully, being positive in the way we think and speak about them and considering all the factors that contribute to their reactive behaviour, we can stack the odds in favour of the positive days and enable our dogs to be at their best when they face difficult situations.

Chapter Five

CHANGING HOW YOU THINK ABOUT OTHER PEOPLE

So far we have considered how we can change how we think about reactivity, ourselves and our dogs but often the real problem seems to lie elsewhere, with other people.

What can we do about the people who sabotage our efforts, either through ignorance or intent? What about our family and friends who may be less than helpful sometimes? What if we feel isolated and alone in our journey with our dog? Surely no amount of work on our thought patterns can protect us from the realities of living every day in a society that seems unsympathetic to our reactive dogs?

Without doubt other people have a huge impact on us and our dogs. We worry about what they think and what they will do. We dread meeting them. We find ourselves fighting even with those we love about the best way forward.

Often our response is to lash out, to rant, to become angry and defensive. These responses are perfectly understandable and natural when we are hurt. They may even make us feel better in the short term. However, they are not going to do anything to make our dog less reactive or help us manage them more effectively. Changing how we think about other people will do just that.

In this chapter we are going to explore how we can change how we think and respond to strangers who we meet out and about and to our family and friends, particularly if they are not yet on board with what we are doing to help our dog.

We will also see that other people do not always put barriers in our way. They can be our allies. We all need a support network to help us on our journey with our dog. We will look at different types of allies that we need and where to find them. You never know, we may even be able to turn some of those awkward strangers into allies as well!

OTHER GUARDIANS AND STRANGERS

Let's face it: other people can be the bane of our lives. Almost all my clients say that they would be just fine if it wasn't for other people! Whether it is the person who insists on approaching your dog, in spite of your protestations; or the one who allows their 'friendly' dog to rush up to yours; or the one who yells abuse at you because your dog objects to theirs 'wanting to play'; other guardians can certainly make life much more tricky.

It is understandable to get angry when this happens. We may become frustrated, we may yell, we may even try to educate. Ultimately, though, we can't control what they do. So who does all our anger and frustration ultimately hurt? It is not the other person and their dog, who will usually move on quickly and without a backward thought. It is we who dwell on it, who nurse the (righteous) indignation, who go off and rant on social media, who turn it over in our minds and then feel increasingly rubbish about it. It is our dogs – not theirs – who know that we are upset and who may feel more stressed as a result.

So what can we do? Raising our awareness of what is really going on and reframing our thinking about it is a good place to start. We need to recognise and accept that we are not responsible for other people and that we can rarely change their behaviour, so dwelling on it is wasted energy. However, we can choose our own responses. So what is going on with these people and how do we deal with the very natural emotional reactions we have to them?

Understanding the people we meet

When we are out with our dogs, we will meet many different types of people. We can learn a lot about them by the way they respond if we ask them to recall their dog or not to approach our dog. Let's consider some typical responses.

Why should I do what you ask?

A very common response is the defensive one. Why should I do what you ask? Who are you to tell me what to do? This can be accompanied by sneering or abuse.

I had a classic example of this a few years ago when I was walking Mirri with my partner in our local meadows, a beautiful area of open parkland, criss-crossed by paths – perfect for walking a 'can-sometimes-be-reactive' dog. Some days earlier Mirri had cut her paw badly and she was sporting a full-length leg plaster in shocking pink! This was our first walk out since her accident, so she was on lead and we were taking it gently.

As we walked, I spotted a group of retrievers heading down the path towards us, so Mirri and I diverted off the path and I focused on keeping her calm while my partner met the approaching group and politely asked their guardian to keep them away.

This simple request was met by a torrent of abuse. We were unfit to own a dog. Mirri had no right to be out in public. His dogs were entitled to do as they pleased. Why should he do what we asked?

We ended up having to physically restrain four large retrievers, one of whom definitely did not have friendly intent, to stop them leaping on our obviously injured, and by now, terrified, dog.

So what is going on here? How do normal, presumably rational people hear a simple, polite request, and become irrational, rude and inconsiderate? Surely anyone could see that, regardless of reactivity, Mirri was not, at that moment, fit to 'play' with four large, boisterous retrievers?

The simple answer is that they don't recall their dogs because they can't. Think about it. If you know your dog will recall, you simply recall them if someone asks. Job done. No issue. I don't think I have ever met someone who was able to recall their dog and refused.

But there is more to it than that. When we ask someone to recall their dog and they can't, we embarrass them. They may believe that, as a responsible dog guardian, they should be able to recall their dog, yet their behaviour conflicts with this. They experience what is known as cognitive dissonance, an uncomfortable inner conflict that occurs when our behaviour is out of step with our beliefs. Their immediate response to these feelings is to attempt to project blame onto others. Instead of having to acknowledge that they can't control their dog, they tell us our dog is the problem. Instead of admitting that they feel they have been irresponsible, they accuse us of being irresponsible. Later, when they have calmed down, they may well recognise they were unreasonable but, of course, we never see this. So it is often we who go away, feeling upset and useless and embarrassed, even though we did nothing wrong.

It's OK, my dog is friendly!
We have all met this guardian. They allow their dogs to race up to yours, even when yours is on a lead and obviously not wanting to play! When you ask them to recall their dog, their response is not angry but light and often blissfully ignorant: it's ok, my dog is friendly!

These guardians also may not be able to recall their dogs, and their response is covering their embarrassment about that with what they see as reassurance. They may not understand that your dog needs space or indeed that their dog is not being friendly at all.

Many people are simply unaware of the impact that their dog's behaviour has on other dogs. They have no knowledge of dog-to-dog communication and think that all dogs like to play with each other. They may believe dogs need to be off lead no matter what their behaviour is like or their dog may pull so much when on the lead that they can't bear to walk them on a lead!

However, on occasion, something else entirely may be going on – see section *I'm so sorry!*

Don't worry, all dogs love me

The 'all dogs love me' response usually comes from those who are trying to greet your dog, even though you have asked them not to. This one is more of a problem for those of us whose dogs are fearful of people, rather than those who are worried by other dogs. Like 'my dog is friendly' they are acting out of ignorance. They don't recognise the signs of distress that your dog is showing. They may genuinely believe that they are a friend to all dogs and this may blind them to the fact that not all dogs want to be friends with them. They may also feel they have something to prove.

Nasty, vicious dog, needs to be put down

This is probably the most upsetting response we can have. I remember many years ago being desperately upset when a man yelled this at me when I was out with my first dog Bruno. Bruno was a re-homed Maremma Sheepdog, who struggled with other male dogs. In those days I had never heard of reactivity. I simply knew that Bruno barked and growled at other males. Since he was a big lad, this meant I struggled a lot on walks. One day, walking through the woods, we met someone with a young male collie cross, who ran up to Bruno, who was on his lead. Bruno, of course, erupted and there was a lot of noise, as he lunged and growled. No damage was done and I got Bruno away but the collie's guardian turned to me coldly and said: "That dog should be put down. He's vicious."

I was devastated. Bruno was anything but vicious. He was sweet and affectionate with me and all his friends, including female dogs and people. I was so upset that I put him in the car and drove two hours to my parents' house to spend the weekend, just so I didn't have to risk meeting that man again.

Looking back on that encounter now, it is likely that the man was also upset, perhaps afraid that his dog was going to be hurt. People lash out when frightened. He may also have held the common belief that growling is a sign of aggression, rather than a communication of concern. The combination of fear and ignorance can lead to hurtful comments.

Did you say something?

Sometimes you meet a guardian who is completely unaware of anything. They may be on their phone, chatting or simply distracted. Sometimes they are not even present. They may be half a mile back down the path and their dog is essentially taking themselves for a walk. When guardians are so disconnected from what their dog is doing that they don't even hear you talking to them, then you usually have to take things into your own hands. We will look at ways to do this and specifically how to handle loose or unaccompanied dogs a little later in this chapter.

I'm so sorry!

It is always worth remembering that not everyone whose dog bothers yours is unaware. Sometimes they have been taken by surprise or misjudged their dog's responses. This happened to me in the incident with Martha on the beach that I described in the last chapter. I misjudged her arousal level and was taken by surprise by her behaviour. I ran after her as fast I could to retrieve her, and as I ran I heard the words "She's friendly" come out of my mouth! At that moment I realised that sometimes those words are used to try to reassure, by someone who is fully aware that their dog approaching yours is a problem but wants you to know that the reason they are running full pelt after their dog is not because their dog is intent on eating yours! As I got closer I apologised profusely to the woman whose dog she approached. I am sure this has happened to some of you too!

If someone is trying to retrieve their dog and apologetic about it then give them some slack. They may have made a mistake but they are doing their best and it can happen to any of us.

Of course, no problem!
There is one more group of people that we also meet regularly, but who we often forget. These are the ones whose dogs have good recall. We ask them to recall their dog and their response is a cheery "No problem" as their dog goes back to them willingly and any trouble is averted. Sometimes we don't even notice them because they have already seen us, noticed our dog is on a lead and put theirs on too. Their dog may already be on a lead or long line as they are still working on their recall and know their dog can be a nuisance to other dogs. We may not even have cause to speak to them at all.

Our negativity bias means that we tend not to notice these guardians. They are not associated with trauma and they don't increase our stress. However, the fact that we don't always notice or remember them does not mean they are not there. It can be worth taking a moment to acknowledge them. It can really help us keep perspective.

We have seen that people respond to us out of ignorance, incompetence, insensitivity or simply being in cloud cuckoo land and we cannot change that. The only thing that we *can* control is our own response. We can do this by understanding and managing our own emotional responses and focusing on making our interactions with others clear, confident and kind. We can also practise strategies to keep ourselves, our dogs and other people as safe as possible. These things are not easy but they are possible. Let's have a closer look at how.

Understanding our own reactions

Just as the people we encounter have their own things going on, so do we. When someone responds negatively to our dog – the dog we love, the dog we wish everyone else could see and understand as we do – we do not always react rationally. We react emotionally. It is worth looking for a moment at the emotions that are likely to be driving our responses.

Fear and Anger

When we are out with our reactive dog fear may be very close to the surface. We are afraid that they will react and upset other people or be difficult to handle. We are afraid that they will hurt another dog or a person. Underlying all of that, if we live in a country with strong dog control laws, is a deep fear that they will be taken from us by the authorities or even killed. None of these fears are trivial.

We react because we are afraid and our reaction can take one of four main forms: fight, flight, freeze and fool around.

We have probably all experienced these responses. We may have tried hard to get out of a difficult situation and move away – flight. We may have felt powerless and unable to act – freeze. We may have tried to laugh it off and make light of the situation – fool around. However, our most common response is often fight: we get angry.

Anger may take different forms. We yell at the person who is there. We rant about them later. We get angry with ourselves. We even get angry with our dogs.

The form our anger takes tends to be learned. We model it on our experiences of anger in our formative years. If we witnessed anger being expressed through shouting, we are likely to shout. If we saw an authority figure belittling or threatening or bullying the object of their anger, our own anger is likely to express itself in similar ways. If anger was never expressed openly, we are more likely to internalise it and turn it on ourselves.

We need to recognise that anger is a response to stress and fear. It is our body's way of preparing us to deal with a threat. It has much of the same physiological impact on the body as fear: heart rate and blood pressure go up, breathing rate increases, muscles tense, attention narrows as the sympathetic nervous system takes control. In this state our rational brain is naturally subordinated. We don't need to think things through rationally when we are fighting for survival. However, our rational brain is powerful and we can train it to override these emotional responses where appropriate. We will look at how a little later.

Embarrassment and Shame
Sometimes our response is not anger or fear but embarrassment and shame. We are not afraid that our dog will get into trouble – we know that they are 'all noise' or perhaps not the type of dog that other people fear. Nevertheless, when our dog lunges or barks at the perfectly well-behaved and under control dog across the park or at the child laughing and smiling as they skip along or at the jogger who is minding their own business on their morning run, we are mortified. For those of us who are dog trainers, that embarrassment is magnified a hundred-fold. The shame can be very real.

Shame, embarrassment and guilt are distinct but inter-related. Shame is one of the most debilitating emotions we have. The fear of being shamed in front of other people, including complete strangers, is paralyzing and can stop us acting at all. Brené Brown, a researcher into shame, defines it as "intensely painful feeling or experience of believing we are flawed and therefore unworthy of acceptance and belonging".[36] It is not about what we do, it is about who we are.

Guilt, on the other hand, is the recognition that we have done something wrong. Embarrassment is a more fleeting feeling that we know will pass, from an experience that we know others have also experienced.

Brown has shown that it is shame that is correlated with depression, addiction, self-harm and bullying. Guilt, perhaps surprisingly, is negatively correlated to these things. Once again making the distinction between 'I am' and 'I did' is critical. Listen to your self-talk when an incident happens. Do you say: "I am useless", "I am such a rubbish trainer" or do you say: "I got that wrong", "I could have handled that better"? The former is shame, the latter guilt (perhaps with a bit of embarrassment thrown in!).

We can feel shame if we do not live up to our own beliefs. We saw in the last section that the people we meet may be experiencing cognitive dissonance, where their actions are in conflict with their beliefs and we can also experience it, of course. We will look at how to address that in the next section.

Reacting emotionally is absolutely understandable: someone we love is being criticised or even threatened. Our brain is designed to respond rapidly to threats so our emotional brain responses are already in motion well before our rational brain kicks in. Managing and changing our emotional responses therefore doesn't come naturally to us but it can be done.

When we manage our emotions we are not negating them or

---

[36] Brené Brown, *I thought it was just me (but it isn't)*, Kindle Edition.

pretending they are not there. We can't turn them off at will, nor would we want to. Emotions are part of being human and are important for our wellbeing.

Emotions are not inherently positive or negative. We tend to see fear or anger as negative emotions but they are there to protect us and we can use them to help us take action in a positive way. So our emotions are not wrong: we just need to think about how we respond to them.

We always have a choice in how we respond. We can sometimes convince ourselves that there is only one way we can react to a particular feeling but it simply isn't true. We always have choices.

Our anger about an incident may be justified but who is it serving? If we get angry or frustrated or think negative thoughts, it is we and our dog who will be affected by it. The person who triggered it will be long gone, but our stress levels will rise, and our dog will pick up on our emotional state. For the sake of our dogs, we need to manage our emotions. We cannot prevent the initial emotional response, but we can choose what we do with it. We can choose whether we act on it, dwell on it, hold on to it, and allow it to fester, or whether we assess it, challenge it, reframe it and channel it. It isn't easy. But it is empowering!

Let's look at some ways that you can start to manage and change how you respond.

Changing our emotional responses

Reframing: Three Accounts Game

Sometimes our anger or embarrassment comes from our assumptions about people. We assume they are judging us. We assume they are rude or careless or arrogant or unsympathetic. We take on the role of mind reader and assume we know what other people are thinking.

However, actions and facial expressions do not always mean

what we imagine they mean. We may assume that the person who turns and stares when our dog barks is disapproving but they may simply be curious as to what the noise was or be a dog lover who can't resist a quick glance at any dog. We may assume that the person who snaps at us is angry with us but they may be in pain or worried about their health or have just received bad news, so be trigger stacked themselves.

Of course they might be rude or careless or arrogant or unsympathetic but who is to say? They may also be embarrassed, struggling with their own dog, just wanting to make conversation with another person, or dealing with their own troubles. The bottom line is that most of the time we will never know. However, when we make assumptions we become angry. Sometimes we become embarrassed ourselves or feel inadequate. We create in ourselves negativity that has nowhere to go and does not help us.

One way to shift our emotional response is to play the Three Accounts game. We can use this with the person who lets their dog run up to us; with the 'my dog is friendly' lady in the park; with the chap who offers unwanted advice on how we should train our dog; with the person who scowls at us in the street when our dog barks; or any other situation where we assign motive to another person.

The Three Accounts game is simple but very powerful. Whenever someone does something that you immediately think of as hurtful, stupid or inconsiderate, come up with at least three alternative accounts: three other possible explanations for the behaviour.

Here's an example unrelated to dogs. You are driving along minding your own business and someone cuts in front of you from a side road. You are forced to brake and they speed off revving their engine. You might assume that they are just an idiot 'boy racer' (and add your choice of expletive) but are there alternative explanations? Perhaps they are rushing their dog to the vet or have just heard that their mother has had an accident. Perhaps they just didn't see you because they are distracted by the fact that they have just lost their job. Perhaps they simply took their eye off the ball for a second, realised their mistake and raced away to avoid inconveniencing you further. Three accounts.

The Three Accounts game really shifts your focus. It reframes your thinking about other people's actions in a way that changes your response. Instead of getting angry with strangers for behaving in ways you can't control, it makes you more sympathetic. It also gives you time to challenge your emotional response and more mental space to focus on the things you can control – your own behaviour and how you work with your dog.

We can even do this when someone has been explicitly rude or said something that upsets us. Here the interpretation of their comments may not be open to question but we can still play the Three Accounts game about their motivation. What are three reasons why they may lack understanding or behave aggressively? Even here the exercise can diffuse our natural feelings of hurt and anger.

Try it. It can be quite fun!

Exercise: Practise the Three Accounts Game
Imagine you are faced with the following scenarios. Come up with at least three explanations for each of these behaviours.

- ☐ A man tells you that you are "doing it all wrong" when you step off the path and treat your dog as he and his dog go past.
- ☐ A woman turns to look at you when your dog barks at another dog.
- ☐ A man does nothing to stop his dog running up to yours.
- ☐ A woman shouts at you when you take hold of her dog's collar to stop him bothering your dog.

Whose emotion is it anyway?

Sometimes we experience emotions that feel alien to us. We may wonder why, when we have done everything right, we still feel shame and guilt. The reason these emotions feel alien is that they do not actually belong to us. After a difficult incident, we can sometimes take on the emotions felt by others.

Remember the incident when Mirri and I were surrounded by four boisterous retrievers? On that occasion I had done everything right. Mirri was on her lead and sporting a vivid pink leg bandage. We were in a wide open space. We had stepped twenty feet off the path and were focused on playing our games together. My partner had politely asked the other guardian to keep his dogs away. There was little more we could have done to avert an incident. Yet I left that situation feeling useless, upset and embarrassed – and it took me weeks before I could bring myself to go back to that meadow. So where did those emotions come from? The truth is they almost certainly came from the other guardian who, as we saw earlier, deflected his own embarrassment by redirecting it on to us. I had effectively taken on his emotions.

The antidote for this is to simply refuse to accept these alien emotions. We can choose whether or not to take on other people's emotions. If you find yourself feeling strong emotions, such as shame or embarrassment, when you have done nothing to be embarrassed about, ask yourself: Where did that come from? Do those emotions really belong to me? Or do they reflect how the other person was feeling?

If the emotions are not ours, we do not have to accept them. We can simply acknowledge that they are not ours and, metaphorically, give them back. Challenging and, where appropriate, rejecting emotions that do not belong to us allows us to move on much more quickly from upsetting incidents.

Challenging our beliefs

Sometimes our emotional responses come as a result of a conflict between our beliefs and our actions: cognitive dissonance. This is particularly the case with shame.

Sometimes it is our actions that need work. If we didn't manage to control our dog as well as we believe we should have, we can focus on improving our management and training skills (more on this later).

However, more often the problem is with our beliefs. We feel shame because our dog is behaving in a way that conflicts with our beliefs about how dogs should be or what a good guardian looks like. Here we need to examine and change these beliefs.

As we saw in Chapter 3, beliefs are not static and we can discard and replace those that do not serve us well. For example, we may believe that good dog guardians have problem-free dogs. Our dog's behaviour therefore makes us ashamed because we are not living up to that belief and we do not feel worthy of belonging to the 'community' of good dog guardians (or trainers or whatever our focus is). Others may wittingly or unwittingly reinforce our beliefs: "There are no bad dogs, just bad owners" is a classic (but completely false!) comment that increases this feeling of shame. So challenging these beliefs, as we challenged our limiting beliefs in Chapter 3, can help here too.

Ultimately, shame feeds on the belief that you are isolated by what you are ashamed of, so simply sharing can help, as long as those you share with are empathetic. Find a safe community where you can share your feelings (see later). If you do feel shame, talk about it. Discovering you are not alone will make all the difference.

Channelling our emotions

Emotions are not inherently good or bad and sometimes it can help to channel our feelings of anger or fear or embarrassment into motivation for change.

If you are angry about loose dogs or careless guardians you can use that anger constructively by campaigning and supporting the creation of safe areas for dogs who need space. Get involved in your local area in educational campaigns like Yellow Dog (see later). Write a short article for your community paper or magazine about the challenges of living with a reactive dog.

If you are fearful about the legal risks to your dogs because of their breed or people perceiving them as threatening, you can campaign against draconian and uninformed dog control laws.

If you are embarrassed because your dog barks at strangers, you can seek help to work on that problem and start training.

Our emotions can be a force for good to drive us to take action to improve the situation, so rather than ranting about how difficult other guardians are, why not channel that anger constructively?

Managing and changing our emotional responses is not easy but it begins with awareness. Start by simply recording your responses for a couple of weeks and writing down how you feel in different situations. You will then be in a better position to assess and manage your reactions.

However, wouldn't it be better if we could reduce the number of negative encounters that we have? We will never avoid these completely, but in the next section we will look at ways we can change how we interact with other guardians so that our interactions become more positive than negative.

Changing how we interact with other guardians

We have looked at how we can manage our emotional responses to difficult encounters with strangers. However, we can also change how we interact with other people, so that we can take more control of the encounters we have.

Instruct, don't ask

Feeling in control is critical for our confidence and well-being. When we are out with our dog we often feel out of control, particularly when we have to interact with other people. One of the reasons we feel helpless is that we struggle to communicate what we need to other people.

It is important to give instructions rather than explanations to the people we meet. Instructions are both clear and to the point. We are not leaving any room for questions or argument. We are not expecting the other person to understand what the issue is or sympathise with us; we are simply telling them what we need them to do.

This often goes against the grain for us, particularly if we come from a culture or an upbringing where being deferential is valued. However, giving an instruction does not have to be rude. We can be polite and use 'please'! However, always start with the instruction and then add the politeness. "Recall your dog, please" is better than "Please would you mind calling your dog?" In the former the action you want the other person to do is up front. It is clear and unequivocal but not impolite. With the latter the other dog will be half way towards you before the instruction is actually uttered!

By all means get into more discussion later, if appropriate. If it helps to give some explanation then that is fine but the time to do that is after the instruction has been given and comprehended. If you start by getting into an explanation of how your dog is a rescue or was attacked as a puppy or is a bit feisty or doesn't like Spaniels then, again, the other dog will be on top of you before the other guardian knows what you need.

The same, of course, applies if our dog is reactive to people. "Stop, please!" "Don't touch, please" first and then the explanation if you need to give it. If necessary, back up your instruction with a hand signal. People will generally understand if you extend your hand towards them with palm out. This is a universal sign to stop. Be firm and clear with a big and obvious gesture. There is no room for a half-hearted response here.

You will, of course, meet people who ignore your instructions. They may not try to retrieve their dog because they know they can't or they may feel they have a God-given right to do as they please. Sometimes, telling a 'white lie' will encourage some effort on their part. My favourite is "My dog is contagious" followed up with some embellishment about expensive vet bills, if concern for their dog's health is not enough to get them moving! If this doesn't work, you will need to take control of the situation yourself. We will look at how to handle off-lead dogs coming towards you a little later.

If you find it difficult to get the right words out under pressure and you find yourself waffling, it can really help to practise in front of the mirror. Create a script that makes sense to you and that you feel comfortable saying. Make sure it gets your point across quickly and clearly. Now practise saying it, over and over, until it comes out of your mouth automatically. You may feel rather silly giving instructions to your mirror but you will come across as much more confident when you have to do it for real.

Yellow Dogs
At this point it is worth mentioning the Yellow Dog project, an international campaign aimed at raising awareness of dogs who need space, including those who can be reactive. The idea is that dogs who need space wear a yellow ribbon on their lead or harness, or a yellow bandana, or a yellow vest. This gives a visual cue to others not to approach, while the dog is still at a safe distance.

The idea of the Yellow Dog project is excellent but it will only work if it becomes general knowledge what the yellow sign means.

This will obviously take time and education. However, the more of us who use these signs and explain their meaning when asked, the more word will get around.

There are now many variations of the Yellow Dog Project around the world and it is possible to buy yellow lead slips, vests and coats printed with whatever message you prefer, making this another way to communicate your instructions to others, without saying a word. A jacket that clearly says "Stay Away" or "No Dogs" can get the message across before you are close enough even to have that conversation.

There has been some concern about whether using yellow equipment is an admission that your dog is dangerous. Legal opinion[37] is that this is not the case as there are many reasons why a dog may require space, including being in training, being old or infirm, being ill or being fearful. None of these things implies dangerous. You are not warning people to 'beware', you are instructing people to give space. However, a vest saying something like "In Training: Do not Disturb" will get the message across without any implication of danger, if you are concerned about this issue.

Advocate or educate?

When our dog is reactive we sometimes feel that we have a responsibility to 'educate' the people we meet; that they need to know how what they have done or not done has affected you. However, we have very little chance of educating people in the context of a walk and, most of the time, attempts to do so will not only fall on deaf ears but may even entrench opinions. No one likes to be told they are wrong!

Many of the people we meet could certainly benefit from some

---

[37] https://www.yellowdoguk.co.uk/index.php/blog/2-are-you-admitting-liability-by-displaying-a-yellow-ribbon

education, but effective education demands a desire for learning on the part of the other person and some kind of commitment. We might be able to plant a seed of interest but realistically few people are likely to be changed by a brief encounter in a park.

Once in a while we may have an opportunity to explain to someone why allowing their dog to approach ours is so difficult for us or why it is always a good idea to ask before trying to touch someone else's dog. So there is no harm in thinking through what we would say and, sometimes, having easy-to-read information to give them can be helpful.[38]

For the most part, education will happen elsewhere and we can certainly contribute to this in many ways:

- ☐ Talk to friends and family so that they understand the difficulties you and your dog can face.
- ☐ Write a short article for your local parish magazine or your neighbourhood Facebook page about your experiences of living with a reactive dog.
- ☐ Tell people you meet at training classes about appropriate lead and space etiquette (and include this in your curriculum if you are a trainer).
- ☐ Support information campaigns like Yellow Dog.

However, this is not our main role on walks. On walks our role is to speak up for our dog, to act as an advocate for their needs, to make sure they are protected, as far as possible, from things that would be too much for them to handle.

We are the only one who will do this. We can often be too polite, too worried about what people will think of us. We don't want to be rude. But really, who is being rude if you ask someone to stay away and they just keep coming? You are not obliged to talk to

---

[38] Lili Chin has a free downloadable folding mini-booklet⌐ ⌐ which is great for this purpose:
http://blog.doggiedrawings.net/post/161598725951/spaceetiquettebooklet

people if you do not want to and your dog is not required to meet other dogs. Instead of worrying about upsetting a complete stranger, prioritise not upsetting your dog. We have to be prepared to advocate for our dogs, to keep them safe, to refuse to let other people put them at risk. If that offends some, so be it. It is not the end of the world. They will get over it – and probably faster than your dog!

If you find it difficult to be assertive, once again the key is practice! Practise with friends or to the mirror. Think through different scenarios and work out what you would say then practise actually saying it. The more you practise, the more likely it is to come out the way you intend.

This role is important even if our dog is sociable with people. We still need to make sure that they have choice about when and how they interact.

Some dogs seem to have a magnetic effect on some humans! People will reach out to touch them and children will try to cuddle them. Sometimes they will ask first but often they will go straight into touching without asking anyone.

Even when our dogs are sociable, it is important that they are still given a choice in whether or not they interact. Like us, sometimes they will prefer to be left alone and that is their right. It is lovely that people want to admire our dogs but sometimes we need to remind them that our dogs are not public property. Interaction can be requested but the ultimate decision about whether to engage with them should always rest with our dog.

When that interaction is not welcome, it is up to us to step in. As an advocate for our dog, we need to decline attention politely and explain that our dog needs space right now. We do not need to be rude but we do need to mean it and be prepared to enforce it, if necessary removing our dog from unwelcome encounters.

Ultimately, if your dog never wants to interact with any stranger ever, that is a perfectly acceptable choice. There is no rule that says dogs should be sociable with strangers. There is no law that says they must say hello just because a human wants to.

If both parties are willing and enthusiastic there can be nothing nicer than meeting new people and dogs, but it has to be their choice – and it is up to us to make sure they have that choice.

Convey Confidence and Calm

We may not be able to change everyone into positive allies by our own attitude but there is no doubt that people will be influenced by how we respond to a situation. If we are anxious and concerned, they are more likely to be anxious and concerned. If we are angry, they are more likely to become angry.

I know this from experience. Many years ago we had a bite incident with our collie, Jake and, as a result, he was always muzzled in public. Mirri was also muzzled if there was a chance a dog could get up close, as she had a tendency to do a 'lurcher nip' at dogs who ran past and she was also a chaser of small furries. So, for a while, both dogs wore muzzles but I felt completely differently about the reasons why.

Jake had bitten a person. The muzzle was a necessity but it was also a reminder of an incident that had been deeply upsetting and frightening, not to mention challenging for my own self-belief as a professional. Mirri, on the other hand, was pretty much bombproof with people and even her reaction to dogs was largely bluster. Even close up, I knew she would not do serious damage though she might catch a dog's fur with a front teeth nip. So her muzzle had none of these emotional associations for me.

When asked about the muzzle with Mirri I would respond lightly: "Oh, she can be a bit nippy with dogs in her face" or, if they are on their own, "She's fine – it's just to protect the squirrels". I was also able to keep her lead loose and long if the person didn't have a dog, as I trusted her completely with humans. I rarely, if ever, had negative reactions to Mirri and her muzzle.

With Jake I was completely different. I kept myself between him and the other person. I kept him close to me. I was almost certainly more physically tense. When they asked, "Does he bite?" I struggled to find an appropriate response. As a result, people were tended to avoid us or mutter about the 'nasty' dog as we passed.

The reality is that I presented a completely different picture to the people I met so it is not surprising they reacted differently. In one case I was relaxed and treated the muzzled dog lightly, and so did they. In the other, I was tense and treated the muzzled dog as a potential problem, and lo and behold, so did they!

When we have a tight lead and tense body language, when we snap at people and when we are flustered or panicked, we are projecting concern. When we talk lightly to our dogs, when we tell our grumbly dog "Don't be daft" in a gentle, light voice as we pass someone, when we keep leads loose and body language as relaxed as we can, we are projecting confidence and calmness.

If our dog is going to launch themselves at another dog or person, we need to be realistic and increase our distance or, if caught out, use tools like the TTouch balance lead (see Chapter 6) or pattern games (see Chapter 8) to get us past. At least for now.

However, when we can, we can start to work on conveying confidence and calmness by paying attention to how we are feeling. We may need to work on those feelings where they are negative, as mine were to Jake's muzzle. We may also need to work on ourselves, learning new leading techniques to help us in more stressful situations (see Chapter 6) and learning how to be more neutral and relaxed on walks (see Chapter 7).

This will not miraculously turn everyone into an ally, of course, but it can go a long way towards cultivating more positive interactions with the people that we meet.

Be Kind

Kindness is a funny thing. I remember years ago when I was doing my coaching training, being genuinely incredulous when the other participants identified 'kindness' as something they recognised in me. Not only did I not feel kind, but I realised I didn't value it either. It felt a bit 'wussy', weak even. Nice feelings but no more.

Of course I was wrong. Kindness is not how you feel but how you act. It is the things that you choose to say and do and the assumptions that you make. Being kind is both difficult and a sign of strength.

None of us would argue about the need to be kind to our dogs. We understand that responsibility and take it seriously. Even in the moments when we lose our temper or get things wrong, we are very aware of it because being kind to our dogs is a fundamental belief we all share.

However, do we extend the same kindness to other people, especially to those we disagree with and those who inconvenience us or cause us difficulty?

Being kind means being considerate, generous and compassionate. It means giving people the benefit of the doubt. It means assuming that someone is doing their best, with the knowledge they have at the moment. It means putting yourself in their shoes and treating them as you would want to be treated. It does not mean you have to agree with them or condone them, but it does mean you have to consider them.

Treating people kindly is not always easy but when we make the effort to do it, to give them the benefit of the doubt when necessary, they will respond. You never know, that stranger in the park may yet become your greatest ally.

Changing how we interact with other people is one side of the coin but, on its own, it is not enough. We also need to take action to ensure that we, our dogs and other people stay safe. We will look at this next.

Keeping everyone safe

While changing how we interact with other people is important and can have a dramatic effect on how they react to us, sometimes this will not be enough and we have to take further action to keep ourselves and our dogs safe. In this section we will consider how to handle loose dogs and aggressive strangers and how to stay safe and within the law.

Dealing with loose dogs

Sometimes the dogs that are bothering you do not have an active guardian. Their guardian may have ignored your instruction to recall their dog or they may have tried and failed to retrieve their dog. Sometimes they are simply too far away or too distracted to be of any use. In this case, the dog is, in effect, unaccompanied and you will need to take matters into your own hands.

The priority is of course to get your dog away as quickly as possible, so training a "Let's go" cue for your own dog is vital. You don't want to be in a position where you have to drag your dog away, which will increase their arousal. Practise this a lot without distractions so that your dog responds instantly. Leslie McDevitt's whiplash turn game[39] is a great place to start with this. You can also play her pattern games like 123 Treat to get you out of trouble; the structure and pattern gives your dog something familiar to focus on while you get away. We'll talk more about both of these in Chapter 8.

You will need to try to get something between you and the approaching dog. Barriers are your friends. Make a mental note of them as you walk and, where possible, move away to the nearest

---

[39] See McDevitt, L (2019) *Control Unleashed: Reactive to Relaxed*. MA: Clean Run.

environmental barrier and get behind it. Fences, trees, walls and cars can all work well. Dogs are less likely to continue to approach if you put something between you and them, plus your own dog is going to be more relaxed behind a barrier.

If there are no environmental barriers, you can use yourself as a barrier or you can use a pop-up umbrella, as suggested by my friend and TTouch colleague Tracey McLennan in her lovely book *Canine Aggression*.[40] Be sure to practise this in advance so that you can put it up one-handed, even under pressure. Make sure your own dog is used to the umbrella. Start with it open at a distance and let them investigate it. Give them lots of treats so that it has a positive association and gradually build up until they are comfortable with it opening in front of them and standing behind it. Using an umbrella as a barrier has a number of advantages:

- It is portable so you can always have it with you.
- It is unusual and therefore likely to surprise another dog into stopping their approach.
- It provides a physical barrier between you and the other dog, should they not stop.

This may, of course, be mildly aversive to the other dog, so should be used thoughtfully. However, if it is our only choice to protect our dog, then I think it is justified.

Other physical props that you might be carrying, like a walking stick, can also provide a barrier. Hold the stick out in front of you, vertically angled across your body. It doesn't create the physical barrier an umbrella does, but it is definitely better than nothing.

Once you are behind a barrier many dogs will lose interest and go and bother someone else. If they don't, or if you can't find a barrier, what do you do next?

This really depends on the situation. Thankfully most

---

[40] McLennan, T (2018) *Canine Aggression*, Hubble and Hattie: Dorchester, p. 50

approaching dogs are over-friendly, untrained and over-zealous but not aggressive. They do not intend your dog any harm (although, of course, harm is exactly what they do if they bounce on your anxious or fearful dog).

However, the fact that they are not intent on hurting anyone does mean that they can often be deflected or distracted. I have often had success just by standing my ground (in front of my dog), holding out my hand and telling them to "Go Away!" loudly and firmly.

Another trick to buy you time to get away is throwing treats at the approaching dog. If you are going to try this, remember to practise throwing treats one way and running in the opposite direction with your dog. Make sure they gets loads of reinforcement for coming away. Otherwise you could end up with the stray dog and your dog both piling in to the same scattered treats at the same time! Not the outcome you want!

You might think that throwing treats is unlikely to stop an approaching dog but it does work. The dog is momentarily startled and then starts chomping on the tasty treats that have fallen from the sky, giving you and your dog time to get away. Patricia McConnell did a small trial of this method and found that it worked well with a range of different dogs. It is worth watching her video of this to see how to do it properly.[41]

With anything that we use to deal with a bothersome dog, we need to be cautious. Try to avoid making physical contact with the other dog. Of course, hitting another dog, even if it is a pest, is not fair. The dog is not to blame for the fact their guardian is not taking proper care of them. Even catching the dog by the collar is not recommended. You do not know how the dog will respond to this and it may trigger a reaction. Touching their dog can also provoke

---

[41] https://www.patriciamcconnell.com/theotherendoftheleash/it-works-how-to-stop-an-approaching-dog-in-an-emergency-2

an aggressive response from the guardian, which will only make the situation worse.

If you do have to catch an errant dog, whether to return to their guardian, or if you believe them to be a stray, use your lead to make a loop that you can slip round their neck. That way you can keep them secure while still holding them at a little distance.

These methods work with the curious, over-friendly dogs who tend to be the ones who bother us on walks but none of them are likely to stop a highly-aroused, genuinely aggressive dog. There are more aversive tools such as ultrasonic dog deterrents and citronella sprays designed for these situations but there are two main problems with these (as well as the ethical concerns):

1.   You do not know how the other dog will respond if they are uncomfortable or irritated. They may stop or it may make the situation worse.

2.   These tools do not discriminate so your own dog will also experience the disturbing noise or scent. This could have negative consequences for your dog.

Therefore, I do not recommend these. However, if you know that there are genuinely dangerous dogs straying in your area and you are fearful for your own or your dog's safety, then carrying something like Sprayshield or Biteback to use as a last resort is an option available to you. If you feel you have to carry something like this, make sure it is not going to cause lasting damage and that the spray can be directed carefully away from your own dog.

If your dog is actually attacked then your priority is only to get the other dog off. Unfortunately there is no 'force-free' way to do this so do what you need to do. There is no point in telling you to protect yourself because, I suspect, you will just dive in to save your dog anyway, without thought of your own safety! However, try to use props – sticks, coats, bags – rather than your hands to separate them. Call for help if you can and prioritise getting away.

Thankfully serious attacks are much rarer than you would think. Most fights are 'squabbles' which result in little damage though can look and sound awful. In fact, if there is a lot of noise, the likelihood is the dogs will not hurt each other seriously. It is the silent attack that is particularly dangerous.

So be prepared for the worst but do not go out expecting it. Practise for emergencies and you will have the resources you need, should the worst happen.

Dealing with aggressive strangers

We've already looked at how we can change how we think about other guardians but what do we do if a stranger becomes aggressive with us or our dog in a public place?

The first thing is to try to remain calm yourself. Take a deep breath. Remember that there is very likely more to this person's response than meets the eye. They may be afraid. Perhaps they are worried about their dog or felt afraid of yours (even if this is not justified)? They are very likely trigger-stacked themselves. It is not your job to address that but it can help to remember that an aggressive response usually comes out of fear at some level. They are 'reacting' in much the same way our dog reacts.

When someone becomes abusive with us, our natural response is often to retaliate. We want to justify ourselves and to defend the honour of our dog. So we often respond in a like manner – and all that does is escalate the argument.

In situations like this the best thing to do is to walk away. Say as little as possible and walk in the opposite direction. Few people will follow you if you have not engaged with them at all.

You may be tempted to try to argue your case but this is really not the time. There is no point in trying to reason with someone when they are hostile or upset – they are not in a state to change their mind.

If you feel under actual threat of harm, get to where there are other people, call for help or call the police. Always carry a phone for emergencies and, if you are having unpleasant experiences regularly, consider a body-worn camera or chest-cam to record any incidents. Many people will think twice if they believe they are on camera, but it also provides evidence should you need it.

Staying within the law
Sometimes we fear not only what people think but what they might do. Will they make a complaint about our dog or have them seized and put to sleep? In this litigious world and with dangerous dogs legislation being extended in many countries such concern is understandable. In the UK someone only has to feel they are at risk from a dog to make a complaint under the Dangerous Dogs Act and we may know that our dog would bite if pushed, with unthinkable consequences. These fears are based on real risks but, in most cases, these risks can be mitigated.

We can address this fear by taking control of the situation. We can minimise risk of complaint and make sure we keep other people safe. It is also useful to know the law and understand both our responsibilities and our rights. This will obviously vary from country to country so I cannot make any specific comments here but find out what laws apply to you and your dog. Knowledge is power.

Do not take chances that could endanger other people. If you know that your dog chases joggers, don't wait for the jogger to appear before you take action. Make sure that there is no way they can ever do it. Use a lead or long line in any situation where you are not sure your dog will recall reliably and where you might meet a jogger. If you know that your dog might bite if a stranger reaches out to them, muzzle them in any situation where this is possible.

Taking steps like these not only minimises the chances of anyone having cause for complaint but provides you with a defence if the unthinkable happens and the police get involved. Your dog being on a lead and muzzled may not be a full defence but it does demonstrate that you are a responsible and thoughtful guardian.

FRIENDS AND FAMILY

Most of the issues we have with other people are with strangers but what about when our dog's behaviour brings conflict closer to home? What do you do when you have a difference of opinion with friends or family members about how to train or handle your dog? How can you make progress if you have people at home who are sabotaging your efforts? And how do you handle it if a partner or other close family member is dubious about keeping your dog? What do you do if friends no longer want to see you because they are frightened of your dog?

There is no doubt that having a dog with challenging behaviour can put pressure on our closest relationships. If we are lucky, our nearest and dearest love our dog as much as we do and are as committed to helping them using kind and effective methods. When this is the case we have a genuine ally (more about allies later).

However, there can be differences of opinion and, even if our family is committed to helping our dog, these differences can create conflict. So what can we do?

Well, it will depend on the extent of our dog's reactivity and the point at which there is disagreement but there are some principles that will always help you to make progress.

Acknowledge concerns

When we love our dog, it can sometimes be hard to admit that they are difficult to live with. We may feel that we are being disloyal or that it somehow means we love them less. We may resent family members who talk in these terms.

Remember your dog is not their reactive behaviour: it is not what defines them. It is not who they are: it is just behaviour. Acknowledging that this behaviour has an impact on your family life is not the same as saying you don't want your dog in your family.

However, when someone else is finding that behaviour difficult, they need to know that you recognise this and that you understand it. Remember your family members also had their dreams about what having a dog would be like, so listen to their concerns and acknowledge how your dog's behaviour is affecting their day-to-day life. This is particularly important where they are involved in caring for your dog or where they are put at any risk by your dog's behaviour.

Talk to them about their concerns. What are they most worried about? What upsets them the most? It may not be what you imagine and it may be something that you can address through simple changes to the way you do things. Even if it is not, talking to them means you can make sure that your training plan takes account of the concerns of everyone in your household.

Listening is critical. When you live with other people, the decisions you make will also affect them. It is only fair to hear their concerns. In some cases these may be safety concerns: they may be worried about their friends being bitten, or children or elderly relatives visiting, or even themselves or your own children. They may be worried about the legal implications: is your dog going to land them in trouble with the police? They may be concerned about the mounting cost of what is needed to help your dog. We can't deny that having a dog who needs behavioural help comes with a price tag attached. We may end up buying new equipment, books like this one, having to pay more for individual dog walkers or home boarders, or for one-to-one training. They may have more personal concerns: that they can't do the things they'd like to do and that they want to be able to go for 'normal' walks rather than have to plan more carefully.

Remember that these concerns are valid and that expressing them does not mean that your family member does not love your dog or that they want rid of them. It just means that they find it difficult too. So listen and acknowledge these concerns.

Be flexible where you can

When we are our dog's primary care giver or trainer or the one making decisions about how to work with our dog, we need to be clear on our options and choices. In the remaining chapters in this book we will look at some of those options relating to handling, walks and training and give you the information you need to make informed choices. You may also have professional help and be working through an agreed training programme.

There are some elements of all this that are fixed in stone. We do not inflict fear or pain or pressure on our dogs in order to get them to comply with what we want. We don't flood them so that they become overwhelmed and shut down. We do reward the behaviours we want to see and we do listen to what our dog is communicating to us. We are kind to our dogs, to ourselves and to each other. These are principles on which we can't compromise.

However, there are still many areas where we can be flexible. We can be flexible about different training strategies that all use positive reinforcement. We can be flexible about the ways in which we walk our dogs and where we go. We can be flexible about how we manage our dog within our household. We can find solutions that take account of everyone's concerns.

So be flexible where you can. This may include sometimes working towards something that you personally would not prioritise. For instance, imagine your partner wants to have a party to mark a significant birthday but you know your dog will not be able to cope with visitors. One option might be to hold the party elsewhere and leave your dog at home, perhaps with a trusted dog sitter. Another would be to recognise that sometimes you will need to have someone else care for your dog and work on finding a good boarding facility or home boarder, who will take them when needed. This may take time so it is worth starting the process well in advance so you can do some trial overnight runs before the main event.

Being flexible does not mean compromising your ethical position or putting your dog in difficult situations but it may mean having to do extra training to accommodate the needs of everyone in the family.

Involve family and friends

Everyone wants to feel needed and that they have a part to play and being involved will give them more investment in the outcome. So, where you can, and where it is safe to do so, involve your family and friends in your plans to help your dog. The important thing here is that you are all singing from the same hymn sheet otherwise your dog will get confused and your training will be much less effective.

Try these three steps to help you to all work together consistently, effectively and harmoniously:

1.   Make a plan. You may do this on your own or in discussion with your family, if they are interested and, ideally, with a professional. Take on suggestions from everyone if those suggestions are appropriate but be ready to explain why you are not including methods that would be unfair on your dog or ineffective. If you have family members who stick to the "well it has always worked for me" argument, it can be useful to draw on some external authority. This is an added

bonus of consulting a professional. You can 'blame' your trainer for the new rules!

2.   Give everyone a role. The plan will mean you are clear about what you are training and why, and about how you are going to do it. But you also need to be clear about who is going to do what. Try to give a role to everyone who wants to be involved but accept that different family members will want different levels of involvement and be supportive of any involvement however small. Remember positive reinforcement works for people too!

3.   Set up your environment to make it easier for everyone to stick to the rules than not. So, for example, make sure there are always pots of treats placed strategically around the house so that it is easy for your family to reward things that they see your dog do that they like. Set up child gates to make it easier to stop your dog being near the front door when it is opened. Leave walking equipment ready and get rid of anything you don't want to be used with your dog. Try to make it easier for everyone to stick to the plan than to do the opposite.

Of course we all have the odd friend or family member who always knows best, who won't listen, even to a professional, or who simply can't be bothered to change anything to help. Where possible, your best strategy is to gently excuse these people from any involvement in things that could make a difference to the success of your plan. So let them make a fuss of your dog and play with them at home, but avoid them getting involved in any training or walking. It can get a bit tricky, especially if you have family members who are keen to help but take a more traditional approach to training. This is where it is important to know why you are doing what you are doing. Explain that this is the way you are training and why and that what they are suggesting will only confuse your dog. If they take this on board, all good. If not, then you may need to insist that they take a step back, at least from walking and training, for the time being.

The same is true of the friend who wants to go for walks with you and your dog but sees no reason to stop her dog leaping all over yours. If you really want to go for walks together try to explain the need for space and work out a plan to allow the dogs to get to know each other in a controlled way. Parallel walking on lead can be a helpful start. But it may simply be easier just to explain that your dog is not yet ready to walk with other dogs and arrange to do something else with your friend instead. If there is any argument, blame your trainer again!

ALLIES

Having a dog who can be reactive is often a lonely place to be. Our friends may all meet up to walk their dogs but we can't go along because our dog can't cope. We may struggle to have visitors at home or it may require planning of such military proportions that we don't bother much. Our family and friends may not understand why we don't just 'tell them off'; some may even question why we keep them at all.

It's not an easy thing to go through on your own. We all need people who understand what it feels like. But when it comes to our dogs, asking for help can also be hard. We may feel we 'should' be able to solve whatever the problem is. We may not know who to ask. We may feel overwhelmed and not know where to start. We may feel we are admitting failure by asking.

A well-known proverb says that it takes a village to raise a child. The same could be said of helping a reactive dog. It is not a job for one person. We all need support, whether from family, from friends, from professionals, from our community and peers. When we work together and draw on all the expertise surrounding us, the progress we can make is astonishing.

I completely understand the reluctance to ask for help. To say asking for help doesn't come naturally to me is an understatement. I am a helper, a problem solver, the one who 'gets-on-and-does'. I am a coper. I know that asking for help is hard!

A few years ago, my coach challenged me on this. What do I get out of helping others and helping them to solve problems? Is it satisfaction? Fulfilment? Joy? And if I get these things from giving help, have I the right to deny those things to other people who may want to help me? I had no answer to this. It had never occurred to me to think about it in this way: that always helping and always coping can actually be a selfish choice.

So, even if you find it hard, reach out and ask for the help you need. Remember Superbetter? Seek out those allies who can support you.

Allies help us get perspective when everything is looking grim. Allies pick us up and give us a hug when things have gone badly. Allies are there to celebrate all those tiny wins and understand how humungous those tiny wins really are! Allies support us and cheer us on as we push our comfort zone and strive to be the best we can. Allies help us problem solve, give us a second opinion, provide an alternative perspective. Allies walk with us even if they can't see the path ahead for the fog any better than we can – and they point out the way-markers that they can see but we have missed. Sometimes they just let us know we are not the only one; that there is someone else who understands. Allies are essential.

So where can we find allies like this? If we are lucky we will have friends and family who will be our allies. Even if they don't have a dog, they will recognise the work we are doing and help us. But sometimes we need to look beyond this and find allies elsewhere.

Professional allies

We may feel we have the knowledge we need to help our dogs. We have done our research, read a lot, practised, we understand what we need to do, we have the skills – so we just keep plodding on by ourselves. We can see no benefit in getting specialist help. What will they tell us that we don't already know?

This can be a mistake. Even if we are doing fine on our own, getting professional help can give us a new perspective. It can introduce new ideas, help us cut through to a better solution, make us more effective and efficient, help us make the best use of our time.

It is not that we can't manage without; we may be able to manage just fine. But a second pair of eyes, with an objective view of the situation brings clarity and focus. It can help us use our time more wisely, can lead to better results, and, perhaps most importantly, it can give us an important ally.

So if you are having issues with your dog, think about investing in professional help, to get that new perspective on the issue, to check that you are going about things in the most effective way. This applies even if you are a professional! We all need a second opinion sometimes.

What that professional help looks like depends on what you need. It may be veterinary or behavioural; it may be help to design a training programme or to move forward in a specific area of performance; it may be seeking support for yourself through coaching or honing your training skills; it may be in developing your dog's physical strength or emotional balance.

Whatever help you need, see it as an investment. Find the right person with the right experience and qualifications. Check that they can deliver what they promise in a way that is positive for both you and your dog. Don't be afraid to ask for testimonials and follow these up if you can. Work out whether you need individual support or a group event or whether you can get the support you need online, through a membership like the Canine Confidence Club.[42]

There is no single solution that will help everyone. We are all at different points with different dogs and different knowledge and skills. But don't struggle on by yourself just because you can cope. Aim to do more than cope: be the best you can be and invest in getting there.

Local allies
Local allies are people that we can meet up with on a regular basis, for moral support or to practise our training. We might meet them through well-run training classes for reactive dogs, through recommendations from our local professional allies or by asking for a local buddy on an online group that supports this service, such as Reactive Dogs UK. We might also meet sympathetic people out walking or at local events where we don't have our dog.

Even just having someone to meet for an occasional coffee can help when we reach the end of our tether. If they are willing, having someone to help you with training practice or to scout for you on walks can be a godsend if you are anxious – and of course you can help them by returning the favour.

Online allies
Even if you don't at the moment have local support, there is still a 'village' available to help you. The internet has made it easier than ever to find allies and we don't even have to meet them to really benefit from having and, of course, being an ally. Joining one of the specialist communities on Facebook can be helpful.[43] Reactive Dogs UK has qualified trainers for advice and tens of thousands of members who will be your allies. My own Your End of the Lead

---

[42] www.canineconfidenceclub.com
[43] Links to some of these can be found at www.yourendofthelead.com.

group on Facebook is much smaller but also provides a supportive community of people who understand – and is open to members regardless of where you live. There are also paid options like the Canine Confidence Club where you can join with others to work together on shared challenges, share progress and problems, and get advice and suggestions. There is a huge amount of experience and expertise in forums such as these, from people who understand about giving and receiving help.

They may be able to make suggestions to help you move forward or find local support or help you join up with people who will understand. At the very least, they will be allies for you on your journey.

Chapter Six

CHANGING HOW YOU THINK ABOUT LEAD-HANDLING

We have looked at how changing how you think about yourself, your dog, other people and reactivity itself can give you a new perspective on the problem and shift you into a more confident, challenge mindset. In the next three chapters we will look at three key elements of your life with your dog – lead-handling, walks and training – and how thinking about them differently allows you to do things differently and become more effective at helping yourself and your dog be successful.

This chapter will challenge some of your assumptions about how you lead your dog and show you alternative approaches that will help you both become more balanced. We are, as always, aiming for comfort at both ends of the lead.

But before we start I want to take a step outside the mechanics of how we walk with our dogs and talk about the importance of being present with them.

BEING PRESENT

Let me start with a story. A few years ago I did a coaching qualification, which included equine-assisted learning: working with the horses helped us to understand things about ourselves.

I was in a small arena with one of the horses, Blackjack, and he was standing by the gate, stamping his feet, focused completely on his pals in the adjoining area. I had been set the task of moving him quietly round the arena, without a halter or rein. As the 'animal person' in the group, I felt the pressure to get it right. My mind was full of the task and the outcome: how I was going to connect with him and, if I am honest, how impressed everyone would be!

As I moved towards him, he tolerated me for a few seconds then headed back to the gate. I could feel myself becoming frustrated and, when I moved again, he kicked his heels and shot off around the arena! So much for my prowess as an animal trainer.

Blackjack arrived back by the gate near his friends, breathing heavily, clearly unsettled and agitated. I moved back to talk to the rest of the group, feeling rather chastened.

My coach reminded me of the importance of being present. So, before going back to him, I stopped, closed my eyes and started a 'body scan'. I concentrated on my breathing, consciously relaxing each part of my body from head to feet. By focusing on the physical, I was able to still my mind, allowing me to be much more present in the moment.

As I opened my eyes, I saw that Blackjack had come over and was standing with me, with his head lowered and leaning into me. He stayed with me for the next few minutes, completely relaxed, completely connected, happy just to be there with me. When I asked him, he walked with me, calmly moving with me around the arena. It was an amazing feeling.

When I had first approached him, my head had been full of interference. What would the people watching think? Would he connect with me? How would it all work? What was I going to do? None of it was about him! It is not surprising that he freaked out – he was embodying the state of my head at that moment! Only when I let go of my ego and the need to achieve an outcome and simply focused on being with him in that moment, was he able to do the same. And once there, completing the task was easy.

Being present is important for our dogs as well. I have no doubt that when our minds are full of interference, worrying about how and what and why, our dogs find it more difficult to connect with us. This is another reason why it is important to practise new things in quiet places. You do not need the added pressure of other people watching, or worrying about whether you can keep everyone safe.

So as you read this chapter, and try out the techniques discussed, try to stay present. Be aware of your dog, of how they are responding, of whether they are engaged. Take time just to be with them. Go to places where you can safely 'hang out' together. Practise building a connection between you that is not a physical lead. It will make your lead-handling much easier.

HELPING YOUR DOG TO WALK IN BALANCE

Handling our dogs when out on walks is one of the biggest sources of tension for reactive dog guardians. We feel the physical tension on the lead when our dog pulls or lunges and the emotional tension of feeling that we are not in control. Our need for control often leads us to more and more close micro-management of our dog and, in some cases, to equipment that is aversive and unpleasant for our dogs to wear. All of this will pull our dogs out of balance, which will in turn make them more likely to pull on the lead, and so the cycle continues. But there are other ways to think about handling that are both effective for us and balancing for our dogs.

What are leads for?

What is the purpose of our dog's lead? That may seem like a daft question. It is so that we can keep our dog under control, right? Control is a concept that is popular among dog trainers and guardians and it is certainly something that we are often urged to strive for with a reactive dog. But as we saw in Chapter 4, control is problematic. It implies restraint and constraint rather than choice and co-operation. We prefer to influence rather than control our dog's behaviour. So control is not what the lead is for. Its purpose is safety.

Leads provide safety for our dogs and for other people. They ensure our dogs cannot run into traffic, chase livestock or interfere with other people and their dogs. They keep us within the law. Even where we are confident that our dog will not leave our side when off lead, there will always be circumstances where a lead is necessary to ensure the comfort of others or to comply with the law.

However, while it may be necessary, there is no doubt that wearing a lead and harness affects our dog's balance. Simply putting a harness on a dog will change their posture and when we add a lead and handler into the mix, our dog has to adjust their weight and position still further. When we look at handling, our aim is to minimise how much the equipment that we use changes our dog's natural balance. We want to enable them to walk in balance, rather than control their movement.

In this chapter, we will look at the principles and practice of kind and effective handling, equipment that can help us, and techniques to keep tension out of our on-lead relationship.

Let's start by looking at why dogs pull.

Why does my dog pull?

We've all asked this question at some point. Whether in exasperation as we come in from yet another walk with aching arms or when seeking help to solve the problem. And people give lots of answers – some sensible, some not so. Among the 'not so' is the idea that our dog is somehow showing they are the 'leader', that our dog is dominating us, or that our dog does not respect us. There is no scientific evidence for any of these ideas.

The truth of the matter is that the answer is multi-fold and depends on how we are looking at it. One observer may say that our dog pulls because they have not been taught to walk on a loose lead. That is quite possibly true but is not the whole picture or a dog, once trained, would never pull at all. Another may say that our dog pulls to get to something they are interested in. That is also likely true and explains why they pull more in some situations than they do in others. And a third may say that they pull because we follow. Also true but not always helpful, particularly when we are trying hard not to follow as we are being dragged down the street!

The simple answer is that our dog pulls because they are attached to us and they walk faster than we do. So they hit the end of the lead pretty quickly when walking at their natural pace. This happens more quickly if they are actively trying to get somewhere.

At that point they will feel tension on the lead, and the natural response to feeling that tension is to move away from it, creating more tension. Our natural response to this is to brace and pull back; ultimately we have to do this to balance ourselves and avoid falling over! This adds still more pressure and it quickly spirals into the drag/yank scenario that is sadly so familiar.

Happily, it does not have to be like this and we will look at some simple ways to change the picture so that we do not fall into the push me/pull you trap! But first, let's consider what this common scenario does to our dog's balance and comfort.

Pressure on the neck

As well as being extremely uncomfortable for all concerned, the drag and yank scenario is potentially very damaging for our dog. If the lead is attached to a collar, the pressure exerted is being applied to a sensitive part of the dog's anatomy: the neck and throat. The neck contains the thyroid gland and lymph nodes, and key parts of the body like the trachea, oesophagus, jugular vein, vagus nerve and spine pass through it!

Pressure on the neck can reduce oxygen to the brain and increase stress and panic. Just try cupping your hand around your neck and pulling back – it is not a pleasant sensation, even though you are in control of the pressure. Now imagine it is someone else's hand on your neck and you start to get closer to how pressure from a collar may feel to a dog.

There is no evidence that dogs have less sensitive necks than we do. In fact, the evidence would suggest that they are at least as sensitive and that pressure, even from flat collars, can cause damage. The thyroid is positioned at the front of the dog's throat, just where a jerk on a collar may put pressure. It can become damaged and inflamed from pressure on the neck. Damage to the bones in the neck is also possible.

When we have a dog who can be reactive, we have the additional concern that pressure on the neck reduces the ability to think clearly, due to reduced oxygen to the brain, and increases panic, neither of which is helpful when we are trying to teach our dog to be calm.

So a key to maintaining our dog's comfort on the lead and overall balance is to remove pressure from the neck and the most effective way to do this, especially while we are training our dog to walk on a loose lead, is to use a well-fitting, non-tightening harness.

Harnesses distribute any pressure across a much larger and less sensitive body area in the chest and flank. A well-fitted harness is therefore more comfortable for our dog than being led by a collar, even if our dog pulls or lunges. However, not all harnesses are made equal so we need to choose an appropriate one for our dog.

Choosing a harness

There are many different types of harness and it can take a while to find the right one for our dog. To some extent this will depend on our own preferences, our dog's size and shape and what is available in our location. But here are six things to look for when choosing a harness.

1. It is vital that the harness does not tighten anywhere on our dog's body. Some harnesses are designed to tighten and be uncomfortable if our dog pulls. These are not recommended. We want to make it enjoyable for our dog to do what we want (walking without tension on the lead) rather than make it painful for them to do what we don't want.

2. We don't want a harness that restricts our dog's movement. Think about how a dog's shoulders move when they walk, trot and run. The shoulder blade moves up and out to the front. A harness must allow for this movement or our dog will be unable to extend their limbs properly, which can lead to more physical tension. So look at the harness. Where do the front straps lie? Do they restrict shoulder movement forwards? In general, it is best to avoid harnesses that have a horizontal piece across the chest unless this can be shown not to impede movement. Instead, choose a harness that has a vertical strap from the neck, down the chest and between the legs, and where the neck piece is designed to lie just above the point of the shoulder. These are sometimes called 'Y' or 'H' harnesses, depending on the shape they make when laid out flat.

3. We need to look at where the ring is on the back. We want to connect the lead behind the shoulder, far enough back that the straps around the belly do not interfere with the elbows or rub under the arms, but not so far back that it encourages pulling or puts our dog out of balance. Look at harnesses designed for racing sled dogs: the lead attaches a long way back on the dog as this makes it easier to pull forward! We want that in a sled dog but not when walking

our dog to the park, so choose a harness where the lead
attaches just behind the shoulder.

4. We need to look at the material. A fleece-harness provides
    for extra comfort, which is particularly important for very
    thin-coated dogs, but it also covers more body area. Dogs
    who are body sensitive can sometimes be more comfortable
    with a soft webbing harness, which may have lighter and
    less intrusive straps. So consider carefully what will work
    best for your dog.

5. We need to think about how we put the harness on our
    dog. If our dog has any concerns about having things over
    their head, we need a harness that opens at the neck as well
    as round the belly. If our dog is an unusual shape, we will
    need lots of room for adjustment or a more customisable
    harness.

6. We want at least a ring on the back and a ring on the chest.
    This will give most flexibility to attach the lead to the back,
    to the front or to both at once, depending on our dog and
    the context we are in.

"My dog won't wear a harness"

Sometimes dogs can find wearing a harness challenging. If you find
that your dog is avoiding the harness or refusing to move when it is
on, consider the following:

☐   Is the fit comfortable? It is well worth trying a different
    style or size of harness as some just don't lie well on certain
    body shapes. Check that there is room to fit a couple of
    fingers flat on both sides and that the harness is not so
    loose that it is sliding about and chafing. Some trainers and
    TTouch practitioners will have a stock of different styles of
    harness so may be able to help you find one to fit.

☐   Does it go over your dog's head? Many dogs can find this a challenge, particularly some of the fleece harnesses that can be quite close-fitting around the head. If your dog is fine once the harness is on but avoids it going on, then it may be the way you are putting it on. Try one that opens at the neck and avoid any pieces hanging around the face and body while you put it on. Hold each strap carefully as you approach the body and close the clips as gently as possible. For some dogs, even the sound that these make can be upsetting.

☐ Has your dog had a bad experience with the harness? If this is the case then change the harness for one of a different style if at all possible. If your dog is still concerned, introduce it gently, pairing its appearance with tasty treats and reinforcing any interest in it. Gradually place the harness closer to your dog, then touch your dog with it, then lay it on your dog briefly without doing it up, until finally you can put it on fully. Pair each step with food and never move on until your dog is comfortable with each step.

☐ Is your dog sensitive to the harness material? If you find your dog is itchy or scratching or at all sore it may be worth trying different materials. Fleece can help with sensitive dogs.

If you have tried all of these and your dog is still struggling with the harness, try getting advice from a TTouch Practitioner. TTouch can often help to change the experience of a harness for a dog, but it is worth getting qualified help to do this.

How to use your lead[44]

Obviously our ultimate aim is to teach our dog to walk on a loose

---

[44] You will find videos to help you with many of these techniques as well as

lead, by our side or wherever we want them to be. But how we use our lead, and indeed the type of lead we use, will have a significant effect on how balanced our dog is able to be and how easy it is for them to walk without pulling. After all, our dog can't learn to walk on a loose lead, until they can at least stand in their own balance on a loose lead!

Assuming you now have your dog in a harness with two points of attachment, there are a number of ways you can connect your lead. The most common way is to simply connect a lead to the back of the harness but this is probably the least effective for encouraging loose lead walking. Attaching a lead to the back of a harness positions you firmly behind the dog – in the perfect position for pulling! Also if the lead does become tight, it is harder to release the tension and allow your dog to rebalance (though not impossible, as we will see!).

You can walk with your dog on a loose lead connected to a single point but it is best suited to ranging-style walking, where your dog is free to sniff, and to dogs who already walk on a loose lead. It is less suitable for walking along a road, where you will want your dog to walk closer by your side, or for dogs who are strong pullers or likely to react.

Two points of connection

An alternative is two points of connection using a lead with a clip on each end, attached to both the front and back rings on the harness. Two points of connection allows you much more influence on your dog's behaviour than a single point, and increases your ability to communicate what you want to your dog. Crucially, it positions you beside your dog rather than behind them. This is a much more comfortable position to walk in and it allows your dog

higher resolution versions of photographs at www.yourendofthelead.com.

to balance themselves more effectively, as there is no pressure from behind.

It can be helpful to think of the connection at the back as your 'brake' and the front connection as your 'steering'. If you feel your dog start to pull you can gently signal upwards rather than backwards on the back connection, pause, then release slowly. This technique, called "meet and melt", will slow your dog without unbalancing them or triggering further pulling.

If you are thinking that will never work with your very pully dog then it is worth noting that this meet and melt technique originated in Connected Riding[45] in horses before being adapted for dogs as a core technique in TTouch. And no matter how strong your dog may be, they are not stronger than half a ton of horse!

Two points of connection on a harness (Photo: Cameron Laing)

Practising meet and melt

We are so used to holding on to our dog's lead for grim death, and

---

[45] Connected Riding is a method for working with animals developed by Peggy Cummings https://www.connectedriding.com

responding to pulling by pulling back or yanking, that loosening our grip and melting to pressure can feel like the exact opposite of what we need to do. But with practice, this will become second nature and you will see for yourself how effective it is for releasing tension in the lead.

TTouch Instructors Robyn Hood and Mandy Pretty[46] suggest the following exercise to get a sense of how meet and melt works:

1. Hold your hands level with your sternum. Hold them horizontally with your right palm and the back of your left hand facing you.

2. Link your finger tips, so that your right thumb and left little finger are upwards and your left thumb and right little finger are closest to the floor.

3. Start with no pressure then engage your right tricep muscles. You will find that your left muscles also engage as you pull back against the pressure. That is you and your dog!

4. Now slowly relax your right arm without releasing your linked fingers. What happened to your left arm? It relaxed too, right?

You can move on to trying this with a lead attached to a solid object. Start by tightening the lead. You will notice that your hands and body are likely to tighten too: braced knees and hips, tight arms and hands. Now slowly and consciously release that pressure. Let your hips soften and your knees bend slightly. See how the tension is released without you letting go of the lead.

---

[46] Their book, *Harnessing Your Dog's Perfection*, is recommended if you want to explore TTouch leading techniques in more depth.

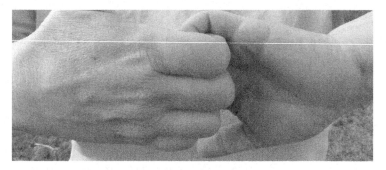

Meet and melt exercise (Photo: Toni Shelbourne)

Try practising this meet and melt technique with inanimate objects and, if you can, another person, before you try it with your dog, and when you do, start in the garden until you get the hang of it. But do persevere, as it is a very effective tool for taking pressure out of the lead.

Stroking the lead

Another technique from Connected Riding, adapted for dogs by TTouch Instructor, Sarah Fisher, is stroking the lead. This is very simple but incredibly effective and can be used with one or two points of connection, on a collar or harness and with pretty much any kind of lead. It will release tension in the lead and help to calm your dog and bring their attention back to you, if they are distracted.

Hold the end of the lead in one hand, avoiding having the handle or any extra clips dangling. Don't worry if it is taut when you start; lead-stroking will release the tension. With your other hand reach along the lead an arm's length and, with the lead between your thumb and fingers (with your thumb on top), slide your hand back along the lead towards you. Repeat this with the other hand, and then again with the original hand, over and over, in a smooth action. Imagine that you are pulling in a rope but with a really light touch.

Stroking the lead with Mischief (Photos: Toni Shelbourne)

Your hands need to be as light as possible on the lead. If your dog is pulling forwards, your pressure will be a little firmer to meet this, as you continue to stroke but, as your dog's pressure eases, your touch on the lead will become lighter and lighter until the lead is flowing over your open hands.

You can stroke the lead when you are standing still with your dog to keep them calm or to ask them to release the tension on the lead. Remember to start in a stand. It is easier when you first start to do the lead-stroking when you are not also trying to walk. Remember the first thing you are aiming for is your dog to be able to stand in their own balance on a loose lead. Don't try to walk before you can stand!

Although you may not be moving forward, you do want to be moving your body. If you stand stock-still and stroke the lead only from your hands, you will find that you will brace your body and the movement will be jerky. Instead, keep your knees and hips soft, keep your feet moving – from side to side or on the spot if necessary – and engage your whole body in the stroking action.

Once you are more practised at stroking the lead you will be able to do it easily while walking to release tension.

Stroking the lead is an excellent technique to help you to keep your hands soft on your dog's lead. Our natural response is to hold the lead tightly but this only exacerbates pulling. Instead, if you practise stroking the lead, it will become a way of clearly communicating with your dog and, once they stop feeling tension in the lead, they will be less inclined to pull.

Your position matters

We can help or hinder our efforts by how we use our bodies. Our body position, what we do with our hands and feet, and where we are looking makes a huge difference in how effectively we can lead our dogs.

We need to position ourselves at or just ahead of our dog's shoulder if we are walking forwards. Being behind your dog will put both of you off balance and make it more likely that your dog will pull. If you find yourself dropping back (or your dog surging forward), then use lead-stroking to slow or stop your dog and reposition yourself before continuing. Don't get into the habit of trying to play catch up with your dog – they will always be faster!

Your hands are also really important. Our tendency – especially with a reactive dog – is to hang on tight, to grip the lead firmly or even to wrap it several times around our hand! This makes us feel secure but makes it much more likely that our dog will experience tension in the lead.

Instead, hold the lead as lightly as possible across your hands, with your palms facing up. This allows you to close your hands when needed but encourages a much lighter touch on the lead.

Remember that your dog is reading your body language as much as, if not more than, your words. If you brace and tense up, your dog will feel it. If you stop and stare at your dog, or if you stop moving your feet, they will find it harder to move forward. But if you keep breathing, move your body in the direction you want to go and look where you are heading, you will communicate your intention to them much more clearly.

Using long lines

So far we have talked about walking on a lead. But one of the problems with standard leads is that they can themselves be constraining for the dog. Many dogs will be more relaxed walking on a longer line and, for some, it can make all the difference in learning to walk on a loose lead. Even if our dog is comfortable on a lead, we may want to allow them more freedom when in a safe environment away from roads and crowds. In these scenarios, a longer line can be very helpful.

It is important to note that a long line is not an extending lead. An extending lead has a line that extends and retracts into a plastic handle, as your dog pulls into it. This in itself encourages pulling. It can also be dangerous if it gets tangled or retracts suddenly and, if you accidentally drop the handle, it can be terrifying for your dog to be 'chased' by the noisy, clanking thing. Most importantly, you can communicate very little to your dog through a hard plastic handle! Extending leads are not recommended.

A long line is a soft, comfortable, long lead, with one clip. I find that a 10-metre length works well for walking – any longer and it gets wrapped around things – and that rope or biothane tangles less than webbing. Obviously you need to choose a line width suitable for the size of your dog, remembering that lines can get heavy especially when wet. My little chihuahua-cross has the thinnest available biothane line, whereas I used to use a horse lunge line for my Maremma Sheepdogs!

Always attach the line to the back of your dog's harness. Never use a long line on a collar or head collar: it is dangerous and has the potential to do serious damage to your dog's neck!

Start in a quiet spot with your dog on the line at normal lead length and the rest of the line held in loops across one hand and use the other hand to guide the line in and out. Avoid winding it round your hand as this will make it harder to let out the line. Instead lay the loops across your hands so you can feed it out easily. Keep your hands as open as possible. This also allows you to stroke the line if you need to slow your dog down or ask for attention.

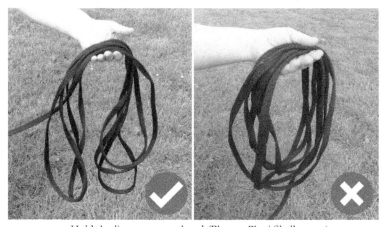

Hold the line over your hand (Photos: Toni Shelbourne)

Gradually let the line out as your dog moves forward and take it in as they come closer to you. Allow your dog to roam and investigate their surroundings; you chose somewhere quiet to practise for a reason! If the line gets taut momentarily then consciously relax your hands and body and let it run through your fingers a little (this is why you need a soft rope – or gloves!) and remember Meet and Melt. As you get more practice, you will be able to do this as you continue on a walk, but start while your dog is investigating a relatively small area.

Sliding lines

A TTouch sliding line is an excellent tool if you have a dog who struggles with the confinement of a lead. Developed as part of the TTouch leading work, a sliding line can be used with one or two points of connection to give your dog a greater experience of freedom, while still staying safe on a line. Because the line is sliding rather than being attached to a fixed connection, there is no jerking and nothing to pull against, so the walking experience is quite different for both dog and handler.

You will need a 10-metre soft cotton rope, the kind that won't hurt your skin. As always start somewhere quiet and practise first. For the simplest sliding line, pass one end of the rope through the ring on the back of the harness then join up with the other end and tie a knot, so that you cannot accidentally lose your dog! Now you have a connection to your dog that slides rather than being fixed. Use two hands, holding one end of the rope in each hand with the knot between.

Mischief walking on a sliding line, with close-up of fit through the harness
(Photos: Toni Shelbourne)

As your dog moves, ask them to come with you by slowly moving your body in the direction you want to go, allowing your hands to go with you. The sliding of the lead will prevent any tension and you may find your dog is surprisingly willing to move with you. You can also stroke the line if you need to communicate where you want your dog to go.

For stronger, more powerful dogs, the TTouch half-butterfly is very effective. This is essentially a sliding line with two points of connection. Pass one end of the rope through the ring on the back of the harness, then bring it round and back through the ring on the front. Centre the rope so that you have the middle of the rope across the dog's shoulder furthest from you and the ends of the rope coming towards you. Tie the ends of the rope together as before. Use both hands on the rope and allow the rope to slide with the dog. As before use your body position and stroking the line to communicate to your dog where you want to go.

Mischief modelling the half-butterfly (Photos: Toni Shelbourne)

The sliding line is very effective but be warned! The chances are you will find it very disconcerting initially. We are used to and often crave being 'in control' of our dog and this can translate into close micro-management on a short lead. A sliding line is the polar opposite of this. It allows our dog to experience being on a lead but with the ability to move quite freely. The idea is not that we micro-manage our dog's movement but that we allow them to experience movement on a line as a positive thing. We *are* quite safe, of course. As long as we have tied our knot and don't drop the line, our dog is not going to escape, and we can always bring the lines in closer if we need more influence.

Using a sliding line is a little different from most things you will have experienced and, like everything new, takes practise. It is a great way to shift from feeling the need to closely control and micro-manage our dogs to thinking in terms of communication and influence. Always practise first in a safe, quiet place.

Three useful additions

There are thousands of gadgets and bits of equipment that you can buy that claim to stop your dog pulling. Most are not needed, so don't get tempted to buy everything that is out there, just in case! You will make most progress using the techniques we have been talking about, combined with a high rate of reinforcement of your dog for being in the position you want.[47] But there are three things that you may not have thought about that can be useful.

Freedom handle
The freedom handle is a soft handle attached to a large ring and is a very effective tool if you find it really hard to keep your hands soft on the lead. Attach the lead to the back of your dog's harness then thread the other end through the ring on the freedom handle before attaching to the front. Hold the handle, maintaining a loose lead wherever possible. Change direction if the lead tightens.

You can try out the concept of the freedom handle using an

---

[47] My favourite technique for doing this is called 300-Peck. There is a brief discussion of how to use this in Chapter 8.

ordinary flat collar or any kind of loop that will allow the lead to flow freely through it. Pass the lead through the ring on the collar if it is big enough or simply though the loop of the collar. This will give you an idea how the handle works. If you find it helps your dog, freedom handles are available to use with your usual double-ended lead or in combination with an integrated lead.

The freedom handle removes tension from the lead in much the same way as a sliding line, but with a normal length lead. It can make a huge difference to many dogs and, in some cases, reduces pulling almost immediately. It is also really useful if you are using two points of connection but walk more than one dog at once as you can put both dogs on freedom handles and hold one dog in each hand. However do work with each dog separately to begin with until they get the hang of loose lead walking!

Freedom handle (Photo: Janet Finlay)

Bungee Extender

A bungee extender is a short piece of elasticated lead with a clip and ring that can be added to your normal lead. If your dog is very strong, using a short bungee extender between the lead and the connection point can reduce the impact of any pulling both for you and your dog. Choose the shortest available extender so that you can still easily stroke the lead and see this as a temporary measure to make you and your dog more comfortable while you work on your loose lead walking.

Walking Belt

A walking belt can be very helpful if you are worried that you might drop the lead if you don't hang on tight or that your dog may escape. You need to choose one that is suitable for the size of your dog, when he is pulling, and that is comfortable to wear around your hips. Ideally, attach a freedom handle to the belt, so that you can still use two points of connection, or use it to tether the end of the long line while you handle it. Don't just attach the dog to the belt and let him pull you! The aim is simply to make you feel more secure, not to change your handling of the lead, so attach the lead in a way that still allows you to keep the lead soft, to stroke the lead when needed and to allow as much freedom as possible.

Walking belt with freedom handle and two points of contact (Photo courtesy of Bernadette Kerbey)

Equipment as cues

One concern that is sometimes raised is whether you can use a harness for loose lead walking, if your dog is used to wearing one to practise a sport that requires pulling into it, such as Canicross or Tracking. The concern is that wearing a harness means "pull" to the dog.

The good news is that dogs are very contextual. They can easily learn to distinguish between different scenarios, so using a harness in two different situations is not a problem for them. You can make it even easier for them by using a different harness for each activity, so that the particular harness becomes a cue for the activity you are doing.

In the same way, you can use the way you connect your lead as a cue to your dog. For example, one point of connection on the back of the harness can cue your dog to explore and sniff, while two points of connection can cue loose lead walking by your side. This is a really easy way to signal to your dog what you expect. But remember you need to be consistent. Always use the same lead configurations in the same way for the same thing and don't allow pulling one day but not the next!

TTOUCH BALANCE LEAD

So you are doing great with your dog's loose lead walking and finding that these techniques are allowing you both to walk much more in balance. But what happens when you suddenly find yourself in a particularly challenging situation, and your normally easy-going dog decides to lunge? Or when you need to bring a dog close without putting pressure on the lead, such as when waiting beside a path for another dog to pass? Or when you need to hold a particularly strong dog in an emergency or in a situation that is initially over-stimulating, such as a new training class or the vet's waiting room? In situations like these, the TTouch balance lead can help.

Note that this is not a replacement for the techniques we have already discussed. Dogs will be most comfortable and most able to balance themselves when they have more freedom to move, so practise allowing this, whenever it is safe to do so. But in situations like those described above, this easy to learn technique, which uses your normal lead, will give you additional support, in a way that is kind to your dog.

The TTouch balance lead is a simple technique that helps bring your dog into balance, keeps pressure off the neck and gives you more influence to keep them from lunging forward.

1. Attach one end of the lead to your dog's harness or collar.
2. Holding the other end of the lead in one hand, take hold of the lead about a foot from the collar or harness with your other hand.
3. Allow the lead between your hands to form a large loop.
4. Pass that loop down the shoulder of the dog, opposite to where you are standing and bring it across in front of your dog's chest.

Be careful not to lean over the dog while you do this. Make sure the lead is positioned across the dog's chest, taking care not to allow it to ride up into the neck. Adjust your hands so that there is no pressure on the point of connection, especially if it is to the collar. You can bring your hands together behind the dog's shoulders if it is more comfortable. Keep the lead light and use the "meet and melt" technique to ask for balance.

You can also create a balance lead if you have the lead attached to two points on the harness if needed. Hold the lead in two hands, keeping your hands apart. Allow the lead that is between your hands to fall into a loop then pass this across the chest as before. This is particularly helpful for very strong dogs.

Mia modelling a balance lead (Photos: Toni Shelbourne)

If your dog backs out of the balance lead, or if the lead tends to ride up as often happens with smaller dogs, the balance lead plus can be helpful.

1. Stand as you would for the balance lead but when you pass the loop across the chest, ask your dog to step over the lead with their offside leg.

2. Bring the lead up between their front legs.

3. If needed, pass the end of the lead up through the collar to secure.

This effectively creates a temporary harness and keeps pressure off the dog's neck so it is also useful for emergency situations where you don't have a harness.

Balance lead and balance lead plus (Image courtesy of Robyn Hood)

The super-balance lead can help in the initial stages of working with a very pully dog. This uses an actual harness but with the additional influence of the balance lead. It works best if you have a harness with a back ring, a front loop or ring and a side ring, but you can adapt it for many harnesses. You will also need a double-ended lead.

1. Attach one end of the lead to the back of the harness.
2. Pass the other end through the loop or ring on the front of the harness. You can also pass it through the harness itself: the aim is to keep the lead in place across the chest.
3. Continue to bring this end round and attach it to the opposite side of the harness to where you are standing.

Use both hands on the lead as you would for two points of connection and always walk so that the side clip is on the opposite side of the dog to you. The super-balance lead can help teach habitually pully dogs where you want them to walk, so that you can begin to reinforce them in that position.

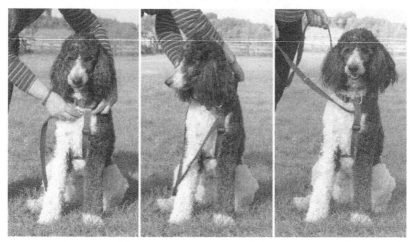

Fitting the super-balance lead (Photos: Toni Shelbourne)

A WORD ON HEADCOLLARS

People often ask about head collars and whether they are suitable for a dog who can be reactive. I have to admit that head collars are not my first choice of equipment for a number of reasons.

1. You are controlling your dog's head, which is not conducive to them being able to communicate appropriately with other dogs or to enjoy calming activities like sniffing. The head collar also tends to keep the dog's head up high, which can create a challenging posture for other dogs.

2. There is no doubt that head collars are aversive to many dogs. If your dog tries to remove the head collar at every opportunity or regularly rubs their face along the ground, then they are really not enjoying the experience, and we need to change that situation.

3. Pulling on a head collar is as damaging to a dog's neck as pulling on a collar, and a sudden jerk may be even more damaging as the dog's neck is pulled sideways. This does not equate to our aim of comfort for our dog.

All that said, all head collars are not equal. Some types work by tightening around the muzzle making it uncomfortable to pull. Many of these fit close to the eyes so that they irritate and some are used to hold the dog's head at an awkward angle. These types are never recommended. However there are one or two styles that are designed to hold their shape on the dog so that they do not tighten around the muzzle or ride up into the eyes. With proper introduction and used carefully, these types can be helpful as a security measure, for those who feel they may not be able to hold their dog in an emergency, such as those with very strong dogs or with physical limitations. In such circumstances, the use of a head collar may be the difference between feeling able to walk the dog or not, and will protect the handler from potential physical harm.

However, there is one unbreakable rule to follow when using a head collar: never, ever attach a lead only to a head collar. Always use a double-ended lead, with one connection to the head collar and the other to a harness, so that you can allow your dog to balance himself.

Get used to thinking of the head collar as emergency controls, and practise keeping the lead to it loose at all times. As you become more practised, try attaching a separate light lead to the head collar and the double-ended lead on the harness, so that you can practise walking without using the head collar at all, while still having the security of knowing it is there. As your dog learns to walk on a harness, you may even find that you can do without the head collar altogether.

THE ONLY THING THAT WORKS...

This is something that all trainers hear sometimes. "I have tried *everything* with my dog, and I have to use... a slip lead/prong collar/choke chain/tightening harness... It is the *only* thing that works for my dog". The problem is that 'only thing' is almost certainly adding to the dog's anxiety rather than reducing it. We can do better than this.

If this is how you feel, have you really tried *everything*? For instance, have you consistently worked through all the suggestions in this chapter, practising them thoroughly in different quiet locations before using them on walks? If not, then you haven't tried everything yet and there are other options.

But why is it important that we don't use equipment that is designed to be aversive with our dogs? It is because we are trying to maintain comfort and balance at *both* ends of the lead.

Obviously using this equipment makes walking easier for you or you wouldn't have chosen it. Your dog may well be quieter, more cautious about 'acting up'. Those difficult behaviours – pulling, barking, lunging – may well have reduced. And you are enjoying your walks much more. So it is fair to say that it succeeds for *your* end of the lead.

But is wearing this equipment really working for your dog? Is feeling pressure, pain or shock when they behave in a certain way really working for them?

When you look at it like this, the answer has to be no. It is not teaching them what you want them to do or how to be successful. At best, it is teaching them what to avoid. At worst, it is teaching them that it is dangerous to try anything so they will shut down. And, ultimately, this type of training is adding to their stress. So it is failing badly for *their* end of the lead. It is not keeping them comfortable or balanced, and it may be physically damaging.

So if you are using any of these things – or anything else that creates discomfort as its mode of operation – go back and look seriously at the other possibilities discussed in this chapter. If necessary, get help from a reliable trainer who understands positive reinforcement, and make a plan to make your handling work well for you and your dog.

Chapter Seven

CHANGING HOW YOU THINK ABOUT WALKS

Learning how to walk our dogs on a loose lead is a critical step to enjoying our walks again, but equally important is examining how we think about walks altogether. How can we change our walks to make them more peaceful? How can we handle the inevitable situations where things don't go to plan? Do we even have to walk our dogs at all? We will look at these questions in this chapter.

WALKS ARE NOT COMPULSORY

"Don't I *have* to walk my dog?"

This is a question that I often hear from clients with very fearful or reactive dogs. I have usually just suggested that they take a short break from walks to let everyone de-stress.

"But isn't that cruel? How will I keep them happy without walks? Don't dogs *need* walks?"

There is a very widely-held belief that dogs must be walked every day, come what may. The pressure to conform to this social norm can be immense. Many people will hold their hands up in horror if you admit that you don't do daily walks – regardless of what exciting things you are doing with your dog instead. I have even heard of rescues refusing to rehome a dog to someone who told them they gave their dogs 'days off' from walks.

We have already seen that the expectations of others can be difficult for us. People tell us we should do this or should do that – or that or our dogs should be a particular way – and we can feel guilty when we don't meet these expectations. Walking our dogs is no exception.

However, the short answer to the question we started with is 'no'. Dogs need physical exercise, they need mental stimulation, they need companionship and social interaction (with you – not necessarily with other dogs), they need access to the outdoors and a natural environment, and they need training. But they don't need walks and can be perfectly happy and healthy without them. All of these things can be provided in other ways.

As a society, we invented the dog walk as a convenient way for us to meet these needs in a simple, enjoyable and efficient package, all in a hour or so a couple of times a day. And it is a model that works really well for many dogs and their guardians, which is why 'walking the dog' is now seen as an essential part of responsible dog ownership.

But what if our dog is not one of those 'many dogs'? For a dog who is fearful of other dogs or unknown people, the standard dog walk can feel like a nightmare for all concerned. Yet many of us still try to use this model to provide for our fearful or reactive dog's needs.

On top of that, we load the model with yet another function: rehabilitation training. So now, not only are we trying to provide exercise, play, stimulation, time to explore, companionship and all that, but we are also trying to help our dog feel better about the things that frighten them. It is a lot to lay on a simple dog walk!

Let me be clear that I am not against dog walks. When they work well they can be one of the most joyful things we can do with our dogs. We get to watch them run and play. We get to wonder at the power of their noses, as they follow the scent of an unseen rabbit. We get exercise ourselves and, most importantly, we enjoy time just being together. If you are both enjoying your walks, fabulous: carry on with what you are doing. However, if you or your dog finds your walks stressful, then perhaps it is time to think 'outside the box'. We can still experience all these joyful things but we need to do things a little differently to get there.

We all have our 'boxes'. The way we have *always* done things. The way things *should* be done. The things that we believe *can't* be changed. The truth is that, almost always, things can be changed. Sometimes, they *need* to be changed for us to make progress.

Here are some examples of thinking outside the 'dog walking box':

- ☐ Choose not to walk your dog every day and do other activities on your 'days off'.
- ☐ Drive your dog to a safe space, to avoid stressful street walking, even if it is only 50 yards from your house.
- ☐ Go somewhere remote to have a quiet walk with just the two of you.
- ☐ Go for a walk without your dog if you need to do that.
- ☐ Employ a good, individual dog walker to give you a break from walking.
- ☐ Rent a field to allow your dog off-lead time.

If you're struggling with progress, think about how you can change your picture. Write down all the options – however foolish they may feel. What do you want to change? What would make it easier? How can you achieve it?

It can take time to find the way that works for us. We need to satisfy our needs and those of our dogs and that can be a delicate balance. It will also change over time so you need to keep assessing whether your solution still works for you.

You may find the options that you come up with are unusual and you may wonder if they are acceptable. I have a very simple way of assessing this, which we will look at next.

Three Golden Rules

Over the years I have realised that what we choose to do or not do with our dogs, and how we train and work with them, boils down to just three Golden Rules. Keep these in mind, and address them honestly, and you won't go far wrong.

When you have to make a decision about something, ask yourself:

1. Are *you* happy with your choice?
2. Is *your dog* happy with your choice?
3. Does anyone else have *legitimate* grounds not to be happy with your choice?

That's it. If you can answer *yes, yes, no* to these three then you are good to go. Just so that it is clear what I am saying, let's unpack this a little bit.

Firstly, are *you* happy with the choice you are making? Note the question is not "Is everything perfect?" or "Are you completely happy with your dog's behaviour?". There may be lots of things you are working on changing. But are you happy that your choice suits you, your family and your life at this moment and that you and your dog are making the progress you want? You may walk your dog on lead or off, every day, some days or rarely. You may be working on training your dog to perfection or just enough to live with easily. You may want them to sleep on your bed or in the kitchen. There is no right or wrong in any of these. What matters is that you have thought about the options and made choices that you are happy with.

However, our own happiness is not the only consideration so the second 'Golden Rule' asks is *your dog* happy with your choice? Too many people stop with their own happiness. They think that the only thing that matters is their convenience and choose techniques that are unpleasant for the dog because they seem to work quickly. When we ask this second question, it stops us picking up choke chains or forcing our dog to 'face their fears'. Our choices also have to safeguard our dog's well being. So your dog is likely to be happiest when your choice results in plenty of positive reinforcement, clarity about what is expected, an environment that is managed to help them get it right, comfortable walking gear, and their physical, mental and emotional needs being met. Our choices need to take these things into account as well.

Finally, we don't live in isolation, so the third question is simply to ensure that no one else has legitimate grounds to be upset by our choices. Note the important word here is *legitimate*. If we let our dog harass people or other dogs, or chase livestock, or destroy other people's property then those people have a legitimate right to be upset. People who do not have legitimate grounds to complain include:

- The amateur dog trainer in park who thinks you should just give them a 'good whack' because that's the way they always did it.
- Friends and strangers on Facebook who swear that it is cruel not to walk your dog ten miles a day.
- The 'dog psychologist' who tells you need to toughen up and "show your dog who's boss".
- The person with the 'friendly' dog who suggests you just let them all get on with it.

You will be able to think of others. These people are actually unaffected by your choices, so simply smile and continue to do what you have decided is right for you and your dog.

You can use these Golden Rules to think through your options around walking your dog, as well as many other decisions you need to make. Explore the options available. Learn to read your dog and see the subtle ways they express their contentment or concern. Talk to those closest to you about what is reasonable and what is not (because 'you' needs to include your immediate family if they are involved in caring for your dog). Make your choices based on what works for you and your dog and keeps everyone else safe.

So why might we choose not to walk our dog? And will that be a permanent or an occasional choice? Let's look at that next.

Stress holidays

The main reason to choose not to walk our dog is because either we or they need a break. As we saw in Chapter 2, our stress response system is designed to protect us when we are under threat. It isn't intended to be constantly activated and, when it is, our health can suffer. The body produces cortisol and adrenaline under stress and this takes hours to leave our system, sometimes even days. So if we experience significant stress on a daily basis, we never get the chance to recover fully and become 'stuck' in a stress response state. Taking a break from walks gives both us and our dogs a chance to relax and regroup. It gives us both relief from the metaphorical storm.

It doesn't have to be forever of course. Just a day or two off after a stressful incident or even an unusually exciting outing can make all the difference to the quality of our walks and our dog's ability to relax. We call it a 'stress holiday' because to gives us a break from stress. It is a really valuable tool to help our dogs to build confidence.

Many people fear that their dog won't cope without a walk: "They'll go crazy! I could never do that with my dog". It is a very common response. If that is you, I would just say, try it. I'm willing to bet that your dog won't go crazy. In fact they are more likely to relax and become more focused. And you will be able to regroup so you can help your dog to make progress.

Of course, it is not as simple as just 'not walking' and this is where some go wrong. We can't just take away an activity; we need to replace it with something else. What you do instead depends on you and your dog. The important thing is you are still meeting your dog's needs.

- ☐ You can do more training with your dog to get them thinking and using their brain.
- ☐ You can give them brain games and enrichment activities to do.
- ☐ You can practise sports, like scentwork, parkour and agility.
- ☐ You can play some physical games and balance activities, so they don't lose muscle and strength.
- ☐ You can spend more time hanging out with them, doing massage or TTouch, so they still have relaxing, quality time with you.

If you do these kinds of activities during your stress holiday, your dog will not have a problem missing the occasional walk.

But what if our dog is so fearful or over-stimulated by the outside world that any walks are too much for them? This needs careful thought. If you have a large garden or live on your own acreage then it is not too much of a problem: you may have room for your dog to get all the interest and exercise they need at home. If, on the other hand, you have no garden or a tiny one, you will need some way to ensure your dog gets sufficient exercise and opportunities to explore the outside world. There are different ways to do this, of course: hiring a field or finding a friend with a large garden that you can borrow a few times a week are two possibilities. But it will take more effort.

There are certainly some situations where this is the right decision for both dog and guardian. I once had a client who lived on a farm with many acres of land. Her dog was very settled at home: happy, confident and welcoming of strangers. But as soon as he set foot off the farm he was a nervous wreck. When I met her, this guardian was dutifully trying to walk her dog off her property a couple of times a day and both of them were completely stressed out as a result. So I asked her whether her dog needed to leave the farm. He didn't. She felt she *should* take him because "dogs need walks" but in fact both of them were much happier walking through their own fields. He was fine going to the vet, when needed, and he got all the exercise and enrichment that he needed at home. She stopped taking him out to walk that day and they both started to relax and make progress.

If we make a decision like this we need to think through the possible implications. Can we consistently provide everything our dog needs? What if our circumstances change? What would we do if we suddenly needed to do things differently? But it is also important to remember that not walking regularly does not have to mean that our dog has to become a recluse. We may still want to work with our dog to help them become more confident, so we may choose to take them out for carefully planned training or desensitisation. We just won't be exposing them to random triggers on a daily basis.

The key to success in this is to think through what our dog needs and then work out how we can provide for those needs. I call this the Deconstructed Dog Walk.

The Deconstructed Dog Walk

Dogs have certain needs in order to be mentally and physically healthy. They need a reasonable level of physical exercise. They need to use their brain and their senses and engage in natural 'doggy' behaviours, like sniffing. They need to play. They need companionship and relationship (whether with humans or other animals). They need to feel safe.

We need a new model to provide these things for those dogs and guardians for whom a standard dog walk doesn't work. This is where the Deconstructed Dog Walk comes in. Think of those fancy desserts on *Masterchef* or in top-flight restaurants that have all the key elements of a Lemon Meringue pie but look nothing like your mum used to make. The Deconstructed Dog Walk has all the key elements of a standard 'walk in the park' but it looks quite different!

For our Deconstructed Dog Walk, we go back to the basic needs and we work out how we will meet each one in a way that is appropriate for us and for our dog. There are two key principles in this:

1. We don't have to meet all the needs through one activity.
2. We don't have to meet all the needs at one time.

Think about providing for your dog's needs over the course of a few days and through a range of activities, some of which might be quite short. Exercise can be achieved through one activity, brain work through another, play and training through still others, though, in reality, most things you do will meet more than one need.

So, for example, the need for physical exercise could be met by:

☐ Running in a secure field or a large garden.

☐ Swimming.

☐ TTouch groundwork, ACE Free Work or other proprioception and balance exercises[48].

☐ Playing fetch or tug.

☐ Using a flirt pole.

☐ Home agility or Parkour.

☐ Walking in a remote location.

☐ Chewing on a good chew or bone.

The need for mental stimulation could be met by:

☐ Scent games and search work.

☐ Problem solving toys.

☐ Trick training.

---

[48] See Chapter 8 for more details of these.

☐   Husbandry training.

☐   Anything training!

The need to explore the environment can be met by any opportunity to spend unhurried time sniffing – remember this is exploration time so don't rush them. These don't have to be pretty places. Your dog is not interested in visual scenery; they only care that there are interesting smells to sniff! Try, for example:

☐   Investigating hedgerows on quiet lanes.

☐   Exploring the scents in a shopping mall car park or industrial estate after hours.

☐   Nosing around an empty field where there has been livestock (with permission).

☐   Sniffing around the garden.

☐   Playing with safe recycling.

Rehabilitation training can also be done separately. We will look at this in more detail in the next chapter. But we can go out specifically to work with our dog around triggers, completely separately from walks.

The great thing about the Deconstructed Dog Walk model is that you shift your focus on to providing what your dog needs, in a way that works for you both, rather than worrying about whether you are doing a particular activity on a daily basis.

If you are meeting all your dog's needs, you have nothing to worry about, whether you are taking time out from dog walks, walking in remote places or indeed choosing to use the standard daily walk within your plan.

Walk alternatives

There are many activities you can do with your dog on the days when walking is not appropriate for you. You will find your own favourites but here are a few ideas to get you started.

All of these are playful activities. Play is important for both mental and physical health. Researchers at Bristol University[49] found that lack of play was strongly correlated with behaviour issues and that increasing play to several sessions a day had a positive influence on behaviour. Play builds confidence. It builds relationship. It gets the brain and body working so can reduce frustration and boredom. It provides a focus in distracting environments. It is a great reinforcer and motivator and it is a stress reliever.

The type of play you choose is important. Play needs to be appropriate for the dog and be empowering rather than demoralising. It needs to engage both of you in the activity, rather than our dog always playing on his own or with other dogs. It needs to be evenly matched so that you can both 'win'. It needs to be managed so that it is not too arousing, which will make your dog over-excited, or too overwhelming, so that your dog disengages. In short, it needs to be great fun for you both.

This kind of play is also valuable when it comes to dealing with environmental distractions. If your dog gets worried or over-stimulated when you do go out and about, play gives you a way of helping them to experience the world as a source of fun and connection to you. Reactive behaviour often reduces as the dog becomes much more focused on climbing the branch, doing tricks, finding the mouse or chasing the tug toy than they are on other dogs.

If you don't already play in this way with your dog, have a think about what would work for you both. There are games you can play with or without props; games that are energetic and games that are more sedate; games that can be played inside or outside or both. There is definitely something for every guardian-dog pair!

Here are some of my favourite playful activities for a day off:

---

[49] Survey results from 4000 dog owners presented as part of Channel 4 series Dogs: Their Secret Lives.

☐ **Parkour** is often called 'urban agility' but can be done in any setting. It is essentially problem solving and exploring objects in the environment in a controlled way: climbing, balancing, jumping, going over and under and through. It is great fun and is practically useful when you need your dog to negotiate obstacles on walks for instance. It develops confidence in your dog. They learn that they can safely explore and solve problems and that their environment provides opportunities for reinforcement. You can find out how to get started with parkour in Chapter 8.

☐ **Interactive Play** includes playing tug or playing with a flirt pole, where you encourage your dog to chase a toy or object. These games are great physical exercise as well as being mentally stimulating. They also help with teaching your dog self-control, as they learn to let go when asked and to wait to restart play.[50]

☐ **Scentwork** is using your dog's impressive sniffing skills to find things. It can be as simple as finding food sprinkled in the grass to more complex tasks like detecting specific scents in large areas or tracking people or other animals. Whatever kind of scentwork you do, remember it is a game to your dog. You can find out how to start searching for a scented article in Chapter 8.

☐ **Trick training** encompasses everything from simple targeting to complex dance moves or helping with jobs around the house. It is fun for you and your dog and really gets you working together and problem-solving. You can learn a trick to impress your family and friends; learn something useful, like how to file their own nails on a

---

[50] To find out more about this kind of play see Craig Ogilvie's work. He does regular workshops and talks internationally and his 2017 book *Interactive Play Guide*, published by First Stone Publishing, is an excellent introduction to it.

scratch-board; or just do it for the fun of learning something new.[51] Here is a very simple trick to get you started: unroll a towel.

1. Sprinkle treats on an old towel or t-shirt and roll it up. Start with one or two treats along the edge.

2. Encourage your dog to push it with their nose to get the first treats. You may need to supervise and guide your dog initially, if they are likely to grab the towel and shake the treats out! But they will soon get the hang of the game.

3. Gradually hide the treats deeper and deeper inside so they have to push more.

Another trick is hunt the treat.

1. Get three or four yoghurt pots or paper cups and place them upside down on the floor.

2. Put a treat under one and ask your dog to find it. As always, start simple by letting your dog see you hide the treat.

3. Once they are confidently finding that, you can move on to hide treats unseen and even move your pots around, once the treat is placed.

Trick training is great fun, gets your dog using their brain and strengthens the bond between you.

☐ **Puzzle toys** are a great way to entertain your dog at home. You can use commercial treat delivery and problem-solving toys or, for a cheaper alternative, try recycling the recycling to make home-made puzzle toys and brain games.[52] Hide treats in a cardboard tube with the ends bent inwards, or

---

[51] The Kikopup YouTube channel is an excellent place to start with ideas for trick training.

[52] You can use anything that is safe for your dog but always supervise and check for sharp edges and remove plastic rings or small choking hazards before use.

use plastic milk bottles, ice-cream tubs and egg boxes – cut some holes in the side if needed – and place a few treats inside. You can make these more challenging by hiding one inside a larger container – but always build up slowly. You want it to be easy for your dog to start. You can make a home-made ball pit by scrunching up pieces of paper into tight balls and putting them in a low box. Scatter some tasty treats in amongst the paper balls. Your dog will love snuffling in the your ball pit to find the food. Whatever you choose, work with your dog. Encourage him to experiment, so he can work out what he needs to do. Go at your dog's pace and make sure he gets rewarded for thinking it through, rather than simply using brute force to get what he wants!

☐ The **TTouch Confidence Course** and **ACE Free Work** will exercise your dog's body through balance and awareness exercises and will provide mental stimulation through non-habitual activity that requires focus and attention. You can set these up in your house or garden, using bits and pieces from your home and garage. For more information on how they work, see Chapter 8.

There are many, many more possibilities: agility, disc-dog, rally obedience, heelwork-to-music are all things that can be practised at home that will exercise your dog in more ways than one. All of these activities will tire your dog as much as, if not more than, a good walk.

If you can't let your dog off lead in public and they need a good run then look out for a secure field that you can visit on a regular basis. A secure field is one that is fully and securely fenced and which can be booked for a set period of time for a fee. They can be a godsend to guardians with reactive dogs as, if they are properly run, you know that your dog can have free exercise without any stress. There are many such fields around the UK.[53] Some are particularly geared towards reactive dogs and have measures in place to make sure dogs do not meet, even by accident on the way in and out. Some include additional facilities such as agility or parkour equipment. Do check any field you use in advance to make sure it is safe and suitable for your dog.

If there are no secure fields in your area then think about other options. A friend with a large garden, a farmer with unused private fields, an equestrian centre with an enclosed manège, a fenced tennis court out of season, are all possibilities if you get permission. Be creative in seeking the opportunities your dog needs.

HOW TO HAVE PEACEFUL WALKS

So we have talked about when we choose not to take our dogs for a walk and how we can provide for their needs in alternative ways, but what about when we do want to walk them? What can we do to ensure our walks are peaceful and enjoyable? There are a few key things we need to think about.

The need for space

The single most valuable thing we can do to make our walks less stressful is to pay attention to space. The reactive dog guardian's mantra should be "Space is our friend". Space makes the difference between our dog being able to watch something calmly and them having a reaction. Space means safety for you both. Space is vital.

It makes sense, of course. When we are afraid of something, whatever that thing is, we will always feel safer when it is further away from us. We know that the danger is not as imminent and we usually still have a range of options available to us. The closer that scary thing gets, the more restricted our options become and the

---

[53] Check here for local, bookable fields: https://www.dogwalkingfields.co.uk

more we panic.

When we are talking about reactive dogs we often talk about *thresholds*. We'll say we need to keep our dog *under* threshold and, if they react, we say they are *over* threshold. But what do we actually mean by 'threshold'? Is it the point at which a dog becomes aware of a trigger or the point where they become concerned about the trigger or is it only the point where they actually react to the trigger?

It is actually all three. Trainer, Eileen Anderson describes three threshold points[54], which give us a really helpful model for thinking about space:

1.   Threshold of *stimulus perception* (the dog sees, hears or smells the trigger: perception).
2.   Threshold of *stimulus aversiveness* (the dog is concerned about the trigger: aversion).
3.   Threshold of *fear response or reactivity* (the dog reacts to the trigger or tries to escape: reaction).

The relative position of these three thresholds varies depending on the dog and the context. Sometimes the points are quite close to each other, when a dog is instantly reactive to another dog at any distance. Sometimes two are close but further from the third, such as where a dog is concerned about dogs at any distance but only reacts when a dog invades their space. Sometimes they are evenly spread, such as when a dog can watch other dogs at a distance without concern, but gets a bit worried when they get closer and reacts when they come closer still.

This model really helps us to think in more detail about how we work with our dogs. Ideally we are aiming not only to keep our dogs under the reaction threshold but also under the aversion threshold, so that they are not concerned about the trigger. If we

[54] Eileen Anderson, *Thresholds in Dog Training…HOW Many?*
https://eileenanddogs.com/2014/02/25/thresholds-in-dog-training/

can do that, then we have the best window for changing how they feel about the trigger, as effectively and efficiently as possible and so reducing our threshold distances.

In many cases, we can do this with a little planning and sufficient space. We are aiming to stay between perception and aversion: where our dog is aware of the trigger without being unduly concerned. Depending on the individual dog, this may not always be possible walking in busy parks or on streets, but may be very doable in more open spaces or those with varying levels. So we need to think about our own dog's need for space and choose the places we walk accordingly. This may mean travelling to a suitable area but it is better to do this and go less often than to go every day to places where your dog is frequently over the second threshold, or even the third.

But what do we do when the three thresholds are really close together and our dog reacts as soon as they see the trigger, at any distance? The first thing to do is test this out – is it really the case? Many people believe that their dog reacts at any distance when in fact they simply have not yet given enough space. So if your dog reacts immediately at the sight of another dog, try moving a football pitch away – or even two or three. Is their reaction the same?

It is likely that you will find a point where your dog does not react instantly and this is the distance you need to separate out the thresholds. Where this is a huge distance, the difficulty is how to manage this practically, in public places. Very few of us can guarantee that we can keep our dog two football pitches away from the next nearest dog!

If this really is your threshold distance then you will need to do some foundation work to reduce stress before you begin to work with your dog out on walks. Review trigger stacking in Chapter 4 and think about how you might address secondary triggers to help lower your dog's reactivity. Then check out the foundation exercises for comfort and calm in Chapter 8. If your dog is reactive to everything as soon as they leave the house, and you have ruled out any physical issues, then they may have more generalised anxiety, and I recommend taking veterinary advice about possible medical interventions to help your dog cope.

In most cases, we find that our dog does have a point where they can watch their trigger without significant concern, but that this point is further away than we had assumed. In this case we need to think about places where we can maintain this kind of distance as we start to work with our dog. The more space our dog requires, the more important it is that we use the Deconstructed Dog Walk to separate out how we meet their different needs. When you work on your dog's triggers you will need to find somewhere where you can watch from a distance, even if you can't walk. For walks, you will need to head out into the wilds or go to 'unconventional' locations, such as industrial estates and retail parks, where you are much less likely to be caught close up. But don't despair. The fastest way to reduce the space needed is to pay attention to space. Give enough space for your dog to learn and you will soon find that the space they need gets less and less.

Individual walks

When you walk more than one dog, you can find that one is a trigger for another to be more reactive. So now, instead of dealing with one reactive dog, you are trying to calm several dogs down. You may also share the problem that I had when I walked Mirri with my other dog, Jake. Mirri reacted to other dogs who approached but Jake liked dogs and wanted to meet them. When I walked them together, Jake had a habit of going to play with other dogs in the park and then bringing them back so we could meet his new buddy! Mirri was never impressed.

Even if your second dog is easy to manage and does not leave your side, you will still have to divide your attention. This will often make things more difficult for you.

There are huge advantages in walking your reactive dog on their own. You can concentrate your full attention on them and their needs. You have fewer distractions and will be able to focus. You can observe your dog more closely and get to know what signals they give. You will be able to respond more quickly and adjust to each situation.

Individual walks are important not only for your reactive dog but for your other dogs as well. When you have a more challenging dog, the 'easy' dog can get less attention. This is not deliberate; it is just that you need to spend more energy on the other. When you walk one dog at a time, each gets what they need as well as your individual attention, which will be very special to them. This is valuable for you too, since you can enjoy a relaxed walk with the easier dog and remind yourself what that is like. When I began to walk Jake on his own, being able to stop and chat to other guardians and enjoy watching dogs playing changed my outlook and helped me feel 'normal' again.

You may be wondering how on earth you will find time to do this. It can certainly be harder to fit in multiple walks as well as work, family and other commitments. But it is worth it finding the time, even if just a few times a week. You will find it easier to train and to relax and your relationship with your dogs will benefit. Reduce the length of the walks if needed – you are focusing on quality not quantity for this. If you walk a couple of times a day, make one walk an individual one and alternate the dogs on different days, giving the others some special play time at home instead on their 'off' days.

If you struggle to leave one dog alone, you may need to build this up slowly, unless there is someone else at home who can be with the one who is left. However, unless your dog has serious separation issues, if you do this slowly they will get used to a new routine. Leave the one at home with some safe, interesting chew and enrichment toys and start going out for just a few minutes with the other dog. Then build it up until you are able to leave one dog at home while you walk the other.

Note that when I talk about individual walks I mean one dog to one person so, if there are two of you, you can still walk together, as long as each handler is absolutely and reliably in charge of their particular dog. If you feel responsible for managing all your dogs, even if someone else is holding one of the leads, then it won't work! And of course, if they spark off each other, or become more reactive with each other's company, take them separately. It will make your progress so much faster.

Practising environmental awareness

Much of our stress on walks comes from being surprised by other guardians and their dogs. In Chapter 5 we looked at how to handle stray dogs and their guardians but we also need to take control and become skilled at responding to our changing environment.

My clients say this is one of their biggest problems – they can't relax on walks because they are always on the alert for other dogs. They get tired of scanning the horizon watching for potential dangers.

We certainly need to be aware of the environment and of potential hazards, but this doesn't have to be stressful. Consider driving. An experienced driver can listen to music and hold a conversation at the same time as operating the car – and still be aware of the road and ready to respond to potential hazards. If you are a driver you do this every day. Yet you probably don't feel stressed every time you get in the car to drive!

The reason is practice: the more you drive, the more automatic the process becomes and the less you have to think about it. You are still aware of the environment and scan the road ahead but it doesn't worry you or dominate your thinking.

This is what we want when walking our dog: awareness of the environment that is so well practised that it no longer interferes with our enjoyment of the walk. But, as with driving, you have to practise to achieve this.

Candidates for the Advanced Driving Test in the UK commentate on a journey as they drive, explaining their thinking and pointing out all the potential hazards along the way:

"Junction coming up on the right. Potential for vehicles slowing suddenly. Cyclist ahead so I will slow down to overtake. Entering a 30-mile-an-hour zone. Parked cars blocking view so watch for pedestrians."

Practising and verbalising in this way helps to develop deep skills, making hazard awareness second nature when driving.

You can achieve greater awareness on walks using the same method. Go for your usual walk without your dog. Instead take a recorder (you'll have one on your phone) and narrate your walk or video what you see and replay it later, identifying the potential hazard spots in real time.

You can also practise with video and photographs of walking environments that you find online – they don't have to be familiar walks. In fact, practising with unknown environments will hone your skills even more. Remember that speaking out loud helps our brains to take things in so don't miss that part out.

We need to be aware of the environment whether or not we have a reactive dog. Even if our dog is not concerned about anything, we need to be aware of things that could harm them. But it can become as natural as it is for a skilled driver. The more we practise, the more automatic it becomes and the less stressful it is.

On or off lead?

So we are giving our dogs space and walking them individually. We are practising hazard perception and becoming more aware of our environment. So should we now let our reactive dog off lead? Like most things, the answer is "it depends".

If your dog has shown signs that they may attack another dog or bite a person, then a lead or a long line is the obvious way to go and this may need to be a permanent solution.

If your dog is generally friendly with people and dogs and will come back reliably even when there are distractions, then there is no reason why they should not be off lead, in places where it is safe and permitted.

But, of course, most of our dogs fall somewhere in between these two extremes.

Some dogs are more reactive on lead than off and will meet other dogs politely or ignore them in most situations, as long as they are off lead. If this is your dog – and they are also friendly or neutral with people – then they may be better off lead. Of course, you need to be able to recall them reliably, especially if they are likely to approach another dog, who may not be comfortable being approached.

It becomes more complicated if they are reactive to people or have any other issues, such as chasing vehicles. It is not worth taking risks with this, when a long line can give you and them security.

However, many of our dogs will behave differently in different contexts, so we need to make a judgement call for our dog in each case. My own dogs both fall into this category.

Martha is generally non-reactive to dogs and people, she stays close to me and her recall is good. So, in normal circumstances, she is off lead. However, I know that she becomes more aroused when there are other dogs walking with us so in those situations I have to be more careful. Most of the time she will still be off lead, but I will reinforce her staying close more often and recall her earlier. I am also aware that if she greets a dog when excited she can be a bit 'full on' so I will often put her on lead rather than let her say hello to another off-lead dog, especially if it is smaller.

Otter, on the other hand, can be more reactive when she is on lead, close up to other dogs. It is mostly frustration and she will meet many of these dogs politely when she is off lead. However, if the other dog does not want to play or if they are too enthusiastic, she can become snappy so I am careful about which dogs she is allowed to meet. Generally, the big, the shy and the exuberant are best avoided. Her recall is very good but can fail when a dog suddenly appears close up so I am careful letting her off in places where visibility is poor or we might meet someone suddenly. She is on a long line anywhere unfamiliar as most fencing is not Otter-proof!

The key to making an informed decision is to know our dog and be honest about the risks. We come back to risk assessment. What is the likelihood of our dog getting into trouble or creating a problem for another dog or human and how serious might the consequences of this be? Whatever we decide, we need to be fair to other people and their dogs in the choices we make. We can all make a mistake once in a while and end up causing alarm to someone else, but it shouldn't be happening on a regular basis.

There are, of course, some situations where all dogs should be on lead, no matter how well behaved or reliable they are. These include when we are on or beside roads, in areas with lead regulations, and when walking in areas with livestock. This is non-negotiable. It is irresponsible to have your dog off lead in these situations.

I would add 'if your dog does not yet have a decent recall' to that list. If you are not confident that you can recall your dog, then a lead or long line is a wise precaution. It is essential if your dog will make a beeline for other dogs, who may not welcome the attention. We should not be risking traumatising other people's dogs to allow our dogs freedom.

So recall is critical core behaviour, especially for dogs who are less reactive off lead but who may still approach others inappropriately. Teaching a solid recall can give you confidence to allow your dog more freedom. We look at how to do this in more detail in Chapter 8.

When to let dogs off lead is a controversial topic. I err on the side of caution and only let my dogs off lead when they have a good recall and in places where it is safe. If they are likely to be distracted by other dogs and not come back, I will keep them on, even if they are friendly. However, there is certainly no blanket rule that says reactive dogs can never be off lead. It has to depend on the context and the individual dog.

Dog walking etiquette

When we have a reactive dog we tend, understandably, to focus on the needs of our dog and expect other people to make allowances. It is perfectly reasonable to expect other people to control their own dogs and not allow them to harass us. However, we also need to be mindful of the expectations associated with different places where we walk and choose the ones that are best suited to our needs. For instance, people using off-lead dog parks and other open dog-friendly public places are likely to have their dogs off the lead and may assume that other off-lead dogs are dog friendly, unless there is an indication to the contrary. Similarly it is reasonable to expect dogs to be on lead on roads, on-lead trails and footpaths, wildlife parks and other places where there are regulations about leads.

Some dogs will be more comfortable in off-lead spaces, others in on-lead spaces and we need to make appropriate decisions for our dog.

But it is worth thinking about dog walking etiquette. Are there some simple rules that we can apply, regardless of whether or not our dog is reactive, to make dog walks easier for everyone? How can you tell whether it is safe to allow your friendly dog to meet another dog?

As with everything, it depends very much on context. But I think we can all help each other by sticking to these three rules:

1. **Your dog is off the lead, the other dog is on the lead.** Don't let your dog approach. Even if both are friendly, it is an unequal meeting and not fair to the on-lead dog. There is usually a reason the dog is on a lead: respect this, give space and move on.

2. **Both dogs are on the lead**. Usually best to avoid a direct meeting: being on leads adds extra tension no matter how friendly the dogs. If you can't avoid, keep leads as loose as possible and only allow a greeting for a few seconds.

3. **Both dogs are off the lead**. Ask permission for your dog to meet the other and wait for a response. If you are not close enough to ask, observe. Are there any obvious resources (toys, balls) that could cause friction? Yes? Then avoid potential conflict and move on. Is the guardian training or playing with the dog? Yes? Then leave them in peace to enjoy their time together. Is the dog reasonably matched to yours in age, mobility, size? Yes? Then the dogs may enjoy meeting. Ask when you are close enough and wait for a response.

Of course, we may feel that it is not us who need to learn this etiquette but it doesn't hurt to have a reminder. The more we model the behaviours we want, the more likely we are to influence others to do likewise.

Muzzles

Muzzling our dogs is another controversial topic. Muzzles are slowly becoming more acceptable but if you suggest to someone that they muzzle their dog, you can get reactions ranging from anger or distress to horror. When you take your dog out in a muzzle, a few people will drag their children across the street and whisper behind their hands. Others assume your dog is 'vicious'. Even among dog professionals, muzzles can be viewed with suspicion or as an indication of a lazy owner. Some argue that if a dog is properly trained, a muzzle is not necessary.

This is all unfortunate as, used properly, muzzles are valuable training tools and can be effective management tools. Sometimes they are a permanent necessity, where there is a legal requirement or an ongoing bite risk. Muzzles can allow safe interaction, training and exercise and they remove significant stress from both owner and dog.

Let me be blunt: if your dog has bitten a person in a public place, a second incident is likely cost your dog their life. A dog may be trained and rehabilitated to a high degree, but are you prepared to bet your dog's life on there not being a repeat incident? That is what you are doing if you don't muzzle your dog, if they already have a bite history of this kind.

Using a muzzle, in situations where we cannot completely control access to people, such as when our dog is off the lead or in a crowded place, allows us to relax and our dog to enjoy freedom, while ensuring that everyone is kept safe.

Muzzles are also great to allow dogs to be assessed and to work with other dogs, without putting the other dogs at risk. They may also allow a dog to play with other dogs, where the issue is inappropriate nipping and grabbing more than serious aggression or fear. Most importantly, using a muzzle stops you feeling anxious, reducing tension for everyone.

Preventing biting is only one reason why a dog might be muzzled. We also use muzzles to:

- ☐ Stop scavenging. If your dog is on a restricted diet, using a muzzle can avoid the risk of picking up and eating unwanted food. If the diet is due to a medical condition or allergy, this can be life-saving or can be a huge help in managing a condition that can increase reactivity.

- ☐ Protect wildlife. Some breeds will instinctively chase and, potentially, kill small animals, such as rabbits, hares and squirrels. A muzzle will mean that, even if your dog chases, this does not end in a kill.

- ☐ Prevent self-harm. If your dog has a wound or a sore area, a muzzle can be used instead of the 'Cone of Shame' to prevent licking or chewing, especially outside or in the car.

- ☐ Allow safe handling in the case of injury. A dog that is injured and in pain might, understandably try to bite those who try to help. A muzzle can enable treatment.

- ☐ Comply with the law. Several countries have muzzle laws which affect specific breeds, regardless of whether they have shown aggression. In some countries, the list includes most bull breeds and a significant number of other large breeds, plus all breeds on public transport.

It makes sense to muzzle train our dogs so that they are comfortable wearing a muzzle if needed, even if it is only in case of injury. It is worth taking a little time to teach your dog to see the muzzle as something positive and unthreatening, so that you will be able to use one if you need to. We do this by introducing it slowly and pairing it with tasty food so that our dog starts to look forward to seeing the muzzle. Teach your dog to target the muzzle (see Chapter 8) and to put their nose into it, rather than you putting it on them.

Muzzles can be very useful but is important that they are not used to put dogs into situations where they are not comfortable. For instance, it is grossly unfair and very frightening for a dog to be muzzled and then put into a space with lots of other dogs. Muzzles are not a way to reduce the space that our dogs get. They are simply a way of keeping everyone safe.

MANAGING MELTDOWNS

We have talked about space and all the things that we can do to ensure our walks are calm and enjoyable. But even the most careful guardians are caught out on occasion.

We are distracted for a moment and take our eye off the ball. Someone appears suddenly or does something unexpected. Our dog is a bit more wound up than we thought and can't cope with something that is normally not a problem.

So our dog has a meltdown. They start barking and lunging at the end of the lead. Their heart rate and respiration is elevated. They are flooded with cortisol and adrenaline. How can we minimise the damage done in these situations?

Managing a meltdown is a critical skill for all of us. We may not always be able to avoid the initial reaction, but we can limit its impact and help our dog (and ourselves) recover as quickly as possible.

I use a three-step method for managing meltdowns to help you and your dog recover quickly: Contain, Calm, Consider.

- **Contain.** The first thing you need to do is damage limitation. The more your dog barks and lunges at the end of the lead, the more they wind themselves up. So your first task is to contain the reaction and move to a safer place.
- **Calm.** Next you need to calm them and yourself. The quicker you can help them calm down, the quicker they will recover completely.
- **Consider.** Once you and your dog are calm and safe, you

can look at the bigger picture. What went wrong? Is there anything you could have done differently? What can you learn from your experience? What can you do to make sure your dog has time to recover?

Let's look at each of these in more detail.

Contain

When our dog reacts we often hold them tighter. We pull them in to us, make the lead short, hold the collar. But the risk with all of these is that they increase, rather than decrease, our dog's level of arousal. Restraint can make our dog feel restricted or even panicked. They can feel frustrated and react more.

The alternative to restraint is to use gentle containment. Containment means 'keeping within limits'. So whereas restraint prevents movement, containment provide safe limits, within which your dog can still move and watch, but which reduce the risk of arousal escalating. You can do this by gently holding the harness or teaching a 'middle' and using your hands gently on the shoulders, but my favourite way to do it is to use the TTouch balance lead. We met the balance lead in Chapter 6 so check back there for full instructions and illustrations, but to summarise:

☐   Hold the lead about a foot from the point of connection with the dog (either harness or collar) in one hand and hold the lead handle in the other.

☐   Let the section of lead between your hands hang in a big open loop (like a smile) then lower this over the opposite shoulder to you and pass it across your dog's chest.

☐   Then bring the two ends together behind your dog's withers.

☐   If you have two points of connection it is even simpler, as you already have a loop between these points. Simply pass this loop across the chest in the same way.

What you end up with is the lead forming a loose loop over your dog's chest and shoulders. They can continue to move within this, so they are not tightly restrained, but they can no longer lunge and pull forwards.

If you practise when things are calm you can put it on in seconds and it allows you to hold even a strong dog much more easily beside you, without them leaping around at the end of the lead. However, they are still able to move and balance themselves. You can also use it to walk your dog away without dragging them.

Guardians of small dogs often ask if it is helpful to pick them up in these situations. I wouldn't hesitate to pick up my tiny dog if I felt she was in danger and I have done it on occasion to calm her down. However, this does depend very much on your dog. If your dog is comfortable being picked up and finds it reassuring, it can be a very useful way to contain a small dog, and allows you to move away easily at the same time. However, if your dog dislikes being picked up then it will not help. We also need to weigh up the risk of another dog jumping at us to get at our dog against any danger they may be in on the ground. Once again, the answer to the question is, it depends!

Calm

Once we have moved away to a safe space, we need to calm both ourselves and our dog as much as we can. The quicker we can do this, the faster our recovery time will be.

Calming our dog
A simple TTouch to use in this situation is the Zebra, a slow, sliding touch, done along the length of the body from the shoulder.
1. Place your hand on the shoulder, fingers together, and slowly slide your hand down (towards the elbow) opening your fingers as you go.

2. Slide back up, closing your fingers, and continue along the body sliding up and down in a zigzag motion.

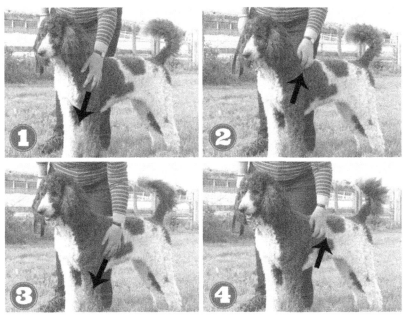

Initial strokes of the Zebra TTouch (Photos: Toni Shelbourne)

There are two variations: do one side first and then the other or do one side, then cross over the back and repeat the slide down the other side. In both, you 'zigzag' along the body from front to back.

Physically moving in simple patterns can also be calming, particularly if these are patterns your dog already knows. An easy pattern to remember is the *Figure of Eight* where you walk with your dog, in the pattern of a large figure of eight on the ground. This pattern encourages movement through the body in both directions, which will help your dog to slow down and become calmer. Practise this movement before you need it so that it comes naturally to you and your dog.

Calming ourselves
It is not just our dog who will need help to calm down after a

meltdown. We can also be left feeling stressed, upset and, possibly, frustrated. So what can we do to calm ourselves down?

- ☐ **Breathe deeply and slowly.** The key is to inhale slowly through the nose and exhale noisily through the mouth. Box breathing is one of the easiest and most effective breathing techniques. Imagine breathing around a square or a box.
  1. Breathe in slowly to a count of 4.
  2. Hold to a count of 4.
  3. Breathe out to a count of 4.
  4. Hold to a count of 4.

  Repeat until you feel yourself calming. Deep breathing will help to lower your heart rate and respiration.

- ☐ **Give yourself a break.** When an incident happens we can become frustrated. We can go over what happened in our minds, dwelling on the bad parts. We can make it seem much worse than it was. We need to reflect on our experience and we do this in the next step, but brooding over it helps no one. So give yourself a break. You did your best. You handled it. Take a deep breath and let it go.

- ☐ **Find a positive and work on that.** There will be something that went well in any situation. Find it and focus on it. Celebrate it. Enjoy it. Be grateful for it. This helps to quiet our Inner Critic and prepares us for the next step.

Consider

The final step is to Consider. What can you learn? Is there anything you need to change? This is not about apportioning blame – far from it. It is about taking what we can learn from a bad situation and then moving on. We may be able to do this immediately or we may choose to come back to it later.

From your point of view, this might be thinking about things that need more practice or whether you could have avoided the situation in the first place. Or you may simply conclude that you did all you could and accept that you can't control everything.

From your dog's point of view you might note what it was that pushed them over threshold or make a decision to give them a rest from walking for the rest of the day or even for a couple of days, so they can fully recover.

The STOP tool

The STOP tool is an excellent way of reflecting on a situation and making strategic decisions. Tim Gallwey describes the STOP tool as stepping out of a battlefield and moving to a higher vantage point to get an overview of all the action[55]. From the battlefield all you can see is what is immediately around you and you are focused on fighting for your survival. From the hillside above you can see the whole picture and take more strategic or tactical decisions.

Gallwey is writing about business decision-making but we can use the same principles to help us with our dogs. We can use this to reflect on what has happened:

- **Step back**. Distance yourself from the immediate situation and your emotional response. Take a deep breath.
- **Think.** What led to the mistake? Were you distracted? Were you already stressed by something else? Was your dog more stressed than you realised?
- **Organise your thoughts.** What could you have done differently? What can you learn from the experience?
- **Proceed.** What do you need to do now? When and how will you do it?

As we become more skilled at using it we can also use this tool to help us make better decisions on walks. When things get

---

[55] Gallwey, WT (2000) *The Inner Game of Work*, NY: Random House.

pressured, we can take a moment to collect ourselves and remember to **S**top and breathe, **T**hink what we need to do, **O**rganise ourselves and **P**roceed.

COMPETENCE IS KEY

We will enjoy our walks again when we feel in control and we will feel in control when we are competent. This is true in any situation.

How confident do you feel when you go to a country where you don't speak the language versus one where you do? When you can't speak the language you have much less control of situations, you are reliant on other people and you can feel insecure. When you can, you have much more freedom and will feel able to do so much more.

The same is true of using new software, learning to ride a bike or drive a car, or learning any new skill. Control and confidence come from competence.

We have little control over the behaviour of others but if we have the skills to handle any situation we face, we will still be more confident. So we need to practise so that the skills we need on walks become automatic, even with distractions. If we only practise the skills we need when a crisis is in progress, we will be like a pilot who only looks at the emergency procedures when the engines start to fail. It is not likely to end well! So practise all these skills at home first.

We will look at practice and how to do it effectively in detail in Chapter 9 but first we need to look at training and how we can help our dog change how they feel and behave.

Chapter Eight

CHANGING HOW YOU THINK ABOUT TRAINING

So finally we reach training. Welcome if you have just joined us for this chapter! Don't worry – you are not alone. Training is where many of us start and stop when it comes to reactivity. Our dog is not behaving as we want so we try to do more training. But if you start here you are missing a lot of the puzzle, so go back and read the previous chapters first. If you have come here by the long route then you know all the other things we need to get in place. The good news is that when we do, the training part becomes much easier.

This chapter aims to get you to think more clearly about your training and work out what you want to do and why. It is not primarily a 'how-to' chapter, although you will find some 'recipes' to get you started training core skills, plus many more pointers to further resources to help once you know what you need to do.

It is easy for us to follow a particular protocol without much thought and, when everything goes to plan, this can work. But when things don't go as expected, we need to be able to take a step back, think about what to do, and have the confidence to adjust our plan appropriately. So we need to know at least a little about learning and training, what our options are, and how we choose what to do to make the best progress. We will look at these questions in this chapter.

WHY TRAIN?

Why do we train our dogs and what do we hope to achieve when we train our reactive dog? Most of us would say we want to stop our dog's reactivity and get them to behave more 'appropriately' around other dogs (or whatever their trigger is). So we want to stop that barking and lunging and teach them to walk calmly beside us or to recall away from other dogs or people. But is that all? I think there is more to it than that.

We train because dogs are always learning

Our dog is always learning whether or not we are intentionally training! We will look in more detail at how dogs learn a little later, but essentially dogs learn by trying something and seeing if it brings them the result they want. If it does, they do it more. If it doesn't, they try something else. In short, they do what works.

This can be quite difficult to understand, particularly in the case of reactivity. How can barking, lunging and getting stressed be 'working' for our dog? Surely this can't be enjoyable for them?

What works is not the same as what is pleasant or enjoyable. We will all sometimes do things that we don't enjoy and, sometimes, that are distinctly difficult because they serve a wider function for us. They may be good for us in the long run. They may make us feel better. They may keep us safe.

Behaviour always has a function for our dog: to get a resource, to be comfortable, to get away from something scary, to satisfy a need or desire. This is not the same as being a deliberate choice. Our dog does not think their way rationally through their repertoire of behaviours and decide that barking and lunging is the way to go! Most of the time the behaviour is driven by an emotional response to the situation: either fear or frustration. But it is still 'working' for our dog in some way:

☐   They get the distance they need to feel safe.

☐   They get an outlet for their frustration.

☐   They feel better.

If a behaviour works for the dog, they will do more of it. We say that the behaviour has been *reinforced*. If it doesn't work, they will do it less. We say the behaviour has been *punished*. We'll look at this in detail in the next section but this is key to understanding why we need to train. Our dogs learn in this way from every interaction they have with us, with other dogs and people, and with their environment. But they may not always learn what we would like them to learn!

I am sure you can think of lots of examples of this. The dog who learns to jump up because they get attention when they do and are ignored when they have four feet on the floor. The dog who grabs the kid's toys because it results in a fun game of chase. The dog who bites without warning because they were told off for growling and learned to avoid that behaviour.

Our dogs are learning all the time so we train to guide what they learn. We train so that we can teach our dogs what behaviours will work in what context. We train so that they do more of what we want. Our dog is going to learn from what we do and how we interact with them. So it makes sense to train deliberately rather than leaving them to learn by accident!

We train to get the behaviours we want

When our dog does something we don't like, we naturally concentrate on stopping that behaviour. We will say: "I want to *stop* my dog barking at other dogs or people or cars" or "I want to *stop* my dog jumping up or growling at the kids".

When we focus on stopping behaviours we almost always turn to aversive training. *If* you do that, *this* bad thing happens. *If* you *stop* doing it, you can *avoid* the bad stuff. It also forces us to set our dogs up to fail. They have to do the behaviour we don't want in order to be 'corrected' with the unpleasant consequence. None of this is the way we want to train.

Of course this doesn't mean we just ignore behaviours we don't like. These behaviours are very stressful both for us and our dog and are sometimes dangerous. So we need to do something about them. But it is kinder and more effective to focus on training a new behaviour to replace the old, rather than only trying to stop the old one. So our mantra is 'train what you want to see'.

If you choose a new behaviour that is not compatible with the old one, then the new one will replace the old. So, for example, if your dog barks at dogs they don't know, if you teach them to pick up a toy when they see a dog then they can no longer bark. If your dog chases bikes, you can teach a solid down stay, which is incompatible with running after a bike. So we will concentrate on training our dogs to behave how we want, rather than trying to stop them behaving in ways we don't want.

- ☐ What do we want them to do when they see the other dog?
- ☐ What do we want them to do instead of jumping up?
- ☐ How do we want them to interact with the children?
- ☐ What do we want them to do when visitors come round?

We need to think carefully about this and be consistent. Once we have decided, we will make it really worthwhile for our dogs to do this and much less valuable to do anything else. Think of it as paying them generously for the behaviours we want to see happen more often.

This involves a bit of effort. We need to be clear what we want our dogs to do so that we can pay when they do it. We need to set up the environment to make it as easy as possible for them to get it right. We want to create lots and lots of opportunities to pay them – being mean is not appropriate here. We need to be ready and able to pay them immediately – no having to run to the kitchen to dig some treats out of the back of the fridge! We need to be watching so we don't miss opportunities to pay them and we need to be willing to interrupt what we are doing to capture those moments. But it is worth it when our dog does more of the things that we like rather than the things we find difficult.

We'll come back to this later when we look at some behaviours we can teach. First let's look at what we do if our dog is too frightened, too anxious or too aroused to be able to respond to our training.

We train to change our dog's mindset

One of the great things about training by reinforcing the behaviours we like is that our dog learns that they can influence their environment by what they do. They can act in ways that bring positive consequences and they know what to do to get the outcome they want. This empowers our dogs.

However, sometimes our dogs are too fearful or frustrated to be able to make good choices, so we first have to focus on changing their emotional responses. We do this by building an association between the currently scary or over-exciting thing and something really positive for our dog, usually really tasty food. We don't wait for a sit or for eye contact or for anything else. We simply feed our dog while the trigger is present and stop feeding when it goes. The food appears not because of anything our dog does but because they see (or hear) the trigger. The trigger will start to predict the tasty food and our dog will start to feel differently about it, because it is associated with something good.

As an example, let me tell you about Otter and the trains. Our local walk skirts a mainline train track on one side. The track is fenced but Otter is tiny and no fence is secure for her. A few months ago she decided trains were fun to chase and began taking off full pelt when one came past on our walk. This is not a behaviour I wanted to encourage. Although it is not a huge risk, there is a chance she could squeeze through plus she was starting to generalise to other vehicles and getting excited by cars. So the alternative behaviour I wanted was for her to come to me when she heard a train.

Initially, Otter was much too excited to respond to me when a train was close, so I started with her on a long line so she was unable to chase: setting her up to succeed. For a while we avoided the path that runs directly beside the line – far too tempting – and instead we started further away where she could hear but not see the train. Whenever she heard a train, I fed her. Sometimes I fed her to mouth, sometimes I threw the treats for her to catch, sometimes I scattered treats on the ground for her to find. But the sound of the train always meant food appeared.

Within a few days, instead of racing off to chase when she heard the rumble of the train, she started to run back to me and look up expectantly: the behaviour I want. Now, I can reinforce that behaviour: I can pay for what I like.

We couldn't do that initially. First we had to change how she felt – in her case reduce her excitement – so she could make good choices. So another reason we train is to change our dog's emotions and mindset. We want our dog to feel more comfortable in the presence of the trigger. We want our dog to be relaxed and happy. We want our dog to be more resilient and more responsive to training.

In the example above, I used *counter conditioning* to do this. We will look at this in more detail later, as well as ways we can help our dogs become more relaxed. However, when we train by reinforcing the behaviours we like, we are also building our dog's resilience, even if the behaviours we are teaching have nothing to do with their reactivity. So how does that work?

Remember the vagus nerve? Our dogs also have one and it

functions in much the same way as ours. So we can assume that the same correlations between vagal tone, positivity ratio and resilience also apply. If that is the case, then we can increase our dog's resilience through ensuring a high positivity ratio, including through positive training.

Several trainers[56] use an accounting metaphor to help us understand this. Imagine your dog has a 'Trust account' or a 'Resilience account'. Every positive experience they have is a deposit into that account. Every negative experience is a withdrawal. Some of our dogs have been dealt a tough hand before they even reach safety with us – physical and genetic issues, poor life experiences and, in some cases, neglect or abuse. Others may come straight to us as tiny puppies but still have the potential for genetic and physical 'withdrawals' and traumatic events in early puppyhood. So our dogs can have low balances or be overdrawn.

While we can't undo what has happened in the past and we can't always prevent bad things happening, we can always make deposits for our dogs – positive deposits that will build up a healthy account balance.

So what counts as a positive deposit into your dog's account? Anything that helps your dog increase trust and confidence. Anything that is helpful to your dog's wellbeing. Anything that your dog enjoys. This includes things like a good diet, pain relief or medicinal support, when needed, as well as help with physical tension through TTouch and physical therapies. It also includes training that shows them that they can control their environment and get positive consequences for their behaviour. It is any training that helps them to be successful.

---

[56] I have heard several great trainers talk about this idea – Steve Martin and Professor Susan Friedman, Chirag Patel and Sarah Fisher. For example, see S. Martin and S. Friedman, The Power of Trust, IAATE Conference 2013 and S. Fisher, Accountability (available from http://www.ttouchteam.co.uk.)

We train to give our dogs tools to negotiate the world they live in. It helps them to know how they can get the outcomes they want. All of this builds confidence as they learn effective ways to handle different situations. We cannot remove all the stress from our dog's life but we can train to give them the mindset they need to handle it.

We train to strengthen our relationship

A fourth reason we train is to build our relationship with our dog. As we problem solve and have fun with our dog, we strengthen the bond between us. We learn to understand each other and to communicate with each other more clearly. The emphasis shifts from training to fix a problem to training for its own sake: to enjoy a shared activity with our dog.

Training is fun! As well as teaching our dogs how we want them to behave, we can also teach them how to communicate with us, letting us know when they are ready to take part in activities with us and what they are concerned about. We often see real change when we shift our focus from thinking about problem behaviours to concentrating on things that build that bond between us or give us highly engaging things we can share together.

There is a practical reason why this helps with reactivity. When we enjoy something, focusing on it is easy. Other things become less important and less threatening. So training activities that we both enjoy strengthen our relationship with our dog and give us additional tools to change mindset and behaviour.

What do you and your dog love to do together? If you're not sure start experimenting with new things: try scentwork, informal agility or parkour, trick training, brain games, Rally obedience. Start at home without distractions and just enjoy it for its own sake. We'll look in more detail at some of the options later in the chapter.

HOW DOGS LEARN

Now that we are clear why we need to train and the benefits it gives us and our dogs, let's look at *how* we train – or, more accurately, how dogs learn – in a bit more detail. This section will use technical language but I will try to make it as accessible as possible. It is important that we understand how our dogs learn so that we can make appropriate choices to help our dogs and understand what the different techniques that we come across are doing. It is worth persevering to get to grips with these principles as, once you do, you will be much more successful as a trainer.

If you are new to this, hang on tight for our whistle-stop tour of the principles and ethics of training. If you are already knowledgeable, forgive me for missing out some of the details of learning theory. My aim is to cover what is needed to understand what is to come and no more.

'Classical' or 'operant' – whaaaat?

There are two names you will hear a lot if you start looking deeper into how animals learn: Pavlov and Skinner. Pavlov came first and is the one who did rather unpleasant experiments on dogs. He demonstrated that if he paired a neutral sound with food, the dogs would start to salivate when they heard the sound, even when the food wasn't present. Skinner is considered the father of behaviour analysis. He did lots of work with rats and pigeons, teaching them to do all kinds of complex behaviour chains by manipulating contexts and consequences. Between them, they discovered two key ways that animals (including humans) learn: classical conditioning (Pavlov) and operant conditioning (Skinner).[57]

Classical conditioning is where something that has no inherent

---

[57] For more in depth coverage of classical and operant learning, I recommend Burch, MR and Bailey, JS (1999) How Dogs Learn, NY: Wiley.

significance to the animal, like a particular sound, becomes associated with something that produces a physiological or emotional response (like food). The neutral stimulus (known as *conditioned*) comes to predict the known stimulus (*unconditioned*) so produces the same emotional response. When your dog gets excited when you open their food cupboard, classical conditioning is at work. The neutral stimulus of the cupboard opening has come to predict known stimulus of the arrival of their dinner.

Classical conditioning has lots of useful applications in training. We have already seen an example of it in *counter conditioning*. Here the same principle is at work but instead of pairing something unknown with something good, we are pairing something scary or worrying with something good. But the intention is the same: to condition a particular emotional and physiological response.

Imagine your dog is frightened of men in hats. We want to change their emotional response so that they start to enjoy seeing men in hats. We can do this by pairing the appearance of any man in a hat with something the dog likes, like very tasty food. Do this often enough and men in hats will start to predict food appearing. It is really important that the trigger appears first: if the food appears first, the process won't work and can even result in the food becoming negative to your dog.

This makes sense if you think about it. As Kathy Sdao says "Emotion spreads backwards".[58] In other words, the emotion associated with the second thing in the sequence connects to the first thing. So excitement about food connects to the man in a hat. However, if you get the order wrong and feed first, then the fear associated with the man in a hat connects to the food. The food starts to mean that a scary thing is coming and your dog will find it aversive.

---

[58] Katy Sdao (2017) Presentation at The weekend with Kathy Sdao, Manchester, UK, 23rd September 2017.

We usually pair counter conditioning with desensitisation, so that we gradually increase the intensity of the trigger in a way that our dog can handle. Here is a summary of the process. You will need very high value treats – real food – whatever your dog will sell their soul for! Start off with a low level version of the trigger so that your dog is not overly concerned: you don't want to trigger the fear response. So, in our example, that might be a man in a hat at a distance where the dog feels safe or a man without a hat or a hat without a man! It depends which part of the scenario is most concerning to your dog. This is the trigger. The steps are then:

1. Present the trigger.
2. Feed your dog while the trigger is present.
3. Continue until the trigger has gone.
4. Repeat until the appearance of the trigger creates happy anticipation in your dog.
5. Gradually make the trigger a little more difficult (e.g. reduce distance or put small hat on man)

If you follow this process methodically and ensure that your dog is not frightened by a 'man in a hat' while you are working on it, you will find your dog starts to respond differently to men in hats.

Classical conditioning also comes into its own when we want to teach our dogs to be comfortable with things that may otherwise be worrying for them. We can use it to condition them to like their muzzle and their harness. We can use it to make equipment like nail clippers exciting rather than scary. And we can use it to create new reinforcers and markers, like the clicker that we will talk about shortly.

The key thing to remember about classical conditioning is that it has nothing to do with what your dog does. It is all about making an association between the conditioned and unconditioned stimuli. Your dog's behaviour is not relevant.

Operant conditioning, on the other hand, is the use of

consequences to train or modify behaviours in specific contexts. Its basic principle is that the dog will link its actions to consequences and that it will choose to do more of the things that bring benefit and less of the things that don't.

Operant conditioning, or learning, is our most useful tool in training our dogs. It allows us to teach our dogs what to do and when to do it. It allows us to give our dogs ways to participate actively in their training. Here our dog's behaviour is vital and they learn that they can control their environment and consequences through what they do. This makes it very empowering to dogs and my go-to choice for working with reactivity. More on that later on.

There are a couple of points to note about operant learning, before we dive in to look at its tools in more detail.

Firstly, with operant learning, your dog's behaviour *does* matter: it is all about what your dog does. Behaviour is reinforced or punished and will become either more or less likely to be repeated. Behaviour has consequences and those consequences drive what behaviours are offered in future.

Secondly, context also matters. Consequences may be what drive future behaviour but context determines what behaviour is offered and when reinforcement (or punishment) is available. This includes:

- Cues. When we give a cue we are telling our dog that reinforcement is available. We are not telling them, you must do as I say or else. This is why we talk about cues rather than commands.

- Environment. Dogs learn to offer certain behaviours in certain places and in response to different environmental cues. A dog approaching is an environmental cue, as is opening the boot of your car. Your dog will learn which behaviours result in reinforcement in these contexts.

So let's look at the tools available within operant learning and how we choose which ones to use.

Why choose positive reinforcement?

We've already met the concept of reinforcing behaviour we like so that we see more of it. This is known as *positive reinforcement*: something is added that results in behaviour increasing. This is one of the four primary ways[59] in which animals learn, the others being *negative reinforcement, positive punishment* and *negative punishment*.

There is a lot of confusion about these terms, which is not surprising because they are all technical terms with specific technical uses. None of these correspond to our normal everyday understanding of the words! As a result, people often scratch their heads, as some of these terms seem to be contradictions.

So let's look at the technical definitions, which should make everything clearer. *Reinforcement* increases the likelihood that a behaviour will be repeated. *Punishment* decreases the likelihood that a behaviour will be repeated. It is the *behaviour* that is 'reinforced' or 'punished' not the animal.

Positive means adding something. *Negative* means taking something away. These are not value judgements: they do not mean good or bad. Think of them mathematically: plus and minus, adding and taking away. This leaves us with these definitions:

- ☐ *Positive reinforcement*: adding something that results in the behaviour increasing or being maintained.
- ☐ *Negative reinforcement*: taking something away that results in the behaviour increasing or being maintained.
- ☐ *Positive punishment*: adding something that results in the behaviour decreasing.
- ☐ *Negative punishment*: taking something away that results in the behaviour decreasing.

---

[59] There is also a fifth – extinction – where the consequence is that nothing happens. This will eventually mean a behaviour will 'extinguish' because it is not reinforced. Extinction is sometimes used to get rid of behaviours but without filling the void with an alternative behaviour, extinction can lead to frustration.

Let's look at a simple example to see how this works in practice: training a dog to walk beside us without pulling. The behaviour we want to see increase is walking on a loose lead beside us. The behaviour we want to decrease is pulling. There are four approaches we could choose to train this behaviour:

1. We can give the dog a treat or similar when they are in the correct position at heel and the lead is loose. If they choose this position more in future, we are using *positive reinforcement*. The food is *added* (positive) and the desired behaviour *increases* (reinforcement).

2. We can use a harness that tightens when the dog pulls and releases when they walk in the position we like. If they choose this position more in future, we are using *negative reinforcement*. The pressure is *taken away* (negative) and the desired behaviour *increases* (reinforcement).

3. We can jerk our dog's collar every time they pull ahead. If they pull ahead less, then we are using *positive punishment*. The jerk to the collar is *added* (positive) and the pulling *reduces* (punishment).

4. We can stop every time our dog pulls. If they pull ahead less, we are using *negative punishment*. The forward movement is taken away (negative) and the pulling *reduces* (punishment).

All of these are, by definition, effective in changing behaviour. However, they are not all equal. Effectiveness is not our only criterion: we also need to consider what is ethical and the emotional response produced by the training we do. We want our dog to enjoy learning and not to experience frustration, fear or pressure.

Only positive reinforcement teaches our dog what we want them *to do* in a way that is entirely non-aversive to our dogs, so this is always our preference. But this doesn't mean we will never use anything else. For example, sometimes we may use negative punishment as well, when we have to stop a behaviour happening, such as stopping forward movement so that our dog does not practice pulling. But when we do this we always combine it with positive reinforcement of the behaviour we want.

When we take an ethical stance, we avoid using things that are aversive to our dog: things that hurt, frighten, shock, startle or pressure them. It is helpful to think about the emotions that tend to result from the use of these four tools.

- Positive reinforcement results in satisfaction and, often, joy. Our dog learns that they can make good things happen through their behaviour and they offer more. Learning is enjoyable and rewarding. Using positive reinforcement not only changes our dog's behaviour but changes how they feel. This makes it a win-win for reactive dogs!

- Negative punishment can result in frustration or anger. They learn that something they want is taken away, but they do not necessarily know what to do to stop that happening.

- Negative reinforcement brings relief, which may seem like a good thing. But to feel relief our dog needs first to feel pressure, which can arise from discomfort, fear or stress. If we escape from a threatening situation we feel relief, but we would still rather not be threatened.

- Positive punishment can result in fear or anxiety. Our dog learns that their behaviour leads to bad things, but they have no way of knowing what to do to avoid this, which makes training stressful. They can only avoid behaviours that have already resulted in bad things but they cannot predict the consequences of new behaviours.

When we look at the tools in this way, positive reinforcement stands out clearly as the most ethical tool to use. However, although positive reinforcement is clearly easiest and most pleasant for our dog, using aversives (through positive punishment or negative reinforcement) is sometimes all too easy for us. We are often frustrated when we are dealing with behaviours we don't like and we just want to stop them at any cost. Aversives can sometimes appear to produce rapid results so they can seem attractive, especially if the aversive is relatively mild. What harm can they do?

The trouble with aversives is that they can have all kinds of fall-out, including suppressing behaviour and damaging the relationship between you and your dog. They may appear to work but they are putting your dog under stress and increasing their anxiety. This will come out at some point. Plus it is not ethical to use fear, pain, shock and pressure to train when there are effective alternatives available.

Sometimes people justify using aversives by saying, *"I tried positive reinforcement and it didn't work"*. When we look at the definition of positive reinforcement, we can see that this does not make sense. If what was done 'didn't work', and the behaviour they were looking for didn't increase, then it wasn't positive reinforcement! It was an attempt at positive reinforcement.

So we need to look at how we are using the tools to make sure they are effective. Sometimes the animal is too fearful or aroused to learn at all and we need to address that first by managing the environment. Sometimes what we thought would be reinforcing was not for that particular animal; it may even have been punishing for that animal. Perhaps we did not make the connection between the behaviour and consequence clear enough. Let's take a closer look at reinforcers and make sure that we are using positive reinforcement effectively.

Understanding reinforcers

As we have seen, a reinforcer is a consequence that leads to a behaviour being maintained or increasing. It is a consequence so it must immediately follow the behaviour and it is only a reinforcer if the behaviour is maintained or increases. This is really important. Reinforcers are not only things that our dog likes: they are things that make behaviour more likely to happen. So they need to be *genuinely* reinforcing for the individual dog and *sufficiently* reinforcing in the context in which the behaviour is happening.

There are different kinds of reinforcer. Primary reinforcers do not have to be learned: they are reinforcing from birth and usually meet a physiological need. Food and warmth are primary reinforcers.

Secondary reinforcers (or learned reinforcers) are initially neutral things that become reinforcing because of their associations. Praise and toys are learned reinforcers. We can use classical conditioning to create endless new reinforcers for our dogs.

Reinforcers are individual. Something can be a strong reinforcer for one dog and have no value as a reinforcer – or even act as a punisher – for another. For example, Martha loves water sprays. If you pick up the hose she goes crazy with excitement. For Martha, playing with a water spray could be a reinforcer. Otter, on the other hand, does not get this at all. She has never been deliberately sprayed but she will beat a hasty retreat if the hose comes out. For her, using a water spray would be a serious punisher. Same consequence but very different outcomes. It doesn't matter what *we* think is a reinforcer. What matters is what our dog thinks!

Reinforcers are contextual. Food may be a strong reinforcer if we are hungry but will have limited or even negative effect if we are feeling full after a heavy meal. Our dog may love their biscuits at home, but may not be interested in them when there are rabbit smells to investigate or other dogs to worry about. We need to choose reinforcers that are valuable in the context in which we are training.

Reinforcers can be environmental. We think of reinforcers as things we add such as food or play but there are many reinforcers in the environment as well, like following a scent trail. We tend to call these 'distractions' but they also reinforce our dog's behaviour and we can use them to reinforce the behaviours *we* want, if we can manage our dog's access to them.

Behaviour can be self-reinforcing. We need to remember that some behaviours can be self-reinforcing if our dog enjoys them. Running, jumping, barking and, even, fighting are all potentially self-reinforcing. This is why it rarely works to ignore these behaviours!

We need to find out what is reinforcing to *our* dog and in what contexts. We need a good range of reinforcers and we need to have access to strong reinforcers in situations where the environment contains competing reinforcers.

Activity:
List as many reinforcers for your dog as you can. Be specific. What kind of food? Which toys? What natural behaviours? Put them in order of value to your dog. How does context change your list?

Now categorise your list into high value, medium value and low value reinforcers. High value reinforcers are those that are still significant when there is plenty of other reinforcement available in the environment. Low value reinforcers are those that will only do when there is nothing much else on offer.

Always use high value reinforcers in situations that your dog finds challenging.

Marking behaviours
If you are finding it hard to make progress with your training, you might be reinforcing too late or not being clear enough about *what* you are reinforcing. Imagine you ask your dog to sit and they do so you go to give them a treat. Meanwhile they stand up and you pop

the treat in their mouth. What have you just reinforced? You've reinforced the stand. It can be tricky to get the timing right especially when our dogs are quick!

The answer is to use a marker so that we can tell our dog precisely which behaviour we want to reinforce. The most common marker is a clicker – a small gadget that makes a very specific sound – but you can use anything that is distinct, precise and available. A specific word said in a specific way, a sound made with the mouth (some people will use a tongue click), a whistle, a flash light and a thumbs up (often used for deaf dogs) all make good markers. It is up to you what you use.

Some dogs will find a clicker too loud: if your dog flinches when they hear the clicker or is cowed by it, then choose another marker. I like to have more than one marker – and at least one that does not require any particular equipment. This means I can mark behaviours even when I have forgotten my clicker or have my hands full!

We will talk about a 'click' but this all applies to whatever marker you choose. When we first start, click is a neutral sound. It means nothing to our dog. So we use classical conditioning to give it value, by pairing it with food.

You will need some small treats, your clicker and your dog. Start in a quiet place without distractions. Click, then give a treat. Note that the food follows the click; it doesn't happen at the same time. Repeat this until you see your dog show a sign of recognition when they hear the click. Their ears may flick or they may look to you. That recognition tells you that the association has been made. The sound now predicts food. For most dogs it happens very quickly – often within half a dozen repetitions. Once you see a flicker of recognition you can move on to use your clicker in training. The association will strengthen naturally through training anyway, as the click is *always* paired with a treat.

The click tells our dog three things:

1.   *That* was the behaviour we wanted. Think of it as taking a snapshot of the behaviour.
2.   Food is coming – and it must – every time!
3.   The behaviour is complete (so it doesn't matter what they do after the click).

It important that every time you click, you follow with food. Even if you click the wrong thing or your dog breaks the behaviour after the click, still follow the click with food.

Only use the click to mark the behaviour you want, never to get your dog's attention. Its only job is to indicate clearly to our dog what behaviour is being reinforced.

Using a marker makes your training much more precise and your intention much clearer to your dog so you make faster progress. It is beyond the scope of this book to do more than get you started but if you want to know more about training this way there are lots of free videos available online for everything from the basics of clicker training to training complex behaviours.[60] I thoroughly recommend you check out some of these.

The role of management

We can facilitate learning through careful management, including avoiding situations that will push our dogs over their threshold, but many people worry whether allowing space in this way is just avoiding the issue. It is a fair question. How can we fix the problem if we don't confront it? How will our dog get used to other dogs if they don't meet them?

Management is also dismissed by some trainers, especially those who promise a quick fix. "We'll show you how to cure your dog, not just *manage* their behaviour." This shows a misunderstanding of

---

[60] My favourite source for ethical and effective clicker training is Emily Larlham's Kikopup YouTube Channel. https://www.youtube.com/user/kikopup.

management and how and why we do it. Management is generally not the end result, but it enables us to get to the end result in a way that is appropriate for our dog.

Management *can* sometimes provide us with a complete solution to a problem without any training at all. Counter surfing is an obvious one. By far the easiest way to stop this undesirable behaviour is not to leave desirable objects on the counters! Another example is using a lead to prevent stock chasing. There is no need to train most dogs not to chase livestock when the most reliable solution is in our hands. A third example is my client's dog who sat and barked at the front window when his guardians were out. We solved this problem very easily by leaving him in the large room at the back of the house when his guardians were not at home. No sight of the goings on at the front of the house meant no barking.

These solutions are quick and complete and there is nothing wrong with using management in this way. It is simple for us, it is simple for our dog and it is effective. So if you can 'manage away' a problem in a way that works for you both, then go for it!

But even when this is not possible, management is still a vital part of every behaviour modification programme. Management sets our dog up to be successful. It scaffolds their learning so that they can concentrate on what we want rather than being distracted by things that are worrying, over-exciting or overwhelming. Management means our dog doesn't practise behaviours we want to stop and makes it easier for them to do the things we like.

Management is a bit like giving your child stabilisers (training wheels) to help them learn to ride a bike or water wings before they go in the pool for the first time. They can learn the mechanics of cycling or swimming without the risk of falling or drowning. We would not send a teenager out to learn to drive on a motorway. If we teach them how to operate the car's controls in an empty car park or on a quiet back street we are not 'avoiding' the motorway!

We are simply saving that experience until our new driver is properly equipped to deal with it safely. This is what we are doing when we give our dogs appropriate space.

So think about how you can make it easier for your dog to be successful in their learning. You might give them more space and teach them some coping behaviours before you take them closer to the things they find challenging. You might use child gates or room dividers to make sure that they can't mug visitors at the door and can learn to meet them in a controlled way. You might use a long line so that you can remind them what you want if things prove to be more exciting than you had expected. There are many, many examples.

Management might be simple but it is not always easy. It demands thought, consideration and flexibility. It can require creativity as you look for ways to make it easier for your dog to learn. It can be inconvenient for you for a time. But good management is core to our success. You will make much faster, more consistent and reliable progress if you remember this one thing.

Training or distraction?

Before we leave this section on how dogs learn, I want to clarify the difference between training and distraction, as this can sometimes cause confusion, particularly with reactive dogs.

When our dog is reactive, it is tempting to shove food in their face as soon as *we* see one of their triggers. We want to distract them from noticing whatever it is they are concerned about.

In an emergency, there is nothing wrong with this. It is far better that our dog be snacking on something tasty than lunging and barking at the end of the lead. So there is a place for distraction when we find ourselves too close to a trigger. But what is our dog learning from this?

If we see the trigger and feed our dog before *they* have seen the trigger, they are not learning anything useful about the trigger. Their attention is redirected. This may be good management – and they will learn that we are a source of good stuff – but they are not learning to feel better about the trigger nor how we want them to behave when the trigger appears.

There is also the potential, if we get it wrong, that our dog will suddenly become aware of the trigger and become scared. This could even 'poison' the food in the mind of our dog: the food becomes a bad thing because it means scary triggers appear.

Distraction, carefully done, is fine as an occasional emergency management tool but it is not effective as a long-term training strategy, as it doesn't change behaviour or emotions. When we are training, we are not simply distracting our dog with food. Food is used very specifically either to create a positive emotional response to something scary (counter conditioning) or to reinforce the behaviour that we like (positive reinforcement).

This is reassuring if you worry about always being reliant on food. When we use food to distract, we always need to have food with us. However when we use it to change emotions or behaviour then, once we see that change, we can start to reduce the food we use. Our dog will feel differently about the trigger and will no longer need us to build that positive association. We never stop reinforcing behaviours we like (any more than we would expect that our pay would stop once we learned the job) but we can reduce the proportion of food reinforcers and replace some with other reinforcement like play, attention, touch and praise.

TRAINING FOR REACTIVE DOGS

When we work with reactive dogs we tend to focus our training on helping them to handle their triggers but, for me, this is only one part of the necessary training. My Reactivity Training Pyramid highlights the different elements that I include when I am working with a reactive dog and their guardian. Each level contributes to the overall solution and builds on the one below.

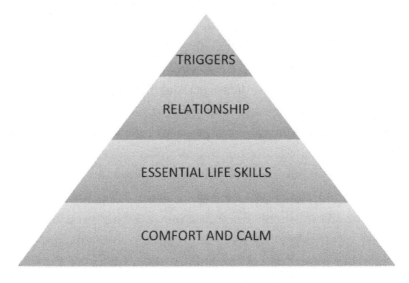

Reactivity Training Pyramid

1. **Comfort and calm.** Reactive dogs are often anxious or easily frustrated and benefit from work to lower their arousal and teach them how to relax. They may also have physical tension in the body, as we saw in Chapter 4, so may need work to address this. I use TTouch bodywork and groundwork for this, as well as Sarah Fisher's ACE Free Work[61], Karen Overall's *Relaxation Protocol*[62] and exercises like *Take a Breath* and mat work from Leslie McDevitt's *Control Unleashed*[63]. This foundation work benefits all reactive dogs but is essential for those who are highly aroused as soon as they leave home.

---

[61] For more information see https://www.facebook.com/tilley.farm.
[62] Overall, KL (2013) *Protocol for Relaxation*, in Overall, KL, Manual of Clinical Behavioural Medicine for Dogs and Cats, MO: Elsevier Mosby, 585-598.
[63] McDevitt, L (2019) *Control Unleashed: Reactive to Relaxed*, MA: Clean Run Productions.

2. **Essential Life Skills.** With any reactive dog, there will be one or two core behaviours that would make life much easier for them and their guardian. This might be a really reliable recall, so they can be called away from entanglements with other dogs. It might be getting (and staying) behind their guardian, so that they can be protected if a dog approaches. It might be walking on a loose lead. It might be maintaining focus on their guardian, even with distractions. The more we practise life skills such as these, the more options we have when we face our dog's triggers.

3. **Relationship.** One of the casualties of reactivity is often the relationship between dog and guardian. The pressure of handling a reactive dog and dealing with incidents that are stressful and embarrassing can lead to relationship damage: the joy seeps out of it. So it is essential that we include in our training at least one thing that both dog and guardian can really enjoy together; something that reminds us what our dog is capable of doing and that is not about 'fixing the problem'. This can be anything – a doggy sport or activity, trick training, interactive play – but it needs to be fun for both parties. My favourites are canine parkour and scentwork, both of which are great fun and can be done anywhere. These have the added advantage of building confidence and providing an absorbing activity out on walks, but the primary objective is to rediscover the joy and build the bond between dog and handler.

4. **Triggers.** Only at the top of the pyramid do we get to specific training to help our dog become more comfortable with triggers and to negotiate the world without becoming over-aroused. Again, my personal 'go-tos' here come from *Control Unleashed*. I use pattern games and *Look at That* to help support dogs and enable them to communicate with us about their level of arousal. But there are many tools we can use here,

including counter conditioning and *Behaviour Adjustment Training (BAT)*[64]. The important point is that whatever you use will be more effective and easier for both you and your dog if we underpin them with training at the other levels.

An important thing about this framework is that most of this training can be done away from the triggers, so if we have a dog who is highly reactive, we can do a lot before we ever need to start working with triggers. We can start at home and build up our foundations so that we are equipped to handle triggers in the world. This may, of course, mean walking our dogs in more remote, quieter locations while we work on the fundamentals or, in some cases, it may mean taking a break from walks while we get these core elements in place.

The idea of this framework is to help us to think about what we want to achieve through our training, rather than worrying about whether we should use this or that technique. Let's look briefly at some of the things that are available to us for each of these levels.[65] Note that these sections are not exhaustive: there are other techniques that you can use. As long as they are kind to you and your dog, that is fine. These are simply the combination of tools that I find to be effective.

Comfort and calm: building solid foundations

When we have a reactive dog we first need to 'turn down the heat' on their arousal and address any issues of physical comfort. Giving them the experience of being calm is very important for their learning. Helping them to release physical tension in the body can

---

[64] For more on BAT see Stewart, G (2016) *Behaviour Adjustment Training 2.0: New practical techniques for fear, frustration and aggression in dogs*, WA: Dogwise Publishing.
[65] Note: it is beyond the scope of this book to give detailed instructions on all of these. My intention here is to give an overview with pointers to further resources.

remove some of the physical triggers for reactivity. Teaching them how to self-calm gives them some control over their own arousal level: they have ways to move themselves from reactivity to relaxation. This is important for all of our dogs but is critical for those who are aroused simply by stepping outside the front door. All of this is work that we can do at home, but it is the foundation for when we start to work around triggers. So what's involved? I use several tools for this: TTouch bodywork, TTouch groundwork and ACE free work, *Take a Breath*, the *Relaxation Protocol* and mat work.

TTouch bodywork
TTouch bodywork can reduce arousal and help your dog to calm. It is also helpful for reducing tension that may be held through the body, helping with physical comfort. There are many TTouches to choose from but these three address key areas of the body that influence emotion and where tension may be held.

Ear slides: There are many acupressure points in the ears and around the base of the ear and this work helps to lower respiration and heart rate, so is very calming. To do the ear slides, support your dog's head with one hand. With the other hand, hold the ear between your thumb (on top) and the rest of your hand (underneath) and gently slide with your thumb from the base of the ear to the tip, covering the whole ear in one or more strokes. Imagine the ear is a green leaf and use the sort of pressure you would use to slide over this without damaging it. Make sure you cover the whole ear and pay particular attention to the tip, especially if your dog is worried.

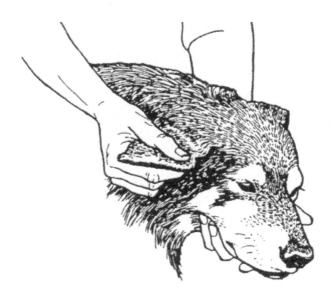

TTouch ear slides (Image courtesy of Robyn Hood)

Turtle TTouch: The Turtle TTouch is excellent for releasing tension through the back, shoulders and hindquarters, which is very common in reactive dogs. Stand behind or beside your dog. Place your hands on each side of your dog's body (e.g. on each shoulder). One hand should be off-set to the other. Do a circle and a quarter with both hands together, so one hand is going up as the other goes down. End by supporting the skin with a pause and then releasing. This touch is excellent for releasing tension.

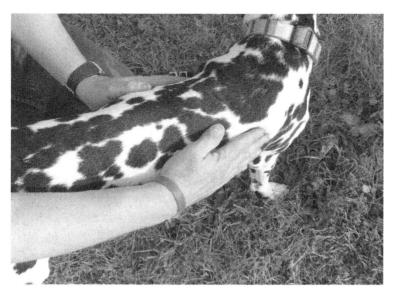

Turtle Touch can be done along the back (Photo: Toni Shelbourne)

Mouth TTouch: The mouth and jaw are strongly linked to emotional expression, through vocalisation, licking, chewing, salivating or through tension or grinding of the jaw. Mouth TTouch is very beneficial in helping to address emotion and release tension. It is a touch that requires trust so take it slowly, building up to working inside the mouth over a period of time. To work with your dog, sit so that you are behind or beside your dog and can support their chin with one hand. Start by doing long slow slides along the side of the mouth with the back of your hand from front to back. Do gentle circular touches over the jaw and muzzle and around the head with your finger tips or knuckles – you are aiming to move the skin under your fingers with a very light pressure. Once your dog is comfortable with you touching him all over the outside of the mouth, try sliding one finger inside the mouth and do a circle on the gums. Gradually build this up until you can work all over the gums. Make sure you have water available to keep your hands wet – dry fingers in the mouth are very uncomfortable.

Mouth TTouch (Photo: Kate Sweeney)

TTouch groundwork and ACE free work

A dog's awareness of their body in the space around them is called proprioception and is sensed through receptors in the skin, muscle and joints. Strong proprioception is indicated by awareness of different body parts, being grounded and coordinated. Weak proprioception typically leads to clumsiness and a lack of coordination and balance. This is important because physical balance is linked to emotional balance: improving proprioception will therefore help to improve both. Tension in the body will mean the dog moves less freely and with lower confidence.

If we can raise our dog's awareness of their body, particularly in movement, then we can help to improve their proprioception. Your dog will benefit from any non-habitual movement that will encourage them to flex through their back, walk on different surfaces and balance themselves. This will improve their balance, flexibility, body awareness and confidence.

In TTouch groundwork we use non-habitual movement, leading the dog over elements on the floor, to let the dog experience the world differently. We ask them to slow down, to allow them to process new information, and we give them the opportunity to make appropriate choices.

The TTouch confidence course is designed to encourage slow, thoughtful movement. You can set the poles out as a labyrinth and work through that as well as over the poles on the ground. Other good exercises are weaving round a series of cones or flower pots, walking over (and pausing on) different surfaces (carpet, plastic, wood, rubber matting, bubble wrap, gravel etc.), and walking over a balance board (a plank laid over bricks so slightly raised off the ground works well).

Example confidence course elements (Photos: Esther Dix)

Sarah Fisher's ACE free work[66] combines different surfaces and levels with enrichment elements such as ball pits, snuffle mats and puzzle toys. It differs from groundwork in a number of ways. Firstly, it begins by working with dogs off lead and with equipment like harnesses and collars removed, in a safe environment. These elements, while necessary for safety, undoubtedly affect our dog's movement and posture. So we can observe more in free work and

---

[66] For more information see https://www.facebook.com/tilley.farm or join the ACE Connections Facebook group.

allow our dogs the opportunity to learn without physical handling. We can also work on connection with our dog that does not depend on the lead. Equipment can gradually be replaced, first using sliding lines (see Chapter 6) and then, finally, the lead. This is much easier once the connection between dog and guardian has been established.

Secondly, the elements are primed with food of different types so that our dog is initially motivated to explore. The food used ranges in size and texture and includes crunchy treats to soft food to encourage chewing, licking and working the jaw. As our dog explores the free work area, there will be preferred elements, which we can later use to support our dog and help them to decompress.

Thirdly, Chirag Patel's Counting Game is used to build connection between dog and guardian. This is a simple game where a treat is placed on the floor while the guardian counts "One", inviting the dog to engage. If the dog is not able to do so, the count can continue with another treat placed or the guardian can wait until the dog is ready. The game structure is simple and, like pattern games (see below), provides a familiar pattern to support the dog and build connection. It also gives information to the guardian about whether or not their dog is able to engage at that moment.

As the dog and guardian progress with free work, other elements from groundwork and TTouch body work can be incorporated, but the beauty of this approach is the awareness it brings to how our handling, the equipment we use and the environment all influence our dog's behaviour. By removing all pressure, we enable our dogs to feel safer and to learn to self-moderate.

Another benefit of free work is that it can be done in small spaces such as kennels in rescue centres, living rooms and small yards. You can use it pretty much anywhere where your dog will be safe.

Otter doing ACE Free Work (Photo: Janet Finlay)

Take a Breath

Take a Breath is a simple but profound technique that I learned
from Leslie McDevitt's *Control Unleashed*. We know that breathing
deeply helps us to calm down and control our respiration and heart
rate. It is the same for our dogs. We can teach them how to Take a
Breath, which gives them a tool to self-calm, and we can teach
them to do this in contexts that they find challenging.

Teaching our dogs to Take a Breath is really straightforward but
it takes a bit of practice. The hardest part is spotting the inhalation:
after all we don't need to teach our dogs to breathe! When we, or
our dogs, inhale, there is a movement in the nostrils and the mouth
closes. You may spot a wrinkle on top of the nose or you may see a
very definite flare, what Leslie McDevitt calls "nostril poofs". If
you find it hard to see try videoing your dog then slow down the
replay so you can spot it more easily. Once you have seen it once, it
will become easier to see.

To teach your dog to Take a Breath:
1. Hold a treat so that they can air scent but not reach it. Hold
    it out of reach or in a closed hand if they are a snatcher.
2. Watch for the signs of the inhale: nostrils flare, mouth
    closes.

3. Give the treat.

If they find sniffing the treat too arousing, try breathing deeply yourself. Your dog will often inhale in response to your inhale.

Once you have taught this, use it regularly: when your dog recalls, when they are settling, before you treat them. Make taking a breath a regular part of their daily routine.

Relaxation Protocol

Dr. Karen Overall's Relaxation Protocol (RP) is a way to teach your dog to relax, whatever is going on around them. There are 15 task sets, each of which has a series of things for you to do while your dog sits or lies down and relaxes. Note that task sets are described as 'Days' in some versions of the RP but, in my experience, few complete them in one actual day. You can take as long as your dog needs to complete a task set and you can break them down into smaller chunks if you need to for your particular dog.

Task set 1 starts with taking a few steps away and by task set 15 you are jogging and talking to imaginary friends in another room! The idea is that your dog just stays where they are, relaxed, while stuff happens around them. The important word here is 'relaxed'. We want our dog to adopt a relaxed posture with deep breathing rather than being alert and in working mode. This is what can take time for many dogs and incorporating Take a Breath can help.

Start working in a quiet room at home and work through the 15 task sets, taking as long as you need. Then repeat in another room, in the garden, at the park, at the pub: anywhere you may want your dog to be able to relax. You can also repeat with different members of the family and with other distractions (like another dog or near traffic). But even doing one or two iterations at home will make a huge difference.

The RP takes time and effort but it is worth it. You can download a free copy in written and audio form.[67]

Mat work

Mat work helps by giving your dog a portable, safe place. The mat is associated both with the feeling of relaxation and the behaviour of being still. Once learned, a mat can give your dog a safe place to be in all kinds of contexts: at home when visitors come, at training classes, in the pub or café, even out on walks.

I recommend getting a new mat – don't just use your dog's bed or blanket. Choose something that is comfortable and big enough for your dog to fit on but manageable to carry and firm enough to hold its shape (towels and blankets tend to slip too much). I like bath mats as they are light and soft but non-slip but you will need to choose something suitable for your dog's size.

A good way to start with mat work is to use it for the Relaxation Protocol. This way you kill two birds with one stone. The mat will automatically become part of the context for relaxation.

If you are not doing this, then just start by reinforcing any interaction with the mat, then only settled behaviour – sitting or lying down – and then only calm, settled behaviour. Make sure reinforcement is given on the mat, initially, and that you regularly bring your dog off the mat so they get used to going back to it.

So these are my go-to foundation tools for addressing comfort, relaxation and calming. Note that when I am using food for these I don't use a clicker as it is too exciting for many dogs and encourages 'work mode'. I might use a very quiet, soft "yesss" as a marker or not use a marker at all. I also deliver food calmly, placing it between the feet or putting it on the mat. I don't throw or drop food when the dog is relaxing, as I don't want to encourage the dog to move. The exception to this is when I want to move the dog off the mat, so that they can practise going back to it.

---

[67] The full protocol and an audio version are available at
http://championofmyheart.com/relaxation-protocol-mp3-files/

When you are doing these activities, think too about your own state of mind. Make sure you breathe and release tension you are holding in your body. Try to let go of expectations and take the pressure off yourself and your dog. Be present and mindful about how you are interacting. All of this will help you both learn to relax together.

Essential life skills: making daily life easier

With any behaviour issue there will be some life skills that will make that behaviour easier to live with. An essential life skill is something that is not specifically addressing the reactive behaviour but that will enable you to live with that behaviour more easily. What you consider to be an essential life skill will depend on you and on your dog but it is worth taking time to identify what they might be and to focus time on training them thoroughly.

Remember we are focusing on teaching our dog to do something rather than to stop doing something. So what would make things much easier for you right now? Here are some ideas.

Target your hand

Teaching your dog to target the hand is a foundation behaviour for many things. Once you have this you can use it to help your dog walk close, turn away or get behind. You can ask also them to target your hand rather than barking when they see another dog.

Hand targets are very easy to teach.

1. Hold your hand out near your dog's nose, close enough that they are likely to move towards it to see what you are doing. You can hold your hand in whatever way you find comfortable, but make sure it is different to any other hand signals you use. A flat palm, two pointing fingers (held out in a 'shooting' action) or a fist are all possibilities.

2. When their nose touches your hand, mark and treat.

3. Repeat this until they are actively moving their nose towards your hand, then increase the distance so they have to move a little more each time.
4. Increase duration by delaying your marker by a second, then marking and treating. Build this up gradually.
5. Introduce movement so they have to move while continually touching your hand.
6. Finally, introduce a cue word (for example, "Touch"). Say this as they move their nose to touch your hand to associate the cue with the action.

Recall immediately and reliably

A reliable recall is key if you want to let your dog off the lead and the stronger this behaviour is, the more confidence you will have. You can use a whistle or a word but avoid anything they will hear every day in different contexts – like their name!

There are many ways to teach a reliable recall. I like to build a really strong association between the recall cue and something really tasty, so that the response becomes immediate and automatic. A whistle is ideal for this and these steps assume a whistle but if you are using a word use that instead:

1. With your dog right beside you, blow the whistle and then treat your dog with high value treats. Repeat this rapidly for a minute or so several times a day for a week. You want this foundation to be strong. Your dog should be very attentive when they hear the whistle.
2. Repeat as above with your dog in the room but not paying attention to you. If they don't come straight to you, go back to step 1.
3. Practise when they are further away or out of sight. Whistle from one room to another, from house to garden, from garden to house, and at different distances in the garden.

Any time your dog doesn't come straight away, go back a step and practise more before trying again.

4.   Now repeat steps 1-3 out on walks. This is much more distracting so do it with them on the lead and beside you to start.

5.   Progress to a longer lead, then a long line, then dropping the line, then finally off lead (in a safe space). If your dog is distracted, take a step back.

Note: Recall is one behaviour where I never reduce the value of reinforcement. I want this to be a behaviour that guarantees a big win for my dog. So only practice when you are able to offer high value reinforcement. Make sure each stage is solid before moving to the next: strong foundations make all the difference to this training.

Let's Go (or the "Oh s***" cue!)

Training a "Let's go" cue for your dog is helpful so that you can do an about turn if you need to get out of trouble. Ideally make the cue for this the actual words that are likely to come out of your mouth when under pressure – even if it is an expletive. I sometimes call this the "Oh s***" cue! Teach your dog that this means turn around and walk the other way. Practise it at home, and out and about, when there is nothing happening so that it is automatic when there is an emergency.

Again there are different ways to teach this. I use a version of the whiplash turn from *Control Unleashed* as your dog learns to reorientate to you in any direction.

Initially you will be looking at your dog's neck. You want to mark the instant you see movement through the neck. This is great practice for you in observation and marking behaviour! Ultimately, you want your dog to turn around instantly and move back to you. When you get this, you can add running away with your dog.

1.   With your dog on a loose lead, place a treat on the ground for them to eat then move behind them.

2.   Say their name enthusiastically, mark that movement in the neck, then treat.

3.   Repeat, keeping up a rhythm to the game. It needs to be fun!

Once you have the reorientation, practice reorienting away from distractions: food, toys, people, other dogs. Do this on and off lead (in safe places).

To turn it into Let's Go:

1.   As your dog approaches you, turn in towards them so you end up going in the same direction and take a step with them as you feed.

2.   Gradually build up to multiple steps

3.   Add your chosen cue after their name "*Rover*, Let's Go".

Positive Interrupter

When our dog does something that we can't ignore, our natural response is to say "No" or "Stop" but there are a couple of problems with this. First, it is hard not to make these sound harsh, especially if we are frustrated. So "No" becomes an aversive sound to our dog, albeit a mild one. Second, "No" is not a behaviour. It is not something your dog can *do*.

But, of course, we can't just let our dog run riot. Sometimes we have to interrupt behaviours because they are dangerous or difficult for us or self-reinforcing. It can be useful to teach a positive interrupter or break-off cue for these occasions. You can then use this if your dog is chewing something inappropriate, making off with your shoe, playing too roughly, barking continually and so on. Remember that this is just a way of interrupting unwanted behaviour. You will still need to work out how to manage things so the behaviour doesn't get repeated and to teach an alternative desirable behaviour. But the positive interrupter means we are not tempted to say "No" all the time.

You need to choose a unique sound, ideally one that will carry over a distance. It should be cheerful and easy to make consistently. You will use this sound to interrupt behaviours. I use a fairly high-pitched "Rrrrr" sound, rolling the tongue. Other good sounds are a whistle (as long as you don't use it for recall), a 'kissy' noise or a cheery word like "Yeehah!". Don't use your dog's name and avoid any noise that will sound cross or frustrated (like "uh-uh"). You want an upbeat noise!

We want to teach our dog to look to us immediately they hear that noise. We do that using classical conditioning, by pairing it to really tasty food. As always, start in the house without distractions.

1. With your dog beside you, make the noise then feed.
2. Repeat until your dog turns to you as soon as they hear the noise.
3. When they are consistently looking to you when they hear the noise, repeat when they are doing something else indoors (but nothing too exciting yet).
4. Repeat steps 1-3 in the garden and then elsewhere outside.
5. Repeat steps 1-3 in the presence of minor and then more significant distractions.

This sound becomes a cue for your dog to stop what they are doing and look to you. Once you have their attention consistently, you can cue your desired behaviour instead of what they were doing. However, remember, to set them up to succeed and don't try to 'test' the interrupter too soon. Wait until it is well established.

Loose lead walking
Loose lead walking is a skill that is critical to being able to work with your dog's reactivity and will make walks on lead much more pleasant. My favourite method for teaching this is called 300 Peck[68].

The idea of this approach is to reinforce your dog heavily for keeping the lead loose in the early stages so that you build duration. Start in a quiet environment until you feel confident in the process. Use the leading techniques discussed in Chapter 6 to help your dog to stand beside you on a loose lead. Mark and treat the position you want.

Now you are going to take and count one step. If the lead stays loose, mark and treat. Then count two steps: 1 2. If the lead is still loose, mark and treat. Then count three steps: 1 2 3, mark and treat the loose lead. Build it up incrementally by adding one to the count each time. Count out loud to keep a rhythm and to help your dog (and you!) to focus.

If at any time the lead tightens, restart the count from 1. Initially, you will be restarting a lot and it may take you quite a while to reach 10 steps on a loose lead. But in my experience, once the penny drops progress becomes much faster.

Always start again from one when you move to a new environment to ensure a high rate of reinforcement in the early stages. However, you will find that, as you repeat the process in different places, getting an unbroken sequence of steps will become easier.

It is beyond the scope of this book to go through all the potential essential life skills and how to train them but these are some ideas to get you started. I am sure you will be able to think of more. The Kikopup YouTube Channel provides excellent videos if you are unsure how to train your chosen life skill.[69]

---

[68] The name comes from the fact the technique originates in work with pigeons on variable reinforcement schedules. There is a fuller description of the method here: http://www.druidalegsd.karoo.net/300peck.htm.

[69] See https://www.youtube.com/user/kikopup.

Relationship: rediscovering the joy

In Chapter 7 we highlighted the importance of playful activities that we can enjoy with our dogs and the third level of the pyramid focuses on training that helps to build the bond between us. This is so important, especially where our dog's behaviour is challenging, as this can so often stop us feeling the joy in our relationship. There are literally dozens of activities and sports that you can enjoy with your dog ranging from agility to rally obedience, from flyball to disc dog, from canicross to trick training and many more. You can choose any activity that you both enjoy. I recommend you find a trainer to help you with whatever you choose unless you are confident you can train it safely – many of these activities are definitely risky if you do them wrong! Many trainers will do private lessons if your dog can't cope with a class yet.

But just for fun, here is how I would get started with my two favourite activities: parkour and scentwork.

Parkour
Canine parkour involves you and your dog interacting and problem-solving in the environment. Sometimes known as urban agility, parkour can be done anywhere where there are things to interact with: in towns, in woodland, on the beach, in the garden and at home. There are set parkour moves, such as four-feet on, two-feet on, over, under, through, balance and jumps but you can do them with any obstacle, limited only by your imagination, your dog's capability and, of course, what is safe!

Safety is very important in parkour. Jumping on and off things and balancing on narrow surfaces can be risky so we always need to be aware of keeping our dogs safe, supporting them using a harness when at a height, helping them off obstacles where the jump may damage their joints, and ensuring that there are no spikes or sharp edges on the things we encourage them to interact with.

But done safely parkour is a wonderful sport that you and your dog can enjoy without attending classes or competitions. There are titles to work for but they are awarded on the basis of video submissions so are perfect for dogs who would struggle in a group or show setting. It has the added advantage that you can use it when out and about with your dog to help them focus. If I need to get Otter and Martha's attention, I will often ask them to "get on" a nearby rock or bench or put "two on" a handy log. They immediately get into 'parkour-mode' and are then focused on working with me rather than what is going on around them.

Parkour also builds confidence by improving our dog's balance and proprioception. As they practise different behaviours and interact with new objects, they learn that they can do new things and that they can succeed. As such it is an ideal activity for a reactive or fearful dog as you can work at their pace and help them grow in confidence.

You can start parkour at home with a low stool or a sturdy box – or out on a walk if you can find a low, secure log or platform. When you place something new in front of them, most dogs will at least investigate it by sniffing: you simply mark and treat this interaction. Then gradually hold out for a little more before marking and treating: putting a paw on, two paws, standing on it and so on. Many dogs will jump on straight away. If yours does this, you have a natural parkour dog. Your challenge will be getting behaviours on cue so they don't jump on everything in sight!

But it is all great fun and well worth exploring. If you want to know more then check out the International Dog Parkour Association's website, where you'll find explanations of all the exercises with video links and information about trainers and titles[70].
There are also several Facebook groups where people will be

---

[70] www.dogparkour.org

delighted to help you get started.

Scentwork

There are many kinds of scentwork, including scent discrimination, tracking and search work. One of the easiest ways to start is to teach your dog to find objects scented with a specific odour and to indicate actively by retrieving and playing with the article. The following suggestion is based on Talking Dogs Scentwork[71] and I recommend their courses, books and videos if you want to take this further.

Get some small soft toys that are safe to play with and put them in a glass jar or metal tin with a scent such as catnip, sage or clove. Choose a scent that is not used every day in your home. After scenting the toy in this way for a couple of days, you are ready to get started.

1. Play with your dog with the toy. Let them tug it. Throw it away from you and let them get it then play a bit more.

2. Take your dog out of the room. Hold them by the collar or harness and throw the toy into the room within sight. Say "Find it" and release your dog. Run into the room with them. When they get the toy, make a big fuss and play with it with them. Repeat a few times.

3. Repeat step 2 but this time, throw the toy into the room so it lands out of sight. Repeat a few times.

4. Leave your dog outside the room. Go in and place the toy behind something but not completely hidden. Let your dog into the room and say "Find it". Step back from them so you are not distracting and keep quiet unless your dog needs help. When they find the toy, make a big fuss and play with it with them. Repeat a few times.

5. Take note of how your dog's body language changes when

---

[71] www.scentwork.com

they locate the object. This is what you will use later when you are doing blind searches (where you don't know where the object is). If you think they have found the toy, take a step back to give them space and ask "Have you found something?".

Over time you can gradually increase the difficulty. You can hide the toy in a cardboard box – put a few out to make it harder for them – or just hide it in amongst things in the room.

Once they get the hang of what they are doing, direct them to the area you want them to work, then step back to let them search. They are the experts at this. It can be fun to get someone else to hide the object too so you don't know where it is: then you will understand how good your dog's nose really is!

If your dog is not interested in toys then use food instead: cheese is a good food for scent work. The process is the same whatever they are learning to find so you can use these steps for cheese as well.

Whatever you choose to do with your dog, focus on the fun! It will help you to keep perspective and remember what a great dog you have.

Triggers: resolving reactive behaviour

Finally we reach the top of our pyramid and training around triggers. If we have done our foundation work thoroughly, we will already have made progress here. We will have a calmer dog, who is able to self-calm; we will have core behaviours that help us to stay safe and we will have a stronger bond and connection. All of these prepare us well for working around triggers.

With this preparation in place, I tend to go straight to working with operant learning around triggers. I find, by this point, most dogs are able to offer behaviours even in the presence of a trigger, as long as there is sufficient space. As we saw earlier, operant learning teaches our dogs that they are able to influence their environment, which is crucial to feeling safe and confident. Once they understand that they can make good things happen, they start to feel differently about the triggers and these become less scary. Instead, a trigger becomes an opportunity to play a fun game or engage with you in a familiar and enjoyable way. Using positive reinforcement is effective at changing how our dogs feel as well as what they do. It lets your dog be an active participant in training and gives them the tools they need to handle new situations.

I sometimes use counter conditioning as an initial step to help a dog feel safe or more relaxed, particularly if they are new to training and do not yet have the foundations in place. Done correctly, it also changes how your dog feels about the trigger so that, instead of being a source of fear, it becomes a predictor of good things. Remember, counter conditioning is not based on your dog's behaviour at all. So you can counter condition no matter what your dog is doing, even if they are not paying attention to you.

Once your dog starts to offer behaviours like looking at you or turning away from the trigger, you can move to operant learning. My programme of choice is Leslie McDevitt's *Control Unleashed*. This is by no means the only good programme available but it is the one that I find most useful and use most often. I love the philosophy behind it of a two-way conversation and the way it empowers our dogs. I thoroughly recommend that you read at least one of Leslie's books[72] to understand how Control Unleashed works. But here is my summary of two of the elements that I use a lot in working around triggers, to give you a flavour.

---

[72] The books are *Control Unleashed: Reactive to Relaxed* (2019), *Control Unleashed: The Puppy Program* (2012) and *Control Unleashed: Creating a Focused and Confident Dog* (2007) all written by Leslie McDevitt and published by Clean Run.

Pattern Games

Pattern Games give both guardian and dog a structure in which to operate when faced with a distracting or challenging environment. They are simple behaviours that we can both learn and then default to when we need them. They all involve some movement, which is often easier for dogs than staying still. They give both us and our dog something simple and familiar to do; a structure that is safe and known.

Pattern Games are useful in a number of ways. They bring the security of a known pattern into situations where our dog may be concerned or distracted. Instead of expecting them to learn something new in this context, we can invite them to play a pattern game. Most dogs breathe an almost audible sigh of relief as they engage in the familiar structure. This can get us out of trouble, allowing us to walk past other dogs, for instance, or to wait calmly while other dogs pass us.

The structure also provides a context in which we continue to change how our dog feels about the trigger, through playing a known and loved game. We are changing how our dog feels, while offering them an appropriate way to behave.

One of the beauties of pattern games is their simplicity. Anyone can do them. They require no experience of training and very little practice – just enough for both guardian and dog to get a feel for the rhythm. They are also very forgiving. The important thing about pattern games is not the exact pattern but the fact that it *is* a pattern. So as long as you are repeating a simple sequence and being consistent, you don't need to worry too much if it is the same sequence as the next person. As long as you and your dog understand the pattern, you are good to go.

I always recommend finding a pattern game to play when stationary and one to play on the move. There are lots of possibilities but I will just give two examples here, one for each of these scenarios:

1. **Up and Down.** Use this when you need to let someone go past. Drop a treat on the ground between your feet to start. Your dog will put their head down to find it. Wait until your dog looks back up at you. Click or mark that and drop another treat. Repeat as long as you need. After a few iterations your dog will get into the rhythm of looking up at you then down for the treat. This is the pattern.

2. **1, 2, 3 Treat.** This is perfect for situations where you need to keep moving, perhaps to pass another dog or get further away from a trigger. It couldn't be simpler. Take three steps, counting out loud as you go. Treat on 3. Repeat as you walk. Your dog will start anticipating the third step and focus on you, waiting for the treat. If your dog doesn't slot into this pattern quickly, they may be too distracted. In that case, start by standing still and counting to three, feeding your dog on the third count. This will help them make the association between you saying 'three' and the treat. Once they have that, you can add in movement.

Don't forget that a key to these patterns is their rhythm, so try to pay attention to that. The aim is that you and your dog engage in these games together: we are not forcing our dog to play!

Look at That (LAT)

Look at That (LAT) is also a pattern game but its power comes from the fact that it facilitates a two-way conversation with our dog. The game allows our dog to communicate what they want and how they feel about the environment.

The name Look at That suggests we are telling the dog to look, but this is not the case. We are asking the question: *can* you look? And we are listening for the answer and adjusting what we do accordingly. We are not cuing the specific behaviour of 'looking' but asking: *"Where is the … and are you OK with it?"*

This is much more powerful than simply cuing a behaviour. When we are helping our dog learn to handle novelty or to feel comfortable in particular environments or to stay calm when things are exciting, specific behaviours can be tools to help us on the journey. But ultimately we want our dog to be able to process and respond appropriately, without a specific behaviour being cued. Here, the conversational approach of LAT comes into its own. We ask the question and then look at how our dog acknowledges the trigger: the way they do that communicates a lot about how they feel.

For example, Otter was practising relaxing on a mat outside a ring where other dogs were working. She can find other dogs working a challenge. If the other dog was at the far side of the ring and I asked her "Where is the dog?", her response was a very clear movement of her right ear backwards. She didn't move her head. She was comfortable enough to give a subtle acknowledgement of the question without needing to look. She kept her attention on me, waiting for her treat. However, when I asked the same question when the dog was on her side of the ring, she turned her whole head before she looked back to me. She still answered the question but in a way that told me she was less comfortable.

Playing this game gives our dog control over their environment. They can communicate how they feel and this safe, secure structure helps them relax. Combined with relaxation activities such as mat work, this can make a huge difference to how our dogs engage with triggers. Playing the game calms them down.

So how do we play? Start by teaching them the question. An easy way to do this is to use a soft toy, if they are not too toy-oriented, or another neutral object, if they are.

- With your dog in front of you, hold the object behind your back.

- ☐ Bring out the object and hold it out to your side: you want to see clearly when your dog looks at it. If they are used to looking at you, they may studiously avoid looking at it! If this happens, try making a noise as you bring it out or wave it about a little.

- ☐ Mark the look, then feed as you put the object back behind you, so that they refocus on you for the food.

- ☐ Once you are getting a consistent look, continue to mark the look but keep the object visible while you feed. Your dog is learning that if they look at something and then back to you, great things happen.

- ☐ Generalise to new objects, place objects in new places, such as on a chair, and gradually introduce more challenging things to look at like people and known dogs.

- ☐ Add your cue (I use "Can you see...?") when your dog is glancing casually at the object and then back to you quickly. If they are staring, then the target is too exciting and you need to take a step back.

LAT works by giving your dog another powerful, familiar pattern that they can use instead of reacting to a trigger. It is a two-way conversation that will sometimes be initiated by your dog and sometimes by you. When they see something they need to tell you about, they can play LAT to tell you it is there and how they feel about it, rather than shouting about it. If they are struggling to play, then you know they need more space. We can also start the game. If we see something that we know will be exciting or worrying for our dog, we can start playing LAT. This tells our dog that the scary thing is there and gives them an effective way to handle it. You will often see a LAT-trained dog spot a trigger and then, after taking a moment to process, settle happily into the game, as the trigger becomes less and less significant. The power of the game calms their concerns about the trigger.

Set-ups or stealth training?

When we start working with triggers we have a couple of choices: we can practice with set-ups or we can do what I call *stealth training*, where we find training situations out and about in the world.

Set-ups are situations that we arrange, often in a private space, where our dog can be exposed to triggers in a controlled way. They generally require three people plus a number of calm dogs. You handle your dog, someone else handles the other dog, and the third person (usually a trainer) choreographs proceedings. Depending on the space required you may also need a means of communicating between you!

Set-ups let us manage a training environment so that our dog encounters triggers at the right distance, without risk and with plenty of opportunities for breaks as needed. There is no doubt that they can be very useful. We can work on specific training issues and work with our dogs in a safe situation. However, there are also a some disadvantages with set-ups:

1.   We need access to a steady stream of calm dogs or helpful friends (often both) who are willing to help us.

2.   Set-ups can be stressful for the helper dogs, especially if they do it often.

3.   Set-ups can help us make progress in one context but may not always transfer to less controlled environments, unless this is built into the practice.

All that said if you can find a trainer or class that will help you with set-ups then make the most of the opportunity. You will be able to practise your skills in a safe environment.

The alternative to set-ups is training out and about, whether on walks or on specific outings for this purpose. I call this *stealth training*: using 'real world' situations for specific training sessions, but without actively involving the other parties. A stealth training session will work with dogs or people who are just going about their day, often without them ever knowing. We choose locations where we can create as much security for our dog as possible, within a public space. We go out specifically to train and to expose our dogs to triggers at an appropriate distance. We usually stay in one place and watch people and dogs pass us by so that we can control our immediate environment.

I prefer to separate this kind of training from walks. When I take my dog for a walk I want to spend time with them, enjoy their company and relax. I look for quiet spaces for this, where I won't meet many other dogs or people, and where I can just be with my own dogs.

Stealth training is a different activity altogether and I treat it that way. For this I go to places that I would never choose for a walk. Instead I choose places where:

☐ There will be dogs, who will be on lead or under control.

☐ I can control distance from dogs or people.

☐ There are natural or artificial barriers.

☐ People are going about their business and cannot approach easily.

☐ I am close to my car so my dog can escape or take a break.

☐ I can watch safely from an appropriate distance.

Some of my favourite places for stealth training include:

☐ Service stations on main roads and motorways where dogs are under control, people are focused on other things and you can retreat to your car if needed.

☐ Country parks, deer parks or stately homes that have livestock, where dogs will be expected to be on lead.

☐ Car parks at garden centres, shopping malls with pet stores, pubs and other places that people take their dogs. Your car becomes a safe space you can retreat to or hide behind.

☐ University campuses or village centres, particularly if your dog is concerned about people.

☐   Local shows when your dog is ready.

Natural and artificial barriers are also helpful so look out for these when choosing your stealth training locations.

☐   Watching from the top of a hill or bank while stuff happens below. Finding a park with a higher vantage point is ideal, especially if other dogs can't easily run up the bank.

☐   Watching from across a stretch of water. Mirri and I used to hang out on one side of the river, opposite a spot where dogs played on the other. The other dogs couldn't get to us and distance was controlled.

☐   Watching from behind a fence or across a road.

☐   Watching from your car.

What is appropriate for you will, of course, depend on your dog's needs. If your dog is fine with other dogs but not with people then you will make different choices than if it is the other way around. But all of us can find somewhere to do stealth training with a little imagination. So look at what is around you. Where can you go to watch other dogs or children or men in hats or whatever your dog's trigger is? How can you use the environment to make sure your dog feels safe while you train? Make a plan then go and do some stealth training!

MAKING TRAINING DECISIONS

We've looked at why and how we can train our reactive dogs and some of the options available to us. But how do we know when our dog is ready to move on or when we can be asking more from them? We will look at how we can recognise progress in Chapter 9 but it is worth noting here that our dog's learning is contextual. What they do and what they can handle will depend on the particular context and, as we have already seen in Chapter 4, we need to be aware of all the factors that will influence this for our dog.

We can take at least six possible actions when our dog encounters a trigger. Think of these as our training choices, even though our dog won't learn much from some of them. We can:

1. **Perform damage limitation.** Apply whatever kind and safe emergency measures we have in place to get our dog out of a situation that they can't handle. We are not expecting our dog to learn much – we are just minimising the stress they experience. This is what we do when we caught out and we just need to get out of there. It involves moving out of trouble and then doing what we need to do to help our dog calm down.

2. **Micromanage our dog.** This is where we use food or a toy to distract our dog, perhaps to let someone pass us on a path. Again, we are not teaching our dog much. We are simply getting through a tricky situation without negative fall-out.

3. **Do counter conditioning and desensitisation (CC/DS).** This is the first choice we have where we are helping our dog to learn. We are not teaching a behaviour but changing their emotional response, through associating the thing they are worried about with something positive, like tasty food. Remember, it doesn't matter what our dog is doing and we don't ask for a particular behaviour.

4. **Invite known behaviours.** This is the first choice where we ask our dog for known behaviours, that we have first introduced away from the trigger. You can choose any familiar behaviour: targeting your hand; looking at you; looking at the trigger and then you; going behind you or between your legs; doing an about turn; moving in a simple, known pattern. What you choose will depend on the situation and what you and your dog know and enjoy. But note that your dog will learn most if they are actively

engaging in behaviours that acknowledge the trigger in a safe way.

5. **Engage in play activities.** Here you and your dog are playing a game you love in the presence of the trigger. Scent games, parkour and tug are all great options for this, but training games can also be fun. This can be an excellent way to shift and keep our dog's focus on us around triggers, as well as associating the trigger with the enjoyment of play. The difference is that our focus is on our play. The trigger is simply part of the environment.

6. **Do nothing.** This doesn't mean ignoring a reaction, of course, or leaving a dog to struggle. If our dog is reacting or worried we need to intervene with damage limitation or management. But our aim is to be able to be with our dogs, to hang out, to carry on, without any particular intervention. We may still be conversing about it but the conversation will be subtle and easy and our dog will just carry on with what they were doing. Remember we do not need our dog to engage directly with the trigger; we just want them to be happy to ignore it.

These are all valid choices that we might make in different contexts when out with our dog. The key is to be able to decide which is the most appropriate choice to make for the situation we are in.

In an ideal world, we would never need the first two choices. We would always ensure that our dog was safe and under threshold and focus on changing their emotions and behaviour. This is why we always try to ensure they have enough space to learn and adjust where we are in relation to the trigger so that our dog can be calm.[73]

---

[73] If your dog is over-aroused as soon as you set foot outside your house, consider whether there is somewhere you can take them that would allow them to be calmer. This might involve driving somewhere quieter to begin with. If you

However, most of us don't live in an ideal world! No matter how careful we are we will still sometimes find ourselves in situations that our dog can't handle. This is when we choose the first or second option to keep them safe. These should not be our standard or regular choice, however, as neither will help to change our dog's behaviour or how they feel. If we want our dog to improve, we need to be working with the other options.

So how do we know which of these options is most appropriate for the situation we are in? We learn to read our dog. What is their body language telling us? Are they staring at the trigger or choosing to look away? Is their body tense, alert or relaxed? Is their heart rate and breathing normal or raised? Are they able to take food? Do they snatch or take the food gently? If they have been taught to take food gently, snatching can indicate over-arousal. Are they able to respond to cues? Are they able to offer behaviours? Can they stand and watch on a loose lead? What are they communicating through the way they offer behaviours or respond to our cues?

I will use CC/DS (option 3) when a dog is able to take food but is not offering behaviours. This is particularly valuable for dogs who are fearful, and can be the key option over a long period of time for some dogs.

I will move on to familiar behaviours and play (options 4 and 5) when a dog starts to offer a behaviour in the presence of the trigger. Often the first behaviour offered is to look at you when they see the trigger, in expectation of food coming. When this happens we can move on to cuing or inviting behaviours or play that have been practised at home and, once our dog is really relaxed doing these, we can observe them and sometimes do nothing at all

---

don't drive and your neighbourhood makes it difficult to keep them under threshold, then consider much shorter outings and doing more at home to give plenty of breaks, or walking in less obvious places like industrial estates or commercial areas. If your dog is always reactive, even at home, then you may need to talk to your vet about whether medication would be helpful.

(option 6).

Note, that even when you do reach the point of doing nothing in some situations with some triggers, you are likely to still need other options for other situations and other triggers. The choice you make is always contextual and you may find yourself making a number of different choices on a single outing, depending on the situation and how your dog is responding. That is perfectly normal and shows that you are in tune with your dog's needs.

Let me give you some real life examples from a recent outing with Otter. She can be a little reactive to large dogs but mostly she just wants to run over to see them and we are still working on her recall close to other dogs. She can also be concerned about small children, particularly when they are moving quickly. These are the scenarios we faced and what I chose to do in each case:

1. We meet a couple of dogs for the second time on the walk. The first occasion they met Otter cheerfully but this time they are happily playing ball with their guardian. Otter is relaxed with these dogs but might be tempted to approach them so I opt to play (5) and ask Otter to "get on" as we pass a rock. She is focused on parkour, which she loves, and the other dogs pass without any interruption to their ball game.

2. A family with three small children is coming towards us on the path. The toddler starts running towards us, pointing at Otter, who starts to grumble. I opt for damage limitation (1). She is already aroused and this is too risky to use as a training opportunity. So I pick her up to get her out of harm's way then do some TTouch to calm her down as we walk away.

3. Walking on the beach, we see a couple with two large, off-lead dogs walking the other way. Otter is also off lead but relaxed and interacting with me. I opt for a known

behaviour (4) and ask her to "Walk with me", her cue for walking casually beside me, while asking her "Where are the dogs?" to check that she is still relaxed. She gives them quick, casual glances as she passes and continues to engage with me.

4.   We walk down a lane and someone has left some birthday balloons tied to one of the fences. Otter looks concerned and begins to back off. This is a one-off situation that is unlikely to be repeated, so I opt to micromanage (2) and use food to distract her and get her past.

5.   On the beach there are children playing. Otter is not reacting but is not entirely relaxed, especially when they run. We pause and I feed her each time the children run, stopping feeding when they are still – counter conditioning (3).

6.   We see some dogs running and playing, some distance down the beach. I know they are far enough away for her not to be tempted to join them, even though she has seen them. So I choose to do nothing (6) and just continue with our walk, keeping an eye on her body language in case I need to intervene.

When we are working with our dog's reactivity, we need to adjust what we do according to how our dog is responding. As long as our dog is comfortable, we aim to give them as much autonomy and choice in what they do as we can. We want them to learn that they have the resources to handle the situation and have control over it, without us constantly intervening. Sometimes we need to 'nudge' ourselves outside of our comfort zone and trust our dog to make good choices, once we know that they can.

But it is also important that we do not push our dog beyond what they can handle. Space is our friend and keeping appropriate distance from the trigger is our first priority. If you are unsure what to do in a situation, then opt for more space first. Practise reading your dog, learning the early signs that they are finding a situation difficult or that they are comfortable enough to learn, to engage in a conversation or play with you, or just to get on with things. This will help you choose the training options that will keep you making progress.

Chapter Nine

CHANGING HOW YOU THINK ABOUT PROGRESS

If you have got this far, you have everything you need to make progress with changing your dog's reactive behaviour. You are addressing your own mindset; you are on the way to being able to understand your dog's responses; you are taking control of your responses to other people and learning ways to manage risk. You have new tools for lead handling, a different perspective on walks and an understanding of how to proceed with training.

So there is just one more topic that we need to look at. It is one that is often neglected or misunderstood yet it is vital if you want to be successful. That topic is progress itself.

We need to know what progress with reactivity looks like; how we can make consistent progress; what obstacles we might face and how to address them; and how to make the most of our progress.

WHAT DOES PROGRESS LOOK LIKE?

Potential clients often ask me if I can 'fix' their dog's reactivity. Can I stop their dog being reactive and how long will it take? This framing of progress as absolutes is understandable but it is flawed. The answer, of course, depends on what you mean by 'fix', how much work you put in, what the day-to-day context is like and a whole stack of other variables.

But what I can always say is that we will make progress. Progress is moving forward. Progress is improvement. Progress is being further ahead today than you were last week or last month or last year. Reactivity is resolved by steady progress, not by immediate fixes, so we need to start thinking in terms of what progress looks like.

How do we know when we are making progress? Is there a pace of progress that we should expect? And how do we know when we have arrived?

First we need to understand the nature of progress. Working with reactivity is not always a linear process, where we move steadily from one stage to the next. Of course we can make steady progress at home on the skills we need, and consistent training will make this more likely. We may also be able to arrange 'set-ups' where we can make fairly steady progress in a controlled environment.

But if we are working with our dog through stealth training or as we go about our normal activities, then the progress we see can be very contextual. Our dog learns to handle one trigger in one context, but may need more support to deal with another trigger or another context. There may be days when we feel as if we are going backwards, when things don't go to plan and we are surprised, or when our dog is finding it harder to cope than usual.

However, there are two areas where we will see progress: in our own responses and in how our dog reacts. Let's look at some examples of each of these. Note that these lists are not exhaustive but they will give you an idea of what to look for and the range of different improvements that show we are progressing.

We are making progress when we see improvements in how *we* respond to situations:

- We are quicker to notice that our dog is becoming aroused and intervene sooner.
- We are better at remembering engage our dog in a game or activity when we meet something potentially challenging.

☐   We are faster at delivering reinforcement for the behaviours we want to see more.

☐   We start to deep breathe deliberately whenever we feel ourselves becoming anxious.

☐   We keep the lead loose and our hands soft when we pass a little closer to another dog.[74]

We are also making progress when we see changes in how our dog responds to situations:

☐   They notice and process a trigger but choose to move on.

☐   They can engage with you closer to their triggers than before.

☐   They react less frequently than they did or in fewer situations.

☐   They recover more quickly from a reaction than they used to.

☐   They can watch a dog calmly from a closer distance than last week.

☐   They choose to come to you when the distraction is a little closer or more exciting.

☐   They pass four out of five dogs without comment when it used to be three out of five.

This is what progress looks like and it is important that we learn to notice and celebrate it. Too often we feel we are not making progress because it happens in this quiet, unassuming way rather than with drama and fanfare. Yet when we look back, we are a long way from where we began.

We can also become despondent when something goes wrong. We feel that if we have a bad day then it means that we have to start again from the beginning. We think that all our progress is lost. But it doesn't work like that. There will always be times when

---

[74] Of course you can replace 'dog' with person or child or bike or car or whatever is a trigger for your dog.

things get too much for us or for our dogs and we react. But these don't cancel out all the progress we have made. They don't put us back to 'square one' and they don't mean our dog isn't still improving.

We can compare working with our reactive dog to climbing a mountain. We rarely make steady, consistent progress all the way to the top. The path goes up but then may go down for a bit before it goes up again. But as long as the overall trajectory is up and we keep going, we will eventually reach the top!

And just like climbing mountains, we can do a lot to make our progress easier and faster. First we need a clear idea where we are going and how we are going to get there.

KNOW WHAT YOU WANT

A key to success in anything is to be clear about where you are going and how to get there. This sounds obvious but we often spend little time on it. We don't think in any detail about what we want to achieve, what it looks like and how we are going to achieve it. We think in fairly vague terms about stopping our dog reacting or even our dog being calm around other dogs but we don't have a clear picture of what that actually means. What does it look like? How do we know we have achieved it? Is it passing another dog without barking? If so, at what distance? Would ten feet be a success? Six feet? Or does it mean meeting nose-to-nose?

So it is really helpful to be clear about our goals and where we are in relation to them, so that we can make a plan and know what to do next.

GROW is a coaching model developed by Sir John Whitmore and others.[75] It was originally designed to guide the conversation

---

[75] Whitmore, J (2009) *Coaching for performance: GROWing human potential and purpose: the principles and practice of coaching and leadership.* (4th Edition) Boston: Nicholas Brealey.

between a coach and client to clarify what the client wants out of their situation. But it is equally useful for us to clarify our own goals and develop action plans for what we want to achieve with our dog. Think of it as self-coaching. GROW acts as a framework to help us to understand what we want and to work out how to get it. It gives us a clear process for goal setting and action planning. It has four stages:

- **G**oals: we define our goals and clarify what success looks like.
- **R**eality: we assess where we are now and get a thorough understanding of our current situation.
- **O**ptions: we identify all the options available and evaluate their value for our situation.
- **W**ay forward: we decide on an action plan and commit to exactly what we will do next and when we will do it.

Note that, while it helps to work through these in order, GROW is not rigidly sequential. At any stage you might need to go back and revisit earlier stages. You might also generate new goals when you identify your way forward.

GROW is simple but powerful and can be used repeatedly as you move towards your overall goal. Let's look in more detail at how we can use it.[76]

Goals

Our goal is the thing we are trying to achieve with our dog. We need to be clear about our goals so that we know where we are going, can tell whether we are still on the right path, and will recognise when we have arrived.

First we need to define clear goals for what we want to achieve. These may be about resolving a specific issue (I want to deal with

---

[76] The following sections are adapted from work done by myself and colleagues as part of the JISC-funded *PC3* project at Leeds Metropolitan University.

reactivity towards men in hats. I want to have quiet car journeys. I want to address reactions to visitors at home) or about things that we want to be able to do in future that we can't do now (I want to compete in Rally competition. I want to take my dog on family holidays. I want to walk on the beach without worrying).

Your goal needs to be specific and measurable so that it is clear that you have achieved it. For example, "I want to be able to walk six feet away from another dog, without my dog displaying reactive behaviour, at least 80% of the time" rather than "I want my dog to be less reactive to other dogs".

If you are a long way from your goal, consider setting interim goals so you can succeed sooner. For instance, if your goal is passing at six feet, but you currently have a reaction at 50 feet, start with the goal 40 feet, then 30, then 20. This will keep you motivated and make your goals more manageable and achievable.

Make sure your goals are appropriate. Is it important to you or to your dog? Or is it shared? Ask what your dog's goals might look like if they could tell you. Where are they the same as yours? Where are they compatible and where are they in conflict? For example, our goal might be to take our dog on a family holiday but our dog finds new places and routines difficult and might choose to stay at home with a trusted carer.

What is the real goal?

Sometimes it takes a while to find our real goal. What would really make the difference you want with your dog?

1. Write down what the problem is for you.
2. Re-write this until it is a short sentence that captures the essence of what you mean.
3. What makes this a problem for you? Write this in the form: My issue is...
4. Re-write this personally, using "I want…". Focus on what

resolving it means to you. State it positively: to *do* something rather than *not* to do something.

5.   Now check your goal. Close your eyes, calm your breathing and imagine you have achieved this goal. How do you feel, what you do you see, smell, hear? How do you know you have achieved it? What were the steps that took you there? Is this goal important to you? Do you believe you can attain it?

For example, let's suppose the problem you describe in step one is that you want to let your dog off the lead when it is safe but, if you do, you are in a constant state of panic in case another dog appears. You worry that your dog will run across and get into trouble.

At step 2 you refine this to: I can't relax when out for a walk in case a dog appears when my dog is off lead and my dog goes over.

At step 3: My issue is recalling my dog if there is another dog present.

At step 4: I want to train a reliable recall from distractions.

At step 5, you check that this goal fits and is the right goal. Is it something that makes you feel positive? Would it resolve your initial problem? We'll look at the details of how to achieve the goal later in the process. The Goals stage is about becoming clear on what they are.

Key questions
1.   What do you want to achieve? Be specific.
2.   What would a successful outcome look like?
3.   How will you know that you have achieved it?
4.   What is most important to you about this goal?

Reality

At the second stage, Reality, you explore your current situation. You want to understand where you are now in relation to your goal – where you want to be. You need to be as honest and non-judgmental as possible here. Remember you can only influence yourself and your dog, not other people, so focus on your reality and how things affect you. For example, at what distance is your dog comfortable at present? How often do they react at that distance? What are the triggers? Where are you with your training? What is stopping you from making progress?

Ask yourself some 'what' and 'how' questions:

☐ What do you know already? About yourself, about your dog?

☐ What have you done already? What can you learn from this?

☐ What barriers or obstacles are there to achieving your goal?

☐ How important is achieving this goal to you (scale of 1 to 10)?

☐ How important do you imagine achieving this goal is to your dog (scale of 1 to 10)?

☐ What current activities are good? How do they contribute towards your goal?

☐ What is missing at the moment?

☐ What makes this an issue now? Has it always been an issue?

☐ What are the implications of doing nothing?

Concentrate on what you are doing or have done, not what the results were.

Key questions
1. What have you already tried?
2. What can you learn from that?
3. What is stopping you reaching your goal?

4.   What do you need to learn to move on?

Options

At the third stage, Options, you identify all the things you could do as a first or next step towards your goal. You might need to address issues for yourself and for your dog and you might look at options relating to calming, to management and to training and rehabilitation. Focus on options that will help you overcome the obstacles you have identified when you looked at Reality.

Be creative at this stage and explore all the things you could do. Try not to judge and don't dismiss anything (that you would be willing to use) at this stage. You are looking for your first or next step only so don't let yourself become overwhelmed.

1.   Take a blank sheet of paper and write down as many ideas as you can that might help you reach your goal. If you run out of ideas, go back through the previous chapters and see what inspires you.

2.   Turn over your paper and write down the criteria you will use to choose between your ideas. For instance, you might only be interested in ideas that are suitable for someone working alone or that can be done within a specific budget.

3.   Do your criteria help you prune and prioritise your initial list?

Key questions
1.   What has worked well in the past?
2.   What else could you do?
3.   What obstacles might stand in your way?
4.   How will you decide between the options available?
5.   How does that option help you move towards your goal?
6.   What do you have to change to make this work?

Way Forward

You can now define the Way Forward. What do you need to do or change to make progress? Specifically, what is the first action you need to take and how and, most importantly, when will you do it?

This final stage of GROW is usually the shortest, as you have already done most of the hard work. But it is very important. This stage is about commitment. Identifying actions won't move you towards your goal; you need to commit to actually doing them to do that!

Consider the following questions:

- [ ] What exactly will I need to do to make this work?
- [ ] Who else needs to be involved? When will I inform them?
- [ ] What might stop me from taking the first step? How can I remove those obstacles?
- [ ] How long will this take?
- [ ] When do I want it to be finished?
- [ ] When will I start?

Commit to action and move forward.

Key questions

1. How will you move forward?
2. What specifically is your next step?
3. When will you do it?
4. Who do you need to speak to?
5. When and how will you review your progress?

Plan to be flexible

GROW helps you plan what you need to do and how to get started. But we should remember that, alongside planning, we need flexibility.

You may feel a bit overwhelmed looking at GROW. How can you achieve even one goal, when there are so many things that you need to work on? If so, take a deep breath! GROW is intended to help us think through the problem and come up with possible solutions but we don't need everything mapped out before we can start. The chances are that, even with a detailed master plan, you will have to adjust again and again. You can't always predict how your dog will respond to what you do or what will happen along the way.

Focus on being clear about your intention. Know where you are heading but concentrate on that first step. What strategies do you need for that one step? How can you have success with that?

Once you have successfully taken that first step, you will find each step that follows becomes more and more obvious. With each successful goal achieved, you will have more information and understanding and the next step will be clearer. Soon you will have made more progress than you can imagine.

Always be prepared to change your plan when you need to. Change what you do based on what you observe. Change what you expect based on your dog's response. Change anything that isn't helping and, if necessary, go back to the drawing board.

GROW will help us be clear about what we want to achieve and what we need to do to get there. It helps us to identify the next action. But how do we make sure we have the skills we need to complete this successfully? For that we need practice.

PRACTICE FOR PROGRESS

We are all familiar with practice. We may have memories of practising scales on an instrument or memorising words and phrases to learn a foreign language or spending hours perfecting a particular sporting technique. Most of us have committed significant time at some point in our lives to practising something that we really wanted to learn. Practice is fundamental to becoming skilled in anything. We are not born skilled. Even where there is a natural gift, it is only developed and honed through practice.

So it always surprises me when people expect to be able to train and handle their dogs with little or no practice at all! Dog training and handling is a skilled activity and, like any other skilled activity, requires practice. Observing our dog needs practice. Timing needs practice. Coordination needs practice. Getting the right sequence of actions needs practice. Managing multiple tools needs practice. Specific techniques need practice.

So we need to practise our training skills. We need to practise TTouch techniques. We need to practise lead handling. We need to practise hazard awareness. We need to practise treat delivery. We need to practise breathing and relaxation.

Practise initially in a safe place, where mistakes won't have serious consequences. Usually this is at home, in the garden, in a quiet street or in a private field. Ideally, work up through all of these before trying things out in the busy park or the main road.

We can also benefit from practising without our dog. For example, we can practise marking behaviours without a dog. Find videos of dogs doing different things and practise marking a specific behaviour, such as every time the dog sits or gets up. Choose one behaviour and practise your timing. You can practise hazard awareness by going for a walk without your dog and 'narrating' hazards. You can practise treat delivery by placing a small pot on a stool at the height of your dog's mouth and practising getting treats out of your treat bag and into the pot. You can practise TTouches on yourself, a partner or a soft toy.

Practice is not always the most exciting thing we can do. We have to look at the detail, review our performance and reflect on how we can improve. It can be hard work. But regular practice is essential to develop skills and skills are what will help you cope with any situation you encounter. Knowing you have these skills gives you confidence.

So practice is critical to our progress. But we need to do it effectively. Practice is not about mindless repetition. We need to reflect on what we do and get feedback where we can. Practice works best when we do it regularly – daily where possible – and when we keep records.

Effective Practice

As the old adage goes: "Practice makes perfect". I prefer "Practice makes proficient" so that we don't get hung up on perfectionism (more on that later) but the intent is the same. Practice is critical to us mastering any skill.

There is a physiological reason for this. Our brain produces a substance called myelin that wraps around the connections between our neurons, making them faster and more efficient. This happens most in childhood but adults can also grow new myelin through repeated practice. So the more we practise something, the more efficient the neural connections for that thing become, and the more effective we will be at doing it. So how can we practise effectively?

Regular practice

Practice needs to be regular. Enthusiasm is a wonderful thing and to be encouraged, but sometimes we can start off enthusiastically only to lose momentum a little way down the road. Instead, we need to slow down and recognise that we need our practice to fit into, rather than take over, our lives. Rushing learning is counterproductive: we take in more when we take our time, reflect and focus.

Daily practice is the fastest way to make progress. Take a few minutes each day to do something that moves you forward. Think about how this will fit in with your existing routine. What training can you do on walks? Can you replace some 'walk time' with 'training time'? Is there a time of day when you are always with your dog that you could make more of? What about the times you are relaxing with your dog? Could you incorporate TTouch or relaxation practice into that? Are you making the most of the training time you already have? Would joining a class or group help with structure and accountability?

Piggybacking or pairing your new practice with existing routines will immediately improve your chances of following through. If you always practise when you come in from a walk or first thing in the morning then you are more likely to keep it up than if you try to fit it in as and when. Not only that, but the established routine will become a cue for you to do your practice.

If you need to establish new routines then find a time each day that will work and set a reminder on your phone. Start small. You are much more likely to fit in five minutes' training before you have breakfast than find a half hour slot each day. Anticipate anything that might get in the way and have a back-up plan. Setting yourself (or joining) a daily challenge for a month can be a good way to start to establish regular practice. Just keep it manageable and be forgiving if you need to take time out for whatever reason.

Time out is an important part of our regular practice. We need time to process information and to rest and refresh ourselves. Every now and then, take a step back from your daily practice and give yourself permission not to move forward with new things. Reflect on what you have learned; the journey you are on; how far you have travelled; the progress you have made. And rest. We all need breaks. We need time for our brains to process experiences. We need to allow our bodies to recharge and recuperate. Sometimes the best thing we can do is nothing at all. This also applies to our dogs so make sure they get time out too.

Repeated practice

Practice needs to be repeated. Trying something once does not make you skilled. Going to one course or reading one book does not make you an expert. We need to practise the same things repeatedly, in different situations and at different times. Every time we practise, we come with the understanding we have at that moment and we notice different details. We layer information onto the model that we are developing. We grasp nuances that we missed before.

This is a process that never stops. No matter how experienced and skilled at something we become, we continue to learn from each and every learning opportunity.

Each new dog teaches us something new; each new person we talk to helps us to think differently; each instructor has their own way of presenting the subject. Most importantly, *we* are different each time we practise. So don't make the mistake of thinking that you have done enough practice. There is always more we can learn.

Reflective practice

Practice needs to be thoughtful. Mindless repetition teaches us very little. We need to reflect carefully on what we are doing. What is happening? Did we get the result we wanted? What was our dog's response? What do we need to change next time?

Remember when you observed one thing about your dog in Chapter 4? Did you find that you adjusted your behaviour to compensate for what you were seeing in your dog? Perhaps you saw that your dog's tail went down when they got close to another dog, so you adjusted your distance to keep their tail up. Or you noticed that you held your breath when you saw a dog coming so you started to breathe more consciously and deeply. Our brain makes these kinds of adjustments naturally when we raise our awareness and focus on one thing. So one way to be reflective in your practice is to notice one thing at a time about what you are doing: perhaps how tight you are holding the lead or how your dog is responding. You will find you automatically adjust what you do to optimise that one thing.[77]

We can also video our practice and then watch it in slow motion. This allows us to reflect on one element and then watch again to see another. We will certainly see things that we missed in the moment. Regularly videoing and reviewing our practice in this way is invaluable.

Shared practice

Practice is best shared. We can, of course, reflect on our practice and improve but there is nothing better for speeding up the process than getting feedback from someone with more experience. It can help clarify in moments, things that might take us weeks to work out on our own. It can help us tweak what we are doing well so that we can become even more effective. It can stop us getting into bad habits or even giving up altogether. Feedback is a vital part of effective practice.

So how can we get feedback on how we work with our dogs? We can find a good one-to-one trainer or practitioner. Even a single session can be really helpful in helping us improve what we are doing. We can participate in a hands-on course, where we can practise our skills. We can practise with other people and ask them for feedback.

Face-to-face feedback is direct and immediate but we can also get a lot of valuable feedback online. Getting input on our videos from more experienced professionals or friends can be very helpful and is worth doing, as it allows for much richer and more detailed feedback

---

[77] If you want to learn more about this, a good place to start is *The Inner Game* series of books by Timothy Gallwey.

However you do it, try to share your practice with someone more experienced and get feedback. It is one of the fastest ways to make progress.

Visualised practice

There is one fact that always blows my mind about practice. Apparently, when you visualise doing something, the neural pathways in the brain are activated in the same way as when you actually do it. It is used a lot in sport and those who visualise their practice can make almost as much progress as those who actually practise. How incredible is that? The brain is so powerful that we can develop neural pathways for physical things in our imagination. So why not practise your training skills through visualisation?

You need to visualise yourself in the present moment doing the activity well and focus on what it feels like, what it sounds like, what it looks like.

Start with relaxation: try a relaxation meditation or simply sit still and focus on your breathing. Close your eyes. You might visualise walking your dog calmly past the dog that is coming the other way. You manage your leads and your treats perfectly. Your dog remains focused on you the whole time.

First play out the scenario as if you were watching it happen to someone else. Imagine it is playing in front of you on a TV screen. What do you see? What do you hear? What are the expressions on your face and on your dog's face? How are you interacting with each other? Do you speak to the other person? What do you say?

Once you have watched the scenario through, move inside it and replay it again first hand, as if you are living it. What does it feel like? Can you see it in your mind? Can you feel each step you take? How does the lead feel in your hands? Where are your hands in relation to your dog? What are you doing with your treats and toys? When do you need to intervene to get your dog's attention? Are you using any particular techniques and how are you using them? Make it real. What are you wearing? Where are you walking? What can you see, hear, feel, smell? What is your dog doing on the walk? Sniffing? Playing? On-lead or off?

The key is to visualise detail and use as many senses as you can. It takes practice but it is worth the effort. If you think this all sounds crazy, remember that this technique is widely used by high-performance sports people, where it is called mental rehearsal. It does not replace actual practice but it enhances it and it strengthens performance. Why not try it?

Set ourselves up for success

So we know we need to practise but it is not always easy to fit it in. There are so many demands on our time and energy. Yet the more we do to support our practice, the more likely we are to make progress. So what can we do to set ourselves up for success in our practice?

Make time

One of the most important things we can do is make time. Most of us are time poor and even things that take only a few moments can sometimes seem impossible to fit into our day. Here are some ideas to make the most of your time.

Can you use any small pockets of time that would otherwise be wasted? How many two- or three-minute practice sessions can you slot in while waiting on hold on the phone, cooking, eating dinner, waiting for kettle to boil? Mat training, attention and eye contact and targeting are all simple things you can train in tiny bite-sized chunks of time.

You can even make use of those times when you have to wait around without your dog: on your commute if you have one or in the waiting room for the doctor or even in the car. Use these to support your practice by reading or listening to books to give you ideas, sketching out some training plans or even visualising some practice (though not while driving!).

Learn to say no, not only to other people's demands but to your own. Passive activities like TV and social media can eat up a lot of time. If you are like me and find time slips past as you play a game or browse Facebook, get a Screen time app that tells you how much time you spend each day on each activity. The result might surprise you! Then try giving something up for a week. For example, take a week's holiday from Facebook and use the time to work on your practice.

We can give ourselves much more training time when we remember that our dogs are learning all the time. So we don't always need a specific training session to teach the behaviours we need:

- ☐ I go to the beach. Otter is on a long line because she is still easily distracted by other dogs. I regularly call both dogs back, give them a treat and release them. Training on a walk.
- ☐ I am sitting on the sofa with Otter beside me. I practise touching and handling her feet. Training while relaxing.
- ☐ I am having breakfast. Someone walks past with their dog. Martha alerts. I reinforce her for watching quietly. Training while eating.

You can't do all your training this way but this mindset will make a huge difference, particularly to life skill training. As you go about your day, simply reinforce what you like.

Finally, consider not just when time is available but when you have most energy. We all fluctuate in mood and energy level through the day so it is worth getting an understanding of your own pattern. We can then find our own 'sweet spot' for working on new things and make the most of it. Spend a little time observing when you work best, if you don't already know, and try to make use of your most productive times when you are learning new things.

Be prepared

You will never make progress if, whenever you want to train, you have to track down your clicker, search through your cupboards for the equipment you need and poke around at the back of the fridge for something your dog might consider a treat! We need to be prepared for practice so that we can make use of the few minutes we have here and there.

I have jars of treats in strategic places around the house. My main equipment is readily available in an easy-to-access box. I try to always have a full treat bag at the ready and often wear it around the house. I want to be able to reinforce the behaviours I want whenever I see them and to be ready to do a quick training session when I get the chance. When I have everything ready and accessible, there is nothing to get in the way of my practice.

Get support

We all need support to make consistent progress so make sure you have allies in your corner to help you, and be prepared to be an ally to someone else.

- ☐ Find a practice buddy. Choose someone who is on the same journey and working on similar goals. They will understand the challenges and will be in a great position to cheer you on.

- ☐ Find a teacher or mentor. Whether you need to develop new skills or hone existing ones, a good teacher or mentor can be invaluable to give you guidance, encouragement and inspiration. Whatever stage you are at, find someone who is more experienced, to be your teacher or mentor.

- ☐ Find a community. It is really helpful to have a community to help support what you are doing and who will be there when your other allies are not available. The shared experiences in a good community enrich our learning and make our practice so much more effective. You can find training communities at local clubs or online.

Monitoring progress

It is always a pleasure to catch up with people and their dogs when I haven't seen them for a while, especially when I know they are working with their dogs on particular issues. I invariably see a big change in their dog's behaviour and it is great to be able to feed that back and celebrate their progress with them.

Often they haven't noticed the change until I point it out. When we live with a situation continually, small changes can be imperceptible. We adjust our expectations and these subtle changes are subsumed into what we see as our dog's everyday behaviour.

Yet their behaviour is changing all the time. Recovery time is becoming a little less each day. Tolerance and ability to watch calmly is increasing and space required is decreasing a little each week. We don't notice these changes as they happen and they quickly become part of 'the norm'. But when someone else comes in after a month, or six months, or a year, those small changes have added up to major and very noticeable improvements.

So it is important that we monitor our progress and that involves benchmarking and recording what we are doing.

Benchmarking

Benchmarking means setting a point of reference against which to compare future progress. That point of reference is where you and your dog are right now before you start. So how do you do this?

You observe your dog's responses and write down your observations. Note the distance at which they are comfortable with another dog or person. Note what influences that. Is it the type of trigger or the environment or the time of day or how excited they already are? Note your dog's response to unusual things or to changes in the environment. Note how long it takes them to recover from a meltdown and how frequently these happen. Note how quickly and confidently they respond to cues and in what circumstances. You can also benchmark your own responses and skills. How often do you find yourself going over threshold? How precisely can you mark and reward a specific behaviour? How much of the time are your hands loose on the lead?

Think about your goals, the things you want to change, and benchmark where you and your dog are now with these things.

Keeping records

We also need to keep some kind of records so that we know how we are doing. This can help us to be more consistent and systematic in what we do, as well as boosting our motivation and accountability.

Record keeping needs to work for you so don't try to adopt a complex system that works for someone else, if you know that even the thought of it will put you off doing any training! Think about how you work. I am convinced that the problem with most 'to do' systems is that they are designed by the organised and used by the disorganised: two groups who think very differently! So finding your fit is crucial and it will be different for all of us.

You should record enough information for you to be able to monitor progress and ensure you are on the right track. Some people prefer paper records and some electronic. Some keep a scrapbook with photos and notes of progress. Some fill in training sheets or forms. Some like to keep a diary or blog. Some have spreadsheets with huge amounts of detail on everything they do. Some just record the highlights. Some prefer a visual record and keep a wall chart with gold stars for every successful session. Some use tracking systems, such as the lolly stick system[78] or training bingo[79] to organise and monitor training done. Some share their progress on Facebook or on a forum and some video what they are doing on a regular basis.

What is important is that whatever you choose is easy and enjoyable for you to do and that it lets you see progress from your benchmark. Decide what you need to record and how you are going to do it, then find a way of doing it as quickly and easily as possible.

OBSTACLES TO PROGRESS

Once we know where we are going and how to practise the skills we need to get there, making steady progress will be plain sailing, right? You might think so but sometimes our thinking still gets in the way. We need to be aware of these obstacles so that we can keep moving around them.

Perfectionism

Perfectionism is one of the most common obstacles to practice. We don't practise because we do not feel we will be good enough. We first met perfectionism in Chapter 3. It masquerades as the quest for excellence but it is not. Perfectionism is actually a protective mechanism that prevents us from being excellent by ensuring that we never complete the work we want to do. Brené Brown's work[80] is clear on this. Perfectionism is an attempt to protect ourselves

---

[78] This involves keeping a pot of lolly sticks or plant label sticks with a training task on each. When you have a moment to train, pick one at random: https://raisingageniuspuppy.com/2016/03/09/training-tasks-organizer/

[79] Training Bingo involves putting each training task in square on a bingo card and crossing one off each training session. You can download training bingo cards free at https://www.canineconfidenceacademy.com/reactivity-bingo.

[80] Brown, B. (2010). *The gifts of imperfection: Let go of who you think you're supposed to be and embrace who you are.* MI: Hazelden.

from judgement, shame and hurt, but instead it stops us from taking action. We need to conquer perfectionism.

Many of the positive habits we set out to form with our dogs are 'almost habits'. We start regular training sessions. We plan to do TTouch each day. We want to take part in a doggy sport and set about working on the foundations. We are seeking to develop solid habits.

But at this stage our fledgling habit is vulnerable. We don't have time to do it properly so we'll just leave it till tomorrow. We stop because we don't have head space or energy to do it as well as we want to.

What if instead we committed to *imperfect* action? Perhaps we can't do a ten-minute training session. But can we do three minutes or a minute or a few seconds? Perhaps we can't do everything we had intended. But can we do something?

Any positive action is better than no action at all. So if you want to develop a training or a TTouch habit, commit to doing one action – however imperfect – every day. Sometimes you will have time and energy and will do a lot. Sometimes you will struggle to do a little. But doing *something* is always better than doing nothing and will move you forward.

Doing something better than nothing is not the same as doing a shoddy job. Doing a bad job means someone has to fix it, to make good what I have done. I have left things worse than if I had done nothing. Doing something better than nothing is not an excuse to do things badly.

But it *is* permission to do things partially. To start even if you can't, at that moment, finish (or sometimes even see the finish). To do less than you would do if things were ideal, or if you had all the time and knowledge and skill that you think you need. To choose to act even if you can't achieve all that you hope for.

☐   Taking your dog for a short walk is better than nothing.

☐ Training your dog for a couple of minutes is better than nothing.

☐ Removing just one source of stress is better than nothing.

Taking action, even in a small way, will move you forward and the result will be better than if you had done nothing. It will give you energy to do more – action leads to more action. Eventually all your imperfect action will get you where you want to go.

Everything at once

Another obstacle to progress is being overwhelmed. When our dog is reactive there seem to be so many problems that we need to work on: things that are intertwined so tightly that they can be hard to untangle. We need to work on our dog's reactivity but they pull so hard on the lead so we need to deal with that too. We need to fix it all at the same time. So we go for a walk and we try to practise our counter conditioning, while also practising loose lead walking and recall from distractions. All while trying to keep track of our children and other dogs and fend off stray dogs intent on meeting ours! It is not surprising we are exhausted.

We may have multiple issues to deal with and they may all be important, but we don't have to work on them all at the same time and on the same walk. Choose the most important one or two issues and manage all the others while you do.

Say you want to practise working on your dog's reactivity to other dogs and on loose lead walking. Rather than trying the best you can to address both when you go for a walk, go out specifically one day to do counter conditioning to other dogs. Find a spot where you can control distance between you and passing dogs and hang out. When your dog sees a dog, feed them. When the dog goes out of sight, stop feeding and go back to hanging out. Focus on that one thing.

But what about the pulling on the lead? Surely if we don't

address that as well they'll practise bad behaviour? It's a valid point. So work out how you can prevent them pulling, without actually working on loose lead walking on that outing. You might drive to your counter conditioning spot or you might use a TTouch balance lead to reduce pulling. You might change the context by using one point of connection for 'free' walking (and forgive a bit of pulling) and two points for loose lead walking.

Another time go out just to practise loose lead walking. Go somewhere quiet where you are unlikely to encounter another dog: industrial estates, a quiet street or even your garden are good candidates. Now just focus on practising loose lead walking.

It is natural for us to want to fix it all at once and all by yesterday. But it is a mistake. Focusing on practising one thing at a time will get you there quicker in the long run. As you and your dog become more proficient, you will be able to work on more from your list and then combine them all with ease. But start with taking one thing at a time.

Comparison

Theodore Roosevelt once said "Comparison is the thief of joy" and it is also an obstacle to progress. We lose confidence in what we are doing when we start to compare but we do it frequently.

We compare the dog we have now to our previous dog or our childhood dog. We compare what they can do to our trainer's dog or their behaviour to the quiet, calm dog we see on our walks. We even compare our dog to an imaginary dog: the dog we dreamed of having.

We judge our progress against the stories we read on Facebook or the ideals we are fed by society and media. We compare our skills with the person next to us in class or the videos we watch on YouTube. We imagine that everyone who sees us is making the same comparisons and reaching the same conclusions.

We need to remember that each dog and each guardian is unique. We all have our own context, our own priorities and our own comfort level. We know our dog better than anyone else and we need to move at the pace we are both comfortable with, not at a pace dictated by someone else.

The truth is that the only comparison that matters is comparing where we are now with where we were last week or last month or last year. Are we progressing from where we were? If not, then we need to think about adjusting what we are doing. But if we are making progress then all is well. We can celebrate that progress and look forward to our next steps. They are the only ones that matter.

Change is scary

The final obstacle to progress is fear of change. Most of us are naturally a little resistant to change. We like the safety of what we know. There is nothing wrong with this but sometimes we need to nudge our boundaries a little and do things differently so we can move forward. This can be especially true when it comes to our reactive dogs.

We can find ourselves in a place where we feel safe, where we can cope with how our dog behaves, and we stop making progress. If we are happily settled in that place, and have chosen it as the place we both want to be, then there is absolutely nothing wrong with that. Change is not always needed. But if we have settled there because we are afraid of what is beyond the boundaries, then we are letting fear of change hold us back.

We need to remember that change does not have to be big. In fact, the most effective changes are often small: tweaking what we do to go somewhere new, go out at a different time or do something differently.

Safely trying new things is a key part of making progress, both for us and for our dogs. When we do something that is just a little challenging and we succeed, it boosts our confidence and we learn that we *can*.

'Safely' is the key here. We are not throwing ourselves off a cliff without a safety line! We are simply nudging boundaries. We are exploring what *new* feels like, while ensuring we keep the option to get back to safety or move away. We are examining new possibilities, without putting pressure on ourselves to embrace those possibilities wholeheartedly right away.

So what might this 'nudging' change look like for us? That depends on what change we want to make but here are a few examples:

☐ We feel we need a head collar for control but we would rather use two points of connection on a harness. So rather than ditching the head collar altogether and feeling vulnerable, we use a second lead on the head collar, and start by unclipping it on quiet points on a walk to test out how it feels.

☐ We currently walk in the early hours because we are terrified of meeting other people. So rather than suddenly starting to walk in the middle of the day we might just walk half an hour later and see how we manage.

☐ We never go to our local park because we are worried about other dogs running up to us. So rather than striding out into the middle of everything, we might park up on the edge and just hang out near our car so we have an easy place to get away.

Change can be scary but it doesn't have to be *too* scary if we take things gently. Nudging ourselves out of our comfort zone just a little every now and then will speed our progress.

CELEBRATING PROGRESS

When we make progress, however small, it is worth celebrating. We need to acknowledge our successes and our dog's successes and mark them appropriately. When we do this, we are much more likely to notice the progress we are making and we will maintain our motivation.

There are two kinds of motivation: intrinsic and extrinsic. Intrinsic motivation is where the motivation comes from within; extrinsic is where it comes from an external source, either from other people or the promise of a reward.

We often feel that intrinsic is superior. We should do things because they are worth doing or because we know they are good things to do or because we enjoy them. But the reality is that extrinsic motivation helps, especially when we are getting started, doing something new or doing something difficult.

This shouldn't be a surprise to us. It is exactly the same with our dogs. With them, we use lots of extrinsic rewards early on to train a behaviour, and then we may ease off on those as the behaviour itself becomes intrinsically motivating for the dog. So if we are being consistent, we should apply the same rule to ourselves and reward our progress.

Some may argue that seeing our dog's behaviour improve is our reward, which is undoubtedly true, but this improvement can be slow and so it can help to recognise the smaller wins along the way.

One way of rewarding yourself is to set mini challenges and give yourself a treat when you achieve them. These are your *handler rewards*.[81] Your handler rewards can be anything that you find rewarding, ideally things that you wouldn't otherwise make time for or be able to justify. They can be time-based – reading a book, watching a film, having a pampering bath – or buying yourself something: books or music, nice stationery, a meal out, something new to wear or a new bit of kit. Some rewards will be small for the

---

[81] Thanks to Bernadette Kerbey for instituting handler rewards in the Canine Confidence Club.

small wins along the way; some may be huge for those big wins! But find what motivates and rewards you and use these regularly to celebrate your wins.

Another way to celebrate is to share with others. This also increases motivation as it gives us accountability: it is much easier to persevere with an activity after the initial flush of excitement if we have made a commitment to someone else. Work with your training buddy to share goals and plans and celebrate each other's successes. Join a training class or group. Post your goals on a blog or on Facebook and post your achievements as you go – you will certainly find allies who will celebrate with you.

Remember how much you have achieved. You have worked to develop a challenge mindset. You have tackled long-standing limiting beliefs. You have learned to observe and better understand your dog. You have reconsidered the way you think about other people. You have practised new techniques for lead handling, new enrichment activities in lieu of walks, and new training methods.

And you are making progress in helping your dog become the best that they can be. That is worth celebrating!

Afterword: The Impossible Decision

I didn't want to finish this book without saying a few words to any of you who are really struggling and wondering if you can carry on with your dog. At what point is it fair to say enough is enough? Is it ever justified to rehome a reactive dog? And under what circumstances should the impossible decision of euthanasia be considered? More generally, can we help every dog and is it fair to expect every guardian to live with reactivity, no matter what their circumstances?

There is a lot of judgement around this question. Even raising the possibility can bring huge guilt and shame to people. They love their dog but they are really struggling. Their dog's behaviour is affecting their family life, their relationships, their mental health. They are sometimes living in fear for their physical safety or that of their children or visitors.

I want to say I am in awe, on a daily basis, of the commitment that people have to their challenging and, sometimes, very broken dogs. I see people willingly rearrange their entire lives to accommodate their dog's needs. I see people work tirelessly and spend thousands of pounds getting the behavioural help they need to move their dog forward. I see people patiently working through each of their dog's fears until they reach a point where everyone can live peacefully. And I know from experience, that when they lose that dog, the pain and grief will be massive, and the only thing they want is to have their dog back with them, reactivity and all. If that is you, then you have my utmost and heartfelt respect and gratitude. You are on a path that will challenge you deeply and teach you more than you can imagine.

But what if this is not possible for you? What if life can't be rearranged without damaging other dogs or other family members? What if safety can't be maintained? What if the choice is between your dog and your marriage or your health?

There are no right or wrong answers to these questions. We can all only answer them for the individual situation we are in. What I want to do here is offer a few comments that may help any of you who are struggling to weigh up your options.

Firstly, dogs' lives matter. Dogs are not disposable and when we make the decision to adopt them, whether as puppies or older dogs, we need to do so on the understanding that we are making a life-long commitment. Anything less than this is unfair. We should never get a dog on a whim, or out of misplaced sympathy, or without thinking about possible issues that might arise and how we would handle them. Rehoming should never be done lightly. However, I doubt that if you are reading a book like this, you would ever consider it so.

Secondly, human lives also matter. I am saddened sometimes when I hear colleagues judging guardians who have unwittingly adopted a dog who is completely unsuited to their life or experience level or who, frankly, are dealing with behaviours on a daily basis, that most professionals would struggle with. When someone is coping with a dog who is regularly injuring family members or whose fears are so extreme that they cannot handle any sort of domestic life, they have the right to our respect, whatever decision they eventually make. We cannot expect people to put their families and mental health on the line, especially when the dog's quality of life is also questionable.

Thirdly, people's capacity to handle stress varies, as does their experience and tolerance when it comes to dogs. Not everyone can live with a dog with severe behavioural issues. Not everyone can make the adjustments necessary to live safely with an aggressive dog. We need to be realistic about what we can handle. It may be that we can actually manage more than we think and that what we actually need is more support or respite care of some kind. But we owe it to ourselves and to our dog to be honest about our struggles and get help when we need it.

Fourthly, we cannot save every dog. I wish that was not the case but it is the truth. Some dogs are so damaged, either by illness, experiences or genetics that they cannot live safely in our human-centred world. Where this is the case, the kindest decision is to give them a peaceful death. It has been said that death is not a welfare issue. It is life, where that life is made intolerable by extreme fear or pain, that can compromise welfare. The huge question is, of course, does *this* dog fall into this category?

Fifthly, rehoming may be desirable but it not always possible. We need to be realistic about the prospects of rehoming a reactive dog, if that is what we seek to do. People often talk about finding their dog "a home in the country", hoping that there is somewhere out there where their dog's behaviour will not be an issue, or where it can be managed successfully. The reality is that, in most cases, such homes are mythical. Alternative homes can sometimes be found with experienced handlers, who can manage a challenging dog safely, but they are rare and usually already full to capacity. If we are attempting to rehome our reactive dog, we need to be scrupulously honest about their issues and history. We cannot hide anything or we are simply passing on the problem and damaging our dog in the process. There is no excuse for that.

All that said, sometimes a dog is simply in the wrong home and may thrive elsewhere. A dog who is frightened of children or who does not get on with another dog in the household may be fine placed in a home without children or may get on fine with a different doggy companion. Keeping a dog in a situation where they cannot take a full part in the family or have to be confined or separate most of the time is misplaced. In doing so we may be preventing that dog from living their fullest life, while also putting other family members – both human and canine – under unnecessary stress. Careful rehoming in this situation can be the best solution for everyone.

If you are contemplating these issues what I would say is this. Do not make this decision alone. It goes without saying that it needs to be a decision discussed and ideally agreed by everyone affected in the household. But it is also worth getting professional advice. Talk to your vet. Consult a behaviourist. If you are contemplating rehoming or euthanasia then make sure you get the best advice. Talk to someone who is experienced in the problems you are facing and who is able to talk you through the options. It may be they have a solution that you haven't thought of. It may be that medication could make a difference to your dog. And even if this is not the case, you will at least know that you have exhausted all possibilities.

And if you are a professional confronted with these questions, be kind. Explore the realistic possibilities if it is in your remit to do so. Refer on if this is outside your expertise. But do not judge. No one makes a decision like this lightly.

I want to end by telling you about Ambrose. His short life set me on a quest for answers that has led me to where I am today. He is the reason I now work with challenging dogs and their guardians. He deserves to be remembered.

Ambrose came into my life two decades ago. He was my dream dog, a Maremma Sheepdog with a sparkling white coat and soft expression. I was full of hope. A beautiful puppy and a joyful youngster, with a happy-go-lucky attitude to life, he loved everyone and everything. When he hit adolescence things changed a little but nothing unusual, just the expected hormones. Until one day he bit my partner badly on the hand, a deep bite needing hospital treatment.

We were not professionals at that time but nor was Ambrose our first dog. Initially we assumed he was resource guarding, as he'd had a bone nearby and we took steps to ensure that this couldn't happen again. We also consulted our vet and a local behaviourist. We expected this to be a one-off. We were working hard to sort it out.

But it did happen again. Over the next few months he bit us both several times. Each situation was different and usually there was no obvious trigger that we could identify.

Someone suggested that we have his thyroid checked and our wonderful vet sent his blood samples off to be tested by Dr. Jean Dodds, the world's leading authority on thyroid conditions and aggression. Her response was unequivocal. He had autoimmune thyroiditis and she had no doubt this was the cause of his aggressive episodes. His immune system was destroying his thyroid and his hormone levels were all over the place.

This diagnosis seemed like a gift to us at first. If we knew what was wrong with him, we would surely be able to fix it. We would get Ambrose back again. We started treatment and, for a while, he seemed much better. But it was not to last.

The last attack I saw coming out of the corner of my eye. He had been sleeping on one side of the kitchen and I was working across the other side. I was not looking at him or interacting at all. There was no sudden movement or noise.

As he launched at me I swung round away from him and he bit me between the shoulder blades. If I had been facing him it could have been much worse. I stood stock still and he backed off snarling. As I edged towards the door, making sure I didn't look at him, I knew it was the end. Ambrose was a huge, powerful dog and we could not live safely with him. And I was terrified that he would hurt someone else and the decision be taken out of our hands.

With the agreement of our vet and behaviourist, he was put to sleep, cradled in our arms. It was a terrible decision to have to make and it broke our hearts.

Twenty years on I still ask myself were we right? Was there anything we missed that could have been done? Would I have been able to do more with the knowledge I have now? What if I had found TTouch sooner? What if I had access to the colleagues I now have? Would the outcome have been different?

Of course no one can answer that. Maybe. Maybe not.

All I know is that we did the best we could with the knowledge and resources we had at the time and that we took the only decision we had left to keep us all safe – including Ambrose. There was no magic wand to fix him. There was no safe place that he could go to (and we tried).

Although I still wonder about it, I am at peace with the decision we made. I am grateful to the people who supported us through it, who tried to help and who did not judge. And I will continue to pay that forward.

So if you are facing a decision like this, know that you are not alone, although it will seem like it when you are in that dark place. Take your time and get all the help you can. You want to know all your options because you need to be really sure about this. But if, after that, this is the choice you are left with, be kind to yourself. It is an impossible decision that no one wants to make. You did the best you could.

RECOMMENDED READING AND RESOURCES

My resources
- [ ] https://www.yourendofthelead.com: website supporting the book where you can find videos of many of the techniques as well as downloads and links to other resources.
- [ ] https://www.facebook.com/groups/yourendofthelead: my Facebook group – please feel free to join us.
- [ ] http://www.canineconfidenceacademy.com: my website, including my blog and details of my courses, including several free ones.

Recommended books
There are many helpful books that are relevant to reactivity. I am only including here my favourites here. Not all of these are 'how to' books – some are sharing stories, which are deeply inspirational as well as educational. Sometimes we learn most from the experience of others.
- [ ] Leslie McDevitt (2019) *Control Unleashed: Reactive to Relaxed*, Clean Run. The most recent of the Control Unleashed series and my favourite. This for me is essential reading. It will give you the training tools you need.
- [ ] Sarah Fisher (2007) *Unlock your dog's potential*. David and Charles. Sarah's work has evolved since this but there is still much useful information here on observation as well as TTouch body work and groundwork.
- [ ] Linda Tellington-Jones (2013) *Getting in TTouch with your Dog*. Quiller Publishing. A very practical introduction to

TTouch body work and groundwork with detailed explanations of different techniques.

☐ Grisha Stewart (2016) *Behaviour Adjustment Training 2.0: New practical techniques for fear, frustration and aggression in dogs*, Dogwise Publishing. BAT 2.0 is a very helpful protocol which respects the dog and gives structure to a desensitisation process. It includes useful leading techniques influenced by TTouch.

☐ Sally Gutteridge (2018) *Inspiring resilience in fearful and reactive dogs*. Practical and informative, supportive of guardians and focused on science-based, positive solutions.

☐ Tracey McLennan (2018) *Canine Aggression: Rehabilitating an aggressive dog with kindness and compassion*, Hubble and Hattie. If you feel you can't cope with your dog, this book will help. Tracey was a first-time dog guardian when her lovely bullmastiff Calgacus attacked another dog. Their journey to rehabilitation is both informative and inspiring.

☐ Patricia McConnell (2017) *The Education of Will*, Atria. The beautiful story of a dog and his guardian and their intertwined recovery from trauma from a world-renowned behaviourist. Honest, brave and very inspiring.

☐ Jay Gurden (2019) *Fight or Fright? A reactive dog guardian's handbook*. Another that is sharing experience rather than outlining techniques but no less helpful for that. Very readable and authentic - Jay's experience will be recognised by us all.

☐ Suzanne Clothier (2002) *Bones would rain from the sky*, Warner Books. One of my all time favourite dog books, focusing on deepening our relationship with our dogs. It will help you understand your dog – and yourself – better.

☐ Jane McGonigal (2016), Superbetter: The power of living gamefully, London: Penguin. This book is not about reactivity but it is *highly* recommended. It is the best self-help book I have ever read but is much more besides that. It will change how you think about the challenges in your life, well beyond reactivity.

Recommended resources

- ☐ Reactive Dogs (UK) is a Facebook group for reactive dog guardians based in the UK. If you need support or sound advice to help you move forward, this is a great place to start. Search in Facebook for Reactive Dogs (UK).

- ☐ Dog Training by Kikopup is my go-to channel on YouTube for positive dog training videos. Material is free and reliable. Search on YouTube for Kikopup.

- ☐ TTouch: there are TTouch practitioners around the world so you should be able to get help with TTouch wherever you are. To find your nearest practitioner, check your national TTouch site (Google 'TTouch' and your country to find this). Key sites include: www.ttouchtteam.co.uk (UK, Ireland and some Europe), www.ttouch.com (US), or www.ttouch.ca (Canada), www.ttouch.co.za (South Africa) and www.ttouchaustralia.com.au (Australia and New Zealand). You can also join the public Facebook group Tellington TTouch Training Club to reach practitioners from around the world.

- ☐ Animal Centred Education (ACE): if you want to learn more about observing your dog and using low impact educational activities to help them become more relaxed and comfortable in different environments, then check out Sarah Fisher's ACE techniques. A good place to start is the public Facebook group called ACE Connections.

- ☐ Training: if you are looking for training support with your dog's reactivity, make sure you choose a qualified and experienced practitioner. There are far too many affiliations around the world to mention them all but check what methods they use and what experience and qualifications they have. Always ask what they will do to your dog if they get something right and, as important, if they get something wrong. If you are concerned about anything you hear, move on.